Listen to the Wind

By

David T. Horsley

authorHOUSE™

1663 LIBERTY DRIVE, SUITE 200
BLOOMINGTON, INDIANA 47403
(800) 839-8640
WWW.AUTHORHOUSE.COM

First published by AuthorHouse 11/09/04

ISBN: 1-4184-8952-2 (e)
ISBN: 1-4184-8951-4 (sc)
ISBN: 1-4184-8950-6 (dj)

Printed in the United States of America
Bloomington, Indiana

This book is printed on acid-free paper.

Library of Congress Control Number: 2004095876

Author photo by Matt Horsley

Table of Contents

Dad

Looking Back on Gifts That Can Never Be Repaid

The leader of the band is tired, and his eyes are growing old,
But his blood runs through my instrument and his song is in my
soul.
　　　　　– Dan Fogelberg, "Leader of the Band"

One morning I was standing in the sunshine outside Baptist-St. Anthony's Hospital. As I talked on my cell phone I began to feel pain in the center of my chest, right under the breastbone. It lasted several minutes.

At that very moment, a few hundred feet away, doctors were operating on my dad. We all knew this was coming and had been preparing or trying to prepare ourselves for it for months. Knowing it was coming didn't make it any easier.

Open-heart surgery for an 83-year-old guy is risky. My siblings and I were not of the same mind about whether it was a good idea. In the end, Dad made the decision himself, knowing well the dangers– the worst of which was dying on the operating table or soon after– but willing to risk it for the chance of a few more good years.

His life had become close to intolerable. A faulty heart valve needed repair or replacement. Nobody thinks much about the hundreds of little bodily mechanisms that must work in near-perfect synchrony for us to live, but when one fails it suddenly gets a lot of attention. That little valve had become the focus of intense scrutiny lately.

As I stood outside the hospital feeling sympathetic pains for my dad, scenes from my life played in my mind's eye. One involved a church picnic years ago. People had gotten up a father-son softball game, and someone hit a screaming line drive directly at the young shortstop's head. The shortstop was me.

A split second before that ball made mush out of my face, a huge glove reached down–seemingly from heaven–and pocketed the line drive with a loud *POW*. Everyone laughed but the shortstop. Inside that glove was my dad's hand.

In another scene, a young me learned to read music by following his thick finger across the hymn book page. Neither of us had what could be termed a solo voice, but thanks to innumerable Sunday mornings of watching his finger, I grew to love music.

Another scene was years later. Our church youth group was returning from a mission trip and one of the vehicles broke down somewhere in the middle of Oklahoma, stranding a half dozen teenagers. It was also the middle of the night. My dad was the only parent we could raise by phone, and a few hours later he pulled into the all-night service station to pick us up. He never said a word about it.

Thank you for the music and your stories of the road,
Thank you for the freedom when it came my time to go.

Somewhere around here I have a cassette tape he made years ago which we dubbed "Joe Remembers." He sent it to me after I got married and moved away. It's the story of his life through age twenty-five or so. In it he describes growing up during the Great Depression, which, together with World War II, comprises the historical watershed of his life.

On the tape he described how as a boy he made skis out of an old wooden Philco radio. The top of the case had just the right curve, and he cut out the curved pieces and affixed them to two boards so he and his friends could schuss down the Cincinnati hills.

That kind of resourcefulness is hard for people to understand unless they've lived through the Great Depression. Even so, I value traces of that sort of playful inventiveness in myself and cherish it in my children. The ability to turn something useless into something useful and fun is a great gift.

Last week he didn't die on the operating table. He survived the critical few hours following surgery, then made it past the forty-eight-hour point. The next hurdle is getting off the respirator and out of the trauma-induced delirium. He's not out of the woods yet, but I'm counting on discussing the experience with him some day soon.

Thank you for the kindness and the times when you got tough,
And Papa I don't think I said 'I love you' near enough.

****

Can Joe Play?

My old man has done a lot of things right in his eighty-some years. The first thing that comes to mind was in the early '60s, when our family was the last on the block to get a TV.

That, in itself, was a smart move. Nobody knew then how detrimental TV would become to young imaginations–Dad just resisted getting one because there wasn't space in the budget for it. The extent to which my siblings and I are imaginative people today, I'm convinced, is directly attributable to the fact that we didn't spend our childhoods glued to a TV set.

But when the uproar became too strong to resist, and he broke down and bought a black- and-white TV, we were appalled by the number and intrusiveness of commercials. This was when three commercials back to back was considered an outrage.

It was also before remote controls. To change the channel you had to get up, walk across the room, and twist a knob. Same goes for lowering the sound.

My civil engineer dad took apart the TV and spliced into the wire controlling the speaker. He gave us about a twelve-foot leash with a switch on the end. When commercials came on, a flick of the switch silenced them. Voila! Remote control, '60s style.

Another thing my dad did that impresses the heck out of me was to work in the same profession–most of it for the same company–for all his adult life.

It's beyond me how anyone does this. The longest I ever stayed in one job was seven years, and that was about three years longer than I wanted to. I would get the itchy foot and have to move on.

What prevented his getting the itchy foot might have been the fact that he was the sole provider for a family of six. He took his responsibility seriously and executed faithfully his duty as father. If he ever dreamed of moving on, of getting out from under the crushing burden of mortgages and car payments and college financing, not to mention the chaos four kids can create, he never acted on that dream.

Something he did that rubbed off on me was to get involved in his community. I'm not talking about being on volunteer boards and such, however valuable such service might be. Dad had an elevated sense of "neighborhood," and he made it his business to know everyone on the block. He drew up charts, knew the kids' names, and distributed phone lists so everyone could reach each other.

It wasn't unusual for kids to ring the doorbell and say, "Can Joe play?" He'd sometimes put on a Santa suit and distribute Christmas presents door to door.

Another smart move was when he went to night school and earned a master's degree over the course of what seemed like a decade. Work all day, rush home and eat, bolt out the door to class, study till you pass out, then get up the next day and do it again. But it paid off for him when Boeing Military Aircraft Corporation started slashing its work force. Most of the people with advanced degrees kept their jobs.

Small incidents stick in my mind, too. One time Dad asked me to help rebuild a window frame. I could tell he wasn't having a good day. Maybe the pressures of job and home and family were getting to him.

He cut our last remaining board too short and exploded in anger. As a kid of about ten or twelve, I didn't know what to say so I said nothing. But the incident remained buried under a pile of memories.

One day twenty or so years later, the phone rang. It was Dad.

"Remember that time you were helping me fix a window, and I lost my temper?"

I had to dig around in old files, but I found the memory all right.

"Yes."

"Well, I need to apologize for that. It was uncalled for and I'm sorry."

That's the sort of guy my dad is. He takes relationships seriously. Maybe he'd been doing some mental housecleaning, and found that ugly little pearl and decided to banish it.

Dad used to joke that he wore a size 13 shoe, but a 14 felt so good that he bought 15s. I've got some big shoes to fill.

****

Be Thankful for Simple Gifts

So many small blessings we take for granted, until we lose something and realize what a marvelous thing it was. Our lives probably overflow with such simple gifts, but the one I've been thinking about recently is the gift of speech.

Since my dad's been in ICU, he's needed a respirator in order to breathe, a TV-sized machine that forces air into his lungs. If you've never needed a respirator, thank your lucky stars. If you have needed one, be thankful one was available. Chances are it saved your life.

But, because the respirator tubing passes between the vocal cords and into the trachea, it takes away the possibility of speech. The tiniest request becomes a painstaking and drawn out guessing game of hand gestures, facial expressions, shrugs, and nods. Imagine not being able to tell anyone you wanted another blanket or needed to scratch your nose or had a leg cramp.

We worked out a crude system for communication, though.

With his hand Dad makes a writing sign in the air. This means he wants to say something. At first we tried the sign language alphabet, but his confused state of mind coupled with my poor recognition of some letters made that impossible.

Since he's too weak to write on paper or even to point to the alphabet chart and spell words that way, I hold the chart a few inches from his face and point to the first row of letters. If the letter he wants is on that row, he nods. If not, I move my finger to the next row, and so on.

Once we find the row he wants, I move across it until he nods again, meaning I've touched the needed letter: *F.*

Then it's back to the beginning. This row? Nod. Move finger until he nods on *I.*

I try to think of words beginning *fi* which might refer to some obvious need of his. Nothing comes to mind. Back to the alphabet. The next letter is *N.*

"Finish?"

He shakes his head.

"Finally?" No.

"Fine?" No.

Back to the alphabet for the letter *D.*

"Find?" Nod.

I look around the room.

"Find something?" Vigorous nod.

I start calling out the names of familiar objects, starting with things on the bedside table. He shakes his head. Then I move to the windowsill, the chair, his briefcase. Nothing I name is the desired object.

"Is it in the room?" Nod.

Were he not too frail to lift his head, I'd ask him to look around and point to it. Back to the alphabet.

N is the next letter. Find n–. *N* is next. Find nukes? Find number? Find nudist? Nuts? No to all, with what passes for a chuckle.

Next letter is *R* and I correctly guess *nurse* is the word he's after. Find nurse–I should have guessed that one. I start to call for the nurse, but a shake of his head stops me.

"You don't want the nurse?" He shakes his head again.

"Do you want a particular nurse?" All the nurses we've encountered have been tops, but maybe he has preferences. But he shakes his head no.

Back to the alphabet. *R* comes next. Even though he's said he doesn't want a nurse, I run through all the possible nurse names beginning with that letter: Rhonda, Ron, Regina, Raymond, Rachel, Ramon, Reggie, Roxanne, Roseanne, Rosemary–all wrong.

In exasperation he drops his hand onto the sheet.

Next letter is *E*. I feel we're getting close. I repeat Regina and Reggie.

He shakes his head and rolls his eyes as if to say, "How many times do I have to tell you it's not a nurse?"

M comes next. Remove? Remedy? Remember? No, no, no.

In the hall outside his room, a nurse overhears our one-sided conversation. I look at her and shrug. She thinks for a moment, then comes in, finds the nurse call button ("nurse remote") and hands it to him.

Find nurse remote.

He lays the control in his lap and mimes a clapping motion. The nurse call button is his lifeline to the outside world, the world where people live and move and respond. Without it he's helpless to signal to the world. A simple message that would take you or I two seconds to speak becomes a ten-minute ordeal.

Be thankful for simple gifts.

****

Inevitable But Unexpected

Probably I'm not the first person to rush out and buy a new appliance the day after his father's death. But it felt a little awkward.

"My dad just passed away," I told the guy at the appliance store, "so we need a deep freezer."

Too much food was the problem. Although my family made a valiant effort to keep ahead of the casseroles, desserts, barbecue, side dishes, and deli trays pouring in, we fell behind. We didn't want it to spoil. That food represented the love and nurturing of dear friends and neighbors.

Our own freezers and refrigerators were bulging, so a small freezer seemed like a smart idea. But the necessity for it was totally unexpected.

In fact, almost everything about my dad's death has proven unexpected. Before he died, I had a fuzzy picture of how things might be if he didn't make it, but the reality hasn't lined up with my picture.

Part of the picture's fuzziness was deliberate. It seemed a vote of no confidence in the doctors or in God to plan too carefully for the possibility of death. I just didn't want to think too much about What If He Doesn't Make It? In hindsight, this wasn't wise.

My advice to you, if someone you love is undergoing a risky procedure, is to plan to the nth degree. You can hardly over-plan. I still haven't located, for example, my dad's bank statements, so figuring out what money goes where has been a challenge. I wasn't expecting that.

His death surprised everyone. He was a problem-solver, a civil engineer accustomed to applying resources to problems and arriving at solutions. All his health problems needed was the application of a solution.

I've watched him do this a million times. His engineering group twisted the wing off a B-52 bomber one time, just to see where the structure would fail so they could prevent it happening during flight. Like him, I had near-total confidence that his health problems would yield to the correct application of appropriate technology.

Another unexpected thing was the funeral. Dad always said he didn't want long faces at his service, but privately I didn't think that was possible. From my seat on the front row, there looked to be an overflowing of love and thanksgiving. I shouldn't have been surprised, I guess, but that funeral was darned near perfect.

People who've lost loved ones will tell you that occasionally they'll think, "Oh, I'd better ask Dad about such-and-so" before the realization hits that nobody's asking Dad anything, ever again. Strangely enough, this hasn't happened once to me. I've been extremely aware, almost every waking minute since he died, that Dad is gone.

I don't understand this and didn't expect it. The space he occupied on this planet is not so much empty as *silent*. It's the silence that's unnerving. I can't seem to get it out of my head.

Other little things have been a surprise. In going through his stuff, I found journals dating clear back to the '60s. I found thirty years of jogging logs, showing daily temperature, wind speed, and relative humidity so he could calculate what to wear for his morning run. I found graphs he plotted to show daily high and low temps over the course of a year. There are pages and pages of weight charts, showing the gradual decline of flesh and bone.

What to do with his clothes was an unexpected conundrum. What with the universal depreciation of all physical reality, I fully expected his wardrobe to be worth mere pennies on the dollar at an upscale resale shop. I had braced myself for that. What I didn't expect was the kindness with which the resale shop lady told me that Dad's wardrobe had fully depreciated, probably during the Nixon administration. There was no market for his size 42 blue seersucker suit.

More than anything, a person's clothes retain his essence. Hauling them to a charity, I caught an unexpected whiff of my dad. I didn't know what that scent was, but clearly it was the odor of the man—maybe a combination of aftershave and hair tonic and Lord knows what else. I held one of his sweaters to my face and breathed in deeply. *Joe Horsley.*

A couple of his shirts—ones that seemed the most laced with his scent—I pulled from the pile and kept. I'm not ready to give up those shirts just yet.

****

David T. Horsley

The Right Thing Isn't Always Clear

I'm in the middle of a big job: cleaning out my mom's house in preparation for the estate sale which will liquidate the family . . . belongings.

Just now I had to stop and think a minute before typing the word *belongings.* I almost used *assets,* but that sounds too business like. This isn't about business. I almost typed *stuff,* but that sounds too casual. There's nothing casual about this job.

For the past few weeks I've been emptying drawers and cabinets, hauling boxes down from the attic and up from the basement, cleaning out closets and spreading out everything on makeshift tables. Of all the tasks I envisioned connected with my dad's death, emptying out the house wasn't on the list. I either overlooked it or didn't want to think about it.

Now, every time I reach out and touch something, I face a decision. Tag and sell? Mail to siblings? Haul to Mom's already-bulging apartment? Save for later? Toss into Dumpster? I want to do what's right, both for Mom's sake and to honor Dad, but the right thing isn't always clear.

Take this hideous, orange and black shag afghan, for instance. It should have been set afire in the '70s when it was new. Somehow it's managed to survive all these years as a TV-room wrap, dog and cat bed, general throw rug/foot warmer, and dust collector.

My sister took it to Mom's apartment recently, probably at Mom's insistence. Then, mercifully, it showed up back at the house. (I'm not the only wishy-washy one!) I put it in the take-to-Dumpster stack, then had second thoughts. Usually I'm pretty decisive, but items like this afghan short-circuit my wiring.

Its psychedelic hues clash with every known color, and its snarled fur is a matted mess. Someone might give Mom a dollar for it, but keeping it for the sale runs the risk that Mom will hang onto it. Don't I have a duty to protect her from this afghan? Who am I trying to please–her, myself, or my dead father?

My role as Mom's care-giver and decision-maker is still being defined. What I'm feeling is tension from several directions. I'd be a poor steward of her resources if I didn't get her house liquidated ASAP. But that means deciding about the afghan, then moving on to other conundrums. With each decision, I balance my opinion and her best interest and hope the two coincide. Sometimes they do; sometimes they don't.

If it were up to her, every square inch of wall space in her new place would be plastered with pictures, and that's only a slight exaggeration. Most of the pictures were taken during the middle decades of the previous century, when Mom's brood was still under one roof. I understand the appeal of photos from that era, but does she really need six portraits of every relative–living or deceased? Wouldn't one or two of each be enough?

Surprisingly, my siblings and I have worked harmoniously throughout most of this process, but one brother and I did argue about the pictures. His philosophy was, if it makes Mom happy, then let's hang all the pictures–every gimpy-framed, crooked photo with cracked tape barely holding it together; every faded shot of us in bell bottoms and bleeding madras shirts; every dusty, gild-edged print of indeterminate origin. My philosophy is that six photos of Uncle Skip won't bring any more happiness than one photo would, so let's just use the one.

Parting with many items is bittersweet; each one has a story, and after a while, story upon story tends to paralyze the will. Here's the life-size, outdoor plastic Holy Family I crawled onto an icy roof in the mid-'60s to install. It's a vestige of Dad's Catholic upbringing. Every Christmas for nigh forty years, it has graced the roof or porch or lawn. Joseph is looking a little scratched and haggard, perhaps the result of slipping off the roof numerous times, but Mary is serene as ever. Baby Jesus lost his manger and now sleeps in a wicker basket made in Taiwan.

Dad outfitted them with light bulbs inside, so they could be seen from the street. Mom now has no place to display or store the Holy Family, so I know we must get rid of them, but "getting rid of the Holy Family" sounds sacrilegious, not to mention a bad way to start the new year.

I realize that anyone with elderly parents has either gone through this or is about to, and it isn't the end of the world. But that doesn't make it any easier to dispose of this orange and black afghan.

****

Everything Must Go

Someday an elderly relative might die and leave you with a house full of stuff. You'll have two choices: hire someone to hold an estate sale, or hold it yourself. My family and I chose the latter, and neither annoying early-birds nor daffy collectors nor cunning thieves were able to detract from the aura of celebration that accompanied selling Dad's belongings.

The sale was to begin at 8:00 a.m. At 7:00 I looked out and saw cars lining the street. By 7:30 a crowd filled the porch and spilled out onto the sidewalk. At 7:59 by my watch, the doorbell began to ring. I unlocked the door, swung it open, and barely managed to jump out of the way before the thundering herd swarmed in. This early crowd was determined and perhaps slightly frozen.

What happened during the next few hours is now a blur, but a few things stand out in memory. While I tried to check people out and answer questions and haggle over prices, a 10-year old girl told me how she enjoyed talking to my dad while she walked her dog through the neighborhood. An elderly friend of my folks came just to talk. Another man went straight for the Jewel Tea set and scooped up every piece. At those prices, I expected that.

A word of explanation: If you decide to hold the sale yourself, you have two choices. Either you can price things to make some money and not worry about having things left over at the end of the day, or you can price things to move and not worry about making money. I chose the latter course—pennies on the dollar.

People gathered armfuls of things and dumped them at my feet. "Keep an eye on these?" they'd ask. A woman and her brother came to see the house where they grew up. Another word of explanation: The house was born under a wandering star. It was located at another address when the woman and her brother grew up there, and moved to its present location a few years ago. It already had been moved once before I moved it.

Another woman said she used to live at this address, but not in this house. Rather, she lived in the house which sat on this lot prior to this house's arrival. Then a man came and said he had grown up across the street from this house, but at the original location, not at this location or the previous one. Another man told me I had dated his wife thirty-two years ago, and did I have any old books? My mind reeled.

I watched a teenager take a small item—probably an old Christmas ornament from my childhood—and slip it into his pocket. Of the range of possible responses, I decided the best one was to ignore it. Confrontation would spoil the happy mood. I smiled as he walked out.

When a woman bought the lamp I was using at the checkout table, my solar-powered calculator went dead. Then someone bought the chair I was sitting on, and I had to stand. Then someone bought the rug from under my feet. I thought, "Now this is what I call a SALE!" Antique rattan furniture went for one-third its value. I told the buyer about the real tiger-skin rug which used to lie in front of that furniture in my great aunt's house in Missouri.

"I wish you still had that tiger," she said.

Unbeknownst to me, three crafty men haggled upstairs for two semi-valuable items, apparently slipped them under their clothes when no one was looking, and waltzed past me to freedom. When we discovered the theft several hours later, I felt stupid. It never occurred to me that people might try such a thing. No doubt professional estate sale planners take precautions against it, but my crew and I were all novices.

An old life-size Santa cutout I found in the attic went for twenty bucks (!). The horrid, black and orange afghan I once wrote about went for three bucks (thank you, Lord!). Someone bought several pairs of size 14 shoes. Out went a bowling ball, three floor fans, and the scattergun used to bag a Collingsworth County turkey last fall. The computer on which I created several hundred of these columns: eighty bucks. Stuff was *flying* out the door.

Out went an ancient woodworking lathe given to me by a dear friend who shot himself through the heart. Out went pots and pans used to cook meals for my siblings and me through our formative years. Out went the same bed twice, sold inadvertently to two different people. As the day wore on, empty rooms began to echo. Dust mice swirled on the floors. Square ghosts of pictures decorated the bare walls.

Several large pieces of stuffed furniture hadn't moved by the end of the day, and I was getting concerned. Then a minister of some sort made a lowball offer on all of it. He was setting up a house for his youth ministry.

If he'd known Dad, he'd have known that we would have *given* him that furniture. Helping teens connect to their true selves is something Dad would have approved.

"See those kids sitting on that old sofa down there," I could hear Dad asking from some celestial perch, "learning about the Lord? That was my old sofa."

He would be beaming with pride.

I Was So Much Younger Then

Alley Rats

When I was a kid I spent as much time in the alleys of my town as I did my own yard. There was something primeval and faintly forbidding about an alley overgrown with weeds, choked with trash trees and strewn with piles of debris. Alleys were the secret-kingdom playgrounds of pre-adolescence. Grown-ups might have owned the streets and yards and houses, but kids owned the alleys.

If you wanted merely to get from point A to point B, you took the sidewalks. But if you wanted to get there without being noticed, if you wanted to slink and spy, you took the alleys and relied on stealth to slip past the sharp-eared dogs. We knew the alleys of our town like we knew our own living rooms.

Stuff you didn't want your mother to see, you did in the alley. My gang used to set up a row of bottles, then step back twenty paces and see who could break the most with rocks. We imagined we were Sandy Koufax or Bob Gibson, blistering the plate with fastballs. Each bottle broken became a strikeout. Incredibly, no adult ever came running, alerted by the sound of this entertainment.

Some of my pals learned to smoke in alleys. There was plenty of time to extinguish the cig and crush the butt into the gravel if an adult approached. While cigarettes never interested me, on one occasion during a sleep-over a buddy and I reverted to savages and, under cover of darkness, stripped naked to roam the alleys in our birthday suits. Probably with homemade spears–I don't remember.

I don't know why we did it. I suspect testosterone and developing male psyches were somehow involved.

Maybe I shouldn't admit this kind of thing publicly, but I imagine the statute of limitations has expired on naked alley-roaming.

Another forbidden thing we did in alleys is hard to believe now. Not far from my house was a hospital. We crept down the alley and climbed in the Dumpster behind the hospital and gathered up all the loose syringes we could carry. These were the old-fashioned glass kind, heavy and well-wrought, with needles like four-penny nails and glass plungers machined to glide perfectly in the cylinders.

We brought them home, rinsed out the blood and junk (probably at the kitchen sink), and then roamed the alleys looking for things to inject with water. Soft-tissued flowers like cannas, irises, and gladiolas were our favorite targets. It's a miracle I lived long enough to write these words.

Even today, if I see a kid walking through my alley, I keep an eye on that kid. He's probably up to no good, just like I was at his age. If he glances over his shoulder a lot, I *know* he's up to no good. I make sure he sees me watching him, too, to repress any monkey business: Go do that somewhere else.

When we fenced our back yard a few years ago, I purposely chose chain-link over cedar, just so I could keep watch over goings-on in my alley. Alleys are more interesting than the public, street-side of things, and I'm reluctant to lose that connection to the backside.

While this might sound illogical, I hate to see alleys become too trashy. Every once in a while, someone dumps a pickup load of used roofing or construction rubble in my alley. I consider such behavior alley abuse. Pouring used motor oil onto the ground, piling branches a mile high, or stuffing the Dumpster so full that I can't get my household trash in are other forms of alley abuse. There's a certain alley etiquette which ought to be observed among civilized people. Never do to someone else's alley what you wouldn't want done to yours.

City sanitation people do a decent job of keeping the big items like sofas and tree stumps picked up, but it's the citizens' job to handle the smaller stuff.

If you operate a daycare facility, make sure whoever empties your trash gets all the Huggies into the Dumpster. When discarding, say, a major piece of an automobile, don't try to jam it into the Dumpster. Same goes for refrigerator boxes, six-foot fencing sections, and mattresses. Use your head, man. Large items belong on the ground next to the Dumpster, where the city crews will eventually pick them up.

When you thin out your flowerbeds, try transplanting the leftovers out in the alley. If your alley has grass, mow it every once in a while. Avoid putting dangerous stuff out there. Your alley might be some kid's playground.

****

The Head Man

Summertime always stirs my recollections of bygone summers. Lately I've been thinking about the summer job market and recalling some memorable work I performed during the warm months of my youth.

During the Summer of Love, for example, while other kids my age experimented with sex, drugs, and rock 'n' roll, my life was in the toilet. I mean literally. I drove around town in an orange Ford Econoline van and cleaned commodes for a company owned by the family of a buddy of mine.

That buddy is now a state supreme court justice, but never mind. Back then he was just another skinny kid whose dad was hiring. I guess I was first in line, because I got the job on the spot. Come to think of it, there was no line. That should have been a clue.

Looking back, I now wonder what I gave as my qualifications for cleaning toilets. I might have fibbed and said I had experience, but honestly, I'd never cleaned a toilet in my life. Isn't that what moms were for?

My friend's dad personally gave me orientation and job training. He walked me to a little closet and pulled open the door. The cloying odor of cleaning solutions and deodorizers wafted out.

"Here are your supplies. Let's get you started," he said.

It surprised me to see so much enthusiasm about scrubbing thrones, but I had to admire his commitment to quality and service.

"My customers will expect clean toilets when you leave, so give them clean toilets," he said.

We practiced in the company restroom, the toilets of which already seemed spotless to me. "Here's one that hasn't been cleaned in a while," he said, squatting next to a toilet so clean it looked like a display model at one of your better plumbing supply showrooms.

The first step in cleaning a toilet, I learned, was to flush it. I thought I managed that part pretty well. Then the boss spritzed down the whole shebang with Solution A from a plastic spray bottle. It smelled exactly like a powerful chemical detoxification agent should smell: frighteningly astringent. The idea was that Solution A would kill all the germs within a three-block area. I quickly came to appreciate the germicidal properties of Solution A.

Clad with industrial-quality rubber gloves, I wiped down the porcelain surfaces with paper towels while the boss watched and nodded. Then it was time for Solution B, which went right into the bowl. I swished it around with a brush and flushed again.

Conventional wisdom told me I was finished. But there was nothing conventional about this job.

"Do you consider this toilet clean?" he asked.

As I admitted that I did, the boss took a little mirror on a stick from the supply bucket and held it below the rim of the bowl. He adjusted the mirror so it revealed the underside of the bowl's rim where, to my surprise, I saw a row of little holes where water came out during a flush. I'd never given much thought to where the water came out during a flush. Before the Summer of Love was over, however, I would give it a lot more thought than I ever imagined possible.

"See those scaly deposits around each hole?" the boss inquired.

Sure enough, there were scaly deposits around each little hole.

"Do you think that scale should be there?"

Personally, that scale wasn't bothering me. It was minding its own business and not hurting anything as far as I could see. You had to have a mirror to even see it, for crying out loud. But I correctly deduced that "yes" would be the wrong answer to his question, so I answered in the negative.

He then produced a third plastic bottle, Solution C: hydrochloric acid. It had a curved spout which made squirting under the bowl's lip possible. He demonstrated the correct amount to squirt, waited a half a minute, swished the bowl with the brush, and then crooked the mirror again. The scaly deposit had vanished.

Finally he gave the toilet a few blasts of Solution D, a heavy-duty deodorizer which, I would soon learn, was absorbed through the pores of one's skin and re-released for days.

I was given a dorky company shirt to wear, keys to the dorky orange van, and a list of some of the most horrendously dirty toilets in town. These toilets were so dirty that people were using a bush in the alley. So dirty that they each qualified as a Superfund site. So dirty that flies were afraid of them.

But I wasn't afraid. Accompanied by my four new best friends, Solutions A,B,C, and D, we kicked ass and took names.

I never made it to San Francisco that summer, never wore flowers in my hair. While some of my friends stepped through the looking glass, my little mirror on a stick and I went boldly where no sane person would ever go.

****

Crawdads Thriving, But Kids Have Me Worried

I'm a little worried about my children.

Oh, they're normal, healthy kids. I'm pretty sure they don't do drugs or engage in self-destructive behavior. I'm quite fond of them. But sometimes I worry about what they don't do.

They don't seem to interact enthusiastically with their environment like I wish they would. They don't exhibit as much curiosity about the world as I'd like. It's not just my kids–their friends don't show these traits either. Maybe I'm expecting too much.

We parents must walk a fine line between guidance and coercion. We hope to influence our children's development, but we can't really

19

make them be interested in something. All we can do is show them possibilities and model responsible living. They decide what, if anything, to do with the traditions and values we give them.

My main model for what a kid ought to do is not out of some book or TV show. My main model is my own childhood, which was fairly normal. I think normal adolescent behavior should look a lot like the sort of things I did when I was a kid. I'm willing to admit this might be a faulty assumption, but let's assume for a moment it's not faulty.

When I was a kid, for example, I decided to collect insects. If memory serves, no one told me to collect insects. It was just something that sounded fun. I got library books about insects. I learned what equipment was required, then set about procuring it.

One thing I needed was cyanide crystals. The book said "your neighborhood druggist" could supply cyanide crystals. I went to my druggist and asked for the deadly crystals.

"No way," he said.

I went to a different druggist, then another, until someone gave me the cyanide.

At home with the cyanide, I mixed some plaster of Paris like the book said. I put the cyanide in a big jar and poured the wet plaster on top, then screwed on the lid. When the plaster set, I had a good killing jar which I tested by sniffing a tiny whiff of that cyanide. Once was enough.

Next I needed a butterfly net. I got my mom to buy some gauzy mosquito netting at the fabric store. I cut the handle off an old broom and found some heavy wire to make a hoop, then sewed on the netting into a long cone shape. After fastening the ends of the wire hoop tightly to the broom handle, I had a good net.

Bugs captured with that net and forced into the killing jar died in the blink of an eye. Then I had to mount them.

Mounting insects is tricky. It takes a piece of stiff cardboard and lots of straight pins. Each little leg has to be held in place with pins while the bug's corpse dries. Wings must be stretched to show color and shape. Antennae have to be coaxed into a life-like position and pinned.

After drying for about a week, they could be moved into a glass display case. I must have mounted hundreds of bugs before the urge left me.

My children have never shown the slightest interest in collecting bugs.

This worries me a little.

Actually I don't care if they collect bugs or not. What concerns me is that they and their friends don't seem interested in doing anything remotely *like* collecting bugs. Mostly they watch TV, play on the computer, or talk on the phone.

I worry that we—you and me—are raising a generation of kids who don't ever do much except use electronic devices. At our house we limit computer and TV time, and still my kids don't want to wander the alleys with a butterfly net. All across America I imagine a vast echelon of kids who've never caught a butterfly.

It doesn't have to be butterflies. Another thing I did as a kid was climb into the Dumpsters behind the medical center and collect used syringes. Okay—bad example.

Another thing I did was build cages for the critters my buddies and I scooped from the creek. We'd get our moms to drop us off at the creek in the morning and pick us up in the afternoon. All day we'd seine for fish, snakes, turtles, frogs, salamanders, and anything else unfortunate enough to be in our path.

After each pass up the creek, we'd dump the net on a sandbar and sort through the wriggling, flashing mass of life. Minnows glistened like quicksilver in the sun. Crawdads flapped their tails. Turtles made a beeline for the water. Snakes would try to hide. Whatever we thought we could keep alive, we'd haul home in buckets or tubs. Then we had to build cages or ponds for it. I had the neatest concrete-lined fish pond.

My point is, we were interacting with our world. We were outside doing stuff instead of sitting indoors.

Maybe the world is better off if kids don't kill butterflies or capture crawdads. Maybe sitting in front of a computer monitor, chatting with someone in Belgium, is a better thing for mankind and the planet. I'm sure the crawdads are thankful.

Still, I doubt my children have ever seen a live crawdad. I wonder if they know what a crawdad is.

This worries me a little.

****

Wheel Fever

Now that I'm almost recovered from a bad case of a common malady, I think I'm ready to talk about it. It decked me for the better part of a week. I hope you don't catch what I had, because, among the several unpleasant effects of this syndrome is the fact that getting well will cost some money. Maybe a lot of money.

The disease is called Wheel Fever. It strikes without warning when you wake up one day and realize that everyone you know drives a car newer than yours. Just like that–*POW*–your trusty old car changes from being plenty good enough into a piece of junk.

The symptoms: Looking at your car makes you ache all over. You notice every door ding and carpet stain. You develop an itch under your wallet. When a new car passes you on the road, drool slips down the corner of your mouth. Diagnosis: Wheel Fever.

My first experience with Wheel Fever was during college. Our gang had one car between ten guys, and that car happened to belong to my roommate. He got testier and testier as our junior year wore on. Could it have been the fact that we were liberal about borrowing his car but stingy about buying gas?

At home that Christmas, I began looking through the want ads for a nice used car. I found a deal too good to be true: a "dependable used truck" for $400, well within the credit line extended by my banker, otherwise known as my dad.

En route to the rural community where said vehicle was located, visions began to play in my imagination about the places I'd go and the things I could do once I had wheels. By the time I followed its owner to the spot behind his barn to inspect my new truck, I had a rip-roaring case of Wheel Fever.

Nothing–not missing tail lights, not four flat tires, not the official State of Kansas green paint, nor the fact that it wouldn't start–could make me see anything but beauty in that truck. I lusted after that baby with all my being. Its dull steel hull exerted a gravitational pull on my psyche.

The owner kindly offered to fix it and get it running before I took possession. This included relining the brake shoes. He suggested I help.

"You can reline brake shoes?" I thought.

Naturally I couldn't wait to get my hands on it, so that was me lying in the snow one frigid day with numb fingers but a brimming heart, handing tools to the owner as he pontificated his well-defined political opinions. When darkness fell, he uncoiled a battered troubleshooter light from a nail in the barn and went right on working, cutting thick brake shoe liner from a heavy roll and riveting it onto the shoes. I'd never seen anything so marvelous. All this for only $400!

That truck proved to be the most important machine in my life for the next few years. Possessing it made me a different person. It didn't have a radio or heater, but it did have paint precisely the same color as maintenance vehicles at Texas Tech, so I could drive past the entry stations with a mere wave of an index finger.

Much of what I know about auto mechanics I learn from the Trial and Error School of Truck Repair. Such as: Don't remove the oil pan unless absolutely necessary. And: Removing the oil pan is NEVER absolutely necessary. And also: If, when foolishly removing the oil pan for no better reason than you're curious about what's under it, you find it jammed between the block and the front suspension and resort to kicking it free, good luck finding someone to weld back the little threaded ears holding on the oil pump you just broke off.

A direct chain of cause and effect stretches from that truck to my present life. One bitter evening during a High Plains blizzard, as I prepared to take my date back to her dorm, the truck wouldn't start (drat the luck). I ground the starter until the battery faded. Then I argued that, in light of the storm and the distance to the Tech campus, the sensible thing to do would be to spend a chaste night together. With considerably less enthusiasm than I'd hoped for, my date agreed. Several years later she agreed to marry me.

But I didn't mean to tell you all that. I started out talking about my recent affliction of Wheel Fever. It passed.

But the cure wasn't cheap.

I Hold With Those Who Favor Fire

The Psychic Pull of Packing Heat

Yesterday I did something that seemed out of character.

It all started several months ago when a friend mentioned that she and her husband had signed up for a handgun course. If they successfully completed the course, they could apply for a license to carry a concealed pistol. My friend invited me to join them in the course.

I'm not anti-gun. For most of my life I've owned firearms, hunted when the mood struck, and was even a member of the National Rifle Association back in the days before it was a political organization.

However, I'd always considered handgun owners a bit extreme. Rifles and shotguns are for hunting, target shooting, and plinking. Handguns are for shooting people.

So I was a little surprised that I didn't dismiss my friend's invitation outright. I thought about it for a few weeks, and the more I thought, the more attractive the handgun course seemed. This puzzled me.

My friend took the liberty of having a registration packet sent to me. The packet lay on my desk for several more weeks. Each time I'd see the packet and think about the course, the idea of carrying a loaded handgun seemed more attractive. This surprised me.

As I pondered the psychic pull of packing heat, I came to several possible conclusions. One was that the devil was behind it. All my life I've subscribed to and been shaped by the Christian values of tolerance, forgiveness, and nonviolence. I'm not a fighter. I don't consider my measly possessions worth the life of a doped-up teenager who, after all, is someone's son, so I doubt I would shoot an intruder even if he deserved it. Maybe the devil was trying to recruit me into his culture of death.

Another possible explanation for my spurt of interest in handguns had to do with the seasons of a man's life. Here in my sixth decade, my life trajectory probably has passed its zenith. There's something about holding a loaded pistol that makes a man feel powerful, youthful, and–dare I say it?–potent. Weapons in general and handguns in particular exert complex seductive energies. I don't understand them all, but I feel the results.

But probably the most likely reason I felt drawn to the handgun course had less to do with theology or psychology than with recent history. Between terrorism, serial snipers, urban mayhem, and students mowing down teachers in the classroom, I feel more exposed than I did fifteen months ago. Although I couldn't consciously connect my interest in owning a handgun with 9/11, neither could I swear that the two were unrelated.

I signed up for the course. I talked to friends and even stopped cops on the street to ask their opinions about handgun makes, models, and calibers. Then I bought a handgun. At the practice range I learned how to shoot it. I discovered I was a fair shot.

The course took place on two successive Saturdays. The first was an all-day class covering handgun safety, laws about handguns, and the use of deadly force. The instructor took our fingerprints and mugshots for an FBI background check. We signed affidavits avowing absence of criminal history and psychiatric disorder.

We learned where to shoot an attacker in order to drop him dead in his tracks. We took a test over the material. I passed.

The second Saturday was the shooting test. Again I passed.

By chance, the day of the shooting test also was opening day of the Gun and Knife Show at the civic center. I spent several hours strolling up and down aisles crammed with guns, ammo, hunting gear, and reloading equipment. There was gun-lobby propaganda and survivalist nonsense as well as useful shooting aids and information. Although some of the people at the gun show weren't the sort you'd ask to baby-sit, most seemed like ordinary citizens exercising their constitutional right to keep and bear arms.

I came home and filled out the application for my concealed-carry license, authorizing me to hide a loaded handgun somewhere on my person as I go about my daily business.

What's odd is that I don't intend to carry a weapon. What's interesting is that I could if I wished, assuming the Texas Department of Public Safety grants my license.

Yesterday, after wondering whether or not I would, I dropped the application in the mail. In a way it seemed out of character for me, and in another way, not.

* * *

Responding to my column about carrying a concealed handgun, *Globe-News* reader J.W. wrote, "That was the most pathetic, spineless and quivering article I've ever read in a Texas newspaper. That article was an embarrassment to the male sex. Good God, grow a spine man! Carry the handgun with you and protect yourself and your fellow citizens! Quit being such a [sissy]."

Let the reader note that *sissy* isn't the exact word J.W. used, but it's pretty close.

Then there was this from reader M.M.: "As a retired police officer, firearms instructor, and current high school English teacher, I welcome you to the ranks of those who have recognized that we are each responsible for our own safety.

"As much as the police would love to be present when crimes occur, such serendipity is rare indeed. Realizing that we must defend ourselves–and others who refuse to take up the gauntlet–helps to make all of us safer. Thanks again!"

Interestingly enough, since I "outed" myself two weeks ago as a handgun user, several friends surprised me by mentioning that they, too, carry a concealed weapon. Methinks these are dangerous times for criminals to prey on the unsuspecting citizen.

****

Concealed Carry Redux

A year has passed since I obtained a license to carry a concealed handgun. At the time I applied for the license, I seemed sort of obsessed with guns. It wasn't clear whether 9/11 or middle age or something else caused my sudden enthusiasm for pistols.

Whatever it was, it has mostly passed. I still own guns and enjoy occasional target practice, but I don't spend as much time thinking about them as I did.

Curiously, I pay attention when handguns appear on TV. Say I'm watching a cop show, and somebody on TV bursts through a door carrying a pistol. Suddenly I quit watching the show and start watching that gun instead. Without meaning to, I've come to recognize various makes and models of handguns.

The Glock, for example, is pretty easy to spot. In case you don't know what an engineer named Gaston Glock accomplished in the early '80s, here's the short version: He decided to rethink semi-automatic pistol design, and the result of his rethinking is a pistol that looks, feels, handles, and shoots differently from all other handguns.

That was the easy part. The remarkable part is that many law enforcement and military people now carry Glocks. Gaston Glock singlehandedly changed the culture. It would be like redesigning the flush toilet or the internal combustion engine and having half the nation adopt your new design almost overnight. Pretty impressive.

What I set out to say is that when I see a handgun on TV, I notice it. Each has distinctive, signature features. Formerly, I didn't pay any attention to this sort of thing.

Another difference I notice in myself is an evolving attitude toward gun control. Some people think America would be safer if no one had guns, and they point to low murder rates in countries like Japan—where practically no one owns guns—as evidence.

As a lifelong gun owner, I never agreed with these folks. I think their goal of a safer society is worthy, but I doubt outlawing possession will achieve that. Our culture is awash in guns already, and there's no quick and practical way to reverse the trend.

Some Second Amendment advocates, on the other hand, feel that America would be safer if everyone had guns and carried them whenever possible. This idea seemed ludicrous even when I was a member of the National Rifle Association. Now that I'm a licensed handgun owner and know the magnitude of responsibility involved in carrying a concealed weapon, the "armed America" argument makes even less sense.

America is a big tent, and, for the general welfare, many of our citizens shouldn't be carrying weapons. Most people can't even control their dogs. Think of all the mayhem caused by malicious teenagers, drunk drivers, enraged sports fans, and so on. Adding loaded pistols to that mix doesn't seem a way to make America safer.

I suspect the truth lies somewhere between the extremes. Knowing that many sober-minded citizens might be carrying weapons probably has a deterrent effect on criminals, who prefer easy pickings. Concealed handgun licensees don't make good victims.

The unrestricted proliferation of firearms, however, seems like a path to social chaos. I think society has every right to put reasonable limits on weaponry. In the definition of "reasonable" is where people of good will might disagree.

Is it reasonable, for instance, to pass a law restricting the number of bullets a gun can hold? The magazine of my Glock was designed to hold fifteen rounds, but thanks to the Brady Bill, new magazines can hold only ten. This seems stupid. How is America a safer nation, now that my Glock has ten bullets instead of fifteen?

Well-intended legislation like the Brady Bill seems more symbolic than practical. In the aftermath of the assassination attempt on President Reagan, the public wanted something done. It was a natural reaction.

If we want to effect meaningful change in the murder rate–and who could deny that this would be a good idea?–why not build more prisons and enact tougher laws for criminals? This is what the NRA might ask.

Because, answers my left-leaning side, that is addressing the problem at its expensive tail-end. The simpler, cheaper way to reduce crime is to prevent it, to address the problem at its beginning, namely poverty, illiteracy, and hopelessness.

While Charlton Heston is grinding his teeth over that answer, he can take comfort in knowing that there's a loaded gun at my right hand, against the day when terrorist guerillas parachute onto my front yard.

* * *

I can always count on interesting responses to anything gun-related. R.H. had this to say about my recent column on concealed-carry handguns:

"As most left-leaning gun hypocrites, you hold elitist contempt for the 'common folk' while at the same time you believe their existence would be better if they would only submit to all sorts of benevolent governmental controls upon their lives . . . all for their own good.

"Yes, [you] look down from your lofty, superior, enlightened perch with disdain forall those other inferiors beneath the 'big tent' while you smugly tote your handgun on your hip."

P.R. smelled something rotten in Denmark: "You present yourself as a 'reasonable' gun owner but I'm not so sure. Rather, I smell a sheep in wolf's clothing."

Then there was this from G.L.: "Thank you for your thoughtful editorial on our right to keep and bear arms. I wish that all of those involved in the debate were as rational and even-handed as yourself.

"Self-defense is a fundamental human right, going far beyond anything that the Bill of Rights protects. Reasonable, and I do mean reasonable, restrictions are certainly appropriate and necessary. It's such a shame that those who advocate for a total ban on the civilian ownership of firearms, whether clandestinely or outrightly, haven't learned a damned thing from history, personal experience or human nature.

"I hope that your editorial gets wide circulation in all camps and that more than a few lights get turned on."

I Hear Music in the Air

Hi Kulture with Itzhak Perlman

I was scheduled to attend a performance of the world-famous violinist Itzhak Perlman, but something came up and I couldn't go. My pal Chaw McCuddy, who runs a cow-calf operation on the Canadian River, owed me a favor, so he agreed to attend the concert and write it up for the newspaper. This is his report.

"I'm sorry to admit that I'd never heard of Itzhak Perlman until last Thursday night when I caught his show at the Amarillo Civic Center. Me and Arlene were almost late on account of she wanted to stop on the way to town and watch that lunar eclipse. So we were just gettin' settled in our seats when the audience went dead quiet, a door opened at center stage, and out came a stove-up guy on crutches who I figured for the page-turner, followed by a pretty lady carrying a fiddle and finally a nicely dressed man who the program notes called 'the reigning virtuoso of the violin.'

"Only it turned out the guy on crutches was Perlman the famous fiddler, and the other guy was the page-turner. It was the first of many surprises that evening. Perlman plunked right down in a chair and launched into a sonata by Handel, but I couldn't hear much of the first two movements on account of all the coughing going on all around me. I'm surprised they schedule these concerts smack-dab in the middle of flu season. But Perlman's playing seemed so happy and effortless that the audience almost forgot to cough, especially during the smooth and melodic third section. However, when he fired up the fast and furious fourth movement, it unleashed another chorus of hacking from people who'd been savin' up.

"It surprised me to see a bunch of folding chairs set up on stage, I guess for people who couldn't afford to sit down in the comfortable seats with the rest of us. Those poor folks got a nice view of Perlman's back at least. Another surprise was that the page-turner guy was only turning pages for the lady piano player (who seemed able-bodied enough) instead of for the guy on crutches whose hands were busy playing the fiddle. But then I don't know much about classical music.

"The artist introduced the next piece by saying that composer Max Bruch's concertos are usually accompanied by orchestra, which Perlman said is like prime rib and baked potato, but that this rendition of it with just the one piano is like a roast beef sandwich. Right there he won me over. As a cattleman, my hat is off to any musician who can work beef into a violin concerto.

"The Bruch piece reminded me of the ranch in other ways too. It had dramatic tense parts that sounded somewhat like wind through a barb wire fence. It had delicate trills that reminded me of a spring songbird in a mesquite tree. It had some fast high runs that called to mind the time I accidentally thrust a socket wrench into the moving fan blades of my tractor. And it had a sweet sad melody that sounded sure enough like the music in that scene from the movie *Sergeant York* when Gary Cooper–Alvin York–is trying to decide whether to go fight the Germans. I could almost hear George Tobias drawling, 'Ma wants you, Alvin.'

"During the intermission I got up to stretch and saw a woman crying. Maybe she was thinking of that Gary Cooper movie, too. Or maybe she had a ten-year-old fiddler at home, and was weeping because she was finally hearing how a fiddle is supposed to sound. But I suspect she was crying because of the feeling of joy and happiness that Perlman gave through the seemingly simple act of playing the fiddle. I swear.

"To kick off the second half, he flipped through a music book called 'Five Really Hard Pieces' and chose some doozies. There was a regal-sounding one by Kreisler, an old-fashioned romance by Schumann (which started Arlene to sniffling), then a light and airy and completely 'un-Hungarian' Hungarian dance by Brahms, then another Hungarian dance which still didn't sound like the cancan I expected, but which ended with the highest note I've heard since Arlene's pet goat swallowed my harmonica.

"Two pieces by Pablo de Sarasate followed the Brahms, both of them typically Spanish: emotional, ornamented, faintly Arabian, and playful. I once had a field hand from Ixtapa who could play the guitar that way. I still miss that rascal.

"To wind 'er down, Perlman played a duet with himself on a piece by Dvorak. How he managed it is a mystery, but there were definitely two fiddles going at once. He made the one create a sound like someone whistling for a dog, the other like sleet on a tin roof, then they both made the sound a drill stem makes, hung up in a well casing. It was hyper-fast and the audience loved it.

"The finale was a shortie by Weiniawski, lightning fast and so high only dogs could hear it. I could hear my Sheltie barking out in the cab of our truck, although I was certain I rolled up the windows. Sure enough, when we got outside, the dog was raising Cain. I felt sure it was the music that got him fired up, but Arlene said it was the moon.

It was a mighty pretty moon and a little magical, with the eclipse and all.

* * *

Quite a bit of my recent mail was in response to my column on violinist Itzhak Perlman. I suspect the sentiments of many people were captured by L.L. when she wrote, "How could you??? One of the most famous violinists in THE WORLD comes to Amarillo and you make light of the experience??? This was not some joker with a fiddle. This was Itzhak Perlman!"

Say, THAT explains why he wasn't wearing boots and a cowboy hat! I thought he was Johnny Gimble!

L.L. continued: "Sometimes reading your article is like witnessing an unavoidable highway accident. You see it coming. You want to do something to avoid what is about to happen. You hold your breath, and then you just can't help but stare at the result. . . . A fan stares on with morbid curiosity."

L.L. has a certain flair with words, wouldn't you agree?

But then there was this from R.H.: "A friend forwarded me your review of the Perlman concert at the Amarillo Civic Center. In my forty-five-plus years as an orchestral musician, that is the most enjoyable concert review I have ever read. It also captures the essence of the performance far better than the usual dry laundry list of self-serving tripe served up by the majority of music reviewers.

"I received the forward as one of a long distribution list, and sent it along to my own extensive list; I expect the entire classical orchestral world will have seen it by week's end. . . . Everyone I've shown a copy has said, 'That's the best damn review I ever read.' . . . Anyway, pass along to Chaw my admiration for the musical sophistication he exhibits as a simple cow hand.' "

And this from D.B.: "Chaw McCuddy's review was a riot. You have to tell him he missed his calling!"

From K.S.: "A friend e-mailed me this article. I haven't laughed that hard in quite a while."

And finally, from my brother Paul who is an actual music critic– as opposed to my pal Chaw McCuddy who only reviews Hi Kulture when he has to–I heard that several nationally prominent figures in music critic circles had forwarded the column to him via e-mail, with an apparent sense of disbelief that any newspaper columnist would allow someone else, let alone a hick cowboy, to write a review in his place, let alone a review of a living legend like Perlman. Chaw's review seemed to confirm their belief that Amarillo is a cultural black hole.

In his defense, Chaw had this to say: "I'm not just some hick from the sticks. I've got every record the Sons of the Pioneers ever recorded. I once met Patsy Cline in person. I know a little about music, can play passable harmonica or washtub bass, and I watch *Austin City Limits* every Saturday night on PBS. I'll bet I know more about Itzhak Perlman than those Eastern dudes know about raising beef."

****

The Day the Music Died

Some years back I rescued an old piano from a one-way trip to the landfill. It was a battered upright, heavy as hell's cornerstone. We muscled it into a spare room and there it sat.

The idea was someday to restore it to playing condition. Advice from a piano technician disabused me of that notion–a small fortune would be required. The felt hammers were moth-eaten, the wooden action broken, the soundboard split.

Still, the idea of burying a piano in a landfill under mountains of garbage seemed sacrilegious. To paraphrase Norman Maclean, in our family there was no clear line between religion and piano playing.

Years passed. One day my family went away for Spring Break, leaving me alone with the piano and a case of beer. I decided it was time to look the devil in the eye. I would dismember the instrument and save the wood for reincarnation as a cabinet or desk. It seemed like a simple plan.

Cast into the gold-painted harp–the iron frame holding the strings–were the words "Beckwith, Chicago. All workmanship guaranteed." Serial No. 218132. I guessed it to be eighty years old. Someone named "MW" had tuned it and scribbled his initials and the date: 9/29/51.

Details about the piano's history were sketchy. Depending on whom I believed, it had been in a whore house, a crack house, or just an old house. Maybe all three. I suspected its true history might be revealed during autopsy.

I started by unscrewing the parts held on by fat, slot-head screws, then lifting out the action, a complicated wooden mechanism involving about fifty separate parts for each key. Next came the eighty-eight keys, each meticulously shaped and balanced on its own felt-encased fulcrum. Painstaking labor had gone into building this instrument, and lots of it. Such craftsmanship gave me a sense of almost sacred awe. No wonder pianos are so expensive.

What lay beneath the keys only can be described as a mouse hotel, complete with sleeping quarters, passageways gnawed through solid wood, restroom facilities, and a casino including a yellowed double-six domino and assorted coins etched by rodent urine. The oldest coins were wheat cents and a black silver quarter from the '50s.

A desiccated guest of the hotel lay in skeletal repose atop a riddled ticket stub for the "Gold Sox vs. San Antonio Dodgers," April 12, 1979, Memorial Stadium. Every tiny bone was intact.

After removing everything that would come off, I was still left with a formidable and ponderous hunk of wood and iron. I got out the crowbar and hammer. With each blow, the piano rang with an awful chord, as if from some atonal opera of the damned. Finally the whole left side yielded and came free.

At that point a prudent person might have noted that the only thing propping up the massive back assembly, including its deadly iron harp, was the right side. Which I proceeded to remove next.

My memory of the right side coming free is now only a blur. I don't recall the back beginning to tip, or my attempt to slow its terrible momentum, or exactly how I ended up on the floor with a pulled groin muscle. Piecing it together afterwards, I concluded that the piano had smitten me hip and thigh as I wrestled with it, like Jacob of old. Except this was no angel.

Ministrations of Advil and beer allowed me to continue. The back assembly lay on the floor like flotsam from a shipwreck, myself the sole survivor. I began unbolting the harp from its wooden frame, then stopped. How much tension, I wondered, did all those strings exert against the harp, and what might happen if the harp weren't restrained by the absurdly heavy bolts?

An image flashed through my mind of the harp snapping in two, a hundred-pound chunk of cast iron hurtling across the room at the speed of sound. A pulled groin might be the least of my worries.

Slowly, carefully, I began removing those strings. The bass wires were fat and easy, one per key. Each belched a song as I removed it. The mid-range wires grew more difficult, because there were three per key. I cheated and snipped some with wire cutters, setting off a cacophony of protest. As each unwound end came loose from its tuning pin, a tiny spark flashed.

Finally the last string came loose with a leap of fire and a keening *PING*. Whatever music this piano had made since it rolled off the assembly line, whatever small fingers had caressed its ebony and ivory keys, whatever bawdy or mean or tender songs it had voiced, whatever human tragedies or joys it had accompanied, it was now a silent, dead thing.

Its music was finished.

* * *

A sharp-eyed California reader of the *Globe-News* caught two blunders I committed recently in the same sentence. I hate when that happens. I started a sentence thus: "Then I heard 'Let's Make a Little Magic' by the Starlight Vocal Band. . . ."

As Steve Joiner of Los Angeles pointed out, there is no such singing group as the Starlight Vocal Band. There is a StarLAND Vocal Band, which scored a hit twenty-five years ago with "Afternoon Delight." But they didn't record "Let's Make a Little Magic." That distinction belongs to the group formerly known as the Nitty Gritty Dirt Band, now called merely The Dirt Band.

I kicked myself for getting that wrong, because for one brief, shining moment, I was on the payroll of the Nitty Gritty Dirt Band. The group performed in Lubbock in the early '70s. A friend of mine was supposed to handle all the pre-concert arrangements but had to back out, so he asked if I'd like the job. I totally dropped out of college for an entire week in order to manage that concert.

This was when the Dirt Band's cover of Jerry Jeff Walker's "Mr. Bojangles" was a huge hit, and I was in love with that song. I was also in love with someone named Shellie, and another of the Dirt Band's hits was "Some of Shellie's Blues." I felt the hand of Fate urging me to quit school temporarily in order to oversee the printing of tickets and posters, rent the Lubbock coliseum, hire concert security, purchase radio ads, and give away copies of the band's latest LP, *Uncle Charlie*, to anyone who would stand still.

Looking back, it amazes me that performers of their stature would trust such arrangements to a nobody like me, whom they didn't know from Adam. Maybe back then, everyone had a more relaxed attitude–especially entertainers.

Curiously, I don't remember much about the concert, because by show time I'd been awake for something like seventy-two hours straight and felt numb between the ears. The only thing keeping me awake was a metal cash box full of money, thousands and thousands of dollars of it, more money than I'd ever seen in my life, every penny of which I had to account for when the concert was over.

The Dirt Band paid me $300 for a week's work. It was one of the happiest weeks of my life. I'm truly sorry I gave "Let's Make a Little Magic" to the Starlight Vocal Band.

****

Baby, Why Don't We Go?

I don't know if other people have this problem, but songs sometimes get stuck in my head.

Psychiatrists reading this column who are familiar with the phenomenon and know it's symptomatic of deep psychological disturbance should keep that information to themselves. I prefer to think my habit is a harmless idiosyncracy of my brain.

Some people carry portable CD players and headphones when they walk; I carry nothing but the tune. I can start the tune anywhere, listen to the whole thing or just certain passages, and play it repeatedly without fumbling with buttons or worrying about my batteries running down. That's the good news.

The down side is that certain tunes tend to play over and over, and the only way to shut them off is to start another tune. I've tried imagining myself pushing the "pause" button, pushing the "off" button, lifting the needle, and yanking the plug–but the music plays on. It can be aggravating for a guy who values peace and quiet.

For example, a couple of weeks ago I took a driving trip to New Mexico. Before leaving town I bought a new CD of Bob Dylan's greatest hits. I've never been a Dylan fanatic, but I like his stuff.

I think the man has a gift and uses it well. Anyway, I enjoyed the music all the way to the Land of Enchantment.

Just before Santa Rosa, the song "Things Have Changed" came on. It happens to be the last song on the two-CD set. I listened to it once. The lyrics seemed somehow riveting, mesmerizing. I listened to it again, trying to pick out more of the words. Then I listened to it a third time. Pretty soon a whole dark musical world opened up, to which the song was a creaky-hinged portal: "Standing on the gallows with my head in a noose / Any minute now I expect all hell could break loose."

I couldn't stop listening to that song.

Long about Vaughn I forced myself to quit, but by then it was too late. "Things Have Changed" had copied itself onto my brain's hard drive, and for the next two weeks would play indiscriminately. I guess I should be thankful I liked the song. Apparently other people liked it, too, because it won an Academy Award, but that was small consolation to me. I wanted to get the durned thing uninstalled.

Before the Dylan song started giving me fits, one by a singer named Enya was doing it to me. Late one night I was listening to her *Paint the Sky With Stars* CD and drifting off to sleep when "Marble Halls" came on. I sat up in bed.

There's something about "Marble Halls." Its ethereal melody fits perfectly with its dreamy lyrics: "I dreamt I dwelt in marble halls with vassals and serfs at my side."

I got a sharp mental picture of that place and of its speaker sitting on a gilded chair while suitors came to woo her. I could even smell the waxed floors and the bougainvillea twining up the trellis. It reminded me of a Maxfield Parrish painting, with salmon-colored cumulus clouds building over distant lavender hills.

By the time I'd heard "Marble Halls" a few times, I was ready for a rubber room.

Before that–let the reader note how I have no trouble recalling the songs that have afflicted me, and in correct order–it was Fiona Apple's "Criminal." Another dark, disturbing work. I happen to think Fiona Apple is a demented genius and "Criminal" a triumphant achievement of a troubled imagination, but never mind that. It's a scary song. It latched onto my mind something fierce.

In the song, a woman comes to confess her sins. It's not clear who her confessor is or the nature of their relationship, but I get the feeling it's no ordinary priest: "I've been a bad, bad girl–I've been careless with a delicate man / It's a sad, sad world when a girl will break a boy just because she can."

Later the song includes the line, "What would an angel say, the devil wants to know?"

This suggests a dramatic scenario: a fallen angel consulting with a celestial angel about the former's infidelity. That a nineteen-year-old songwriter could come up with such a vision amazes me. Shades of John Milton.

Lest you think all the songs which bug me are dark or satanic, let me hasten to add that the one before "Criminal" was the Beach Boys' "Kokomo." It got hold of me and shook me like a throw rug: "Key Largo, Montego, Baby why don't we go? Bermuda, Bahamas, come on Pretty Mama."

It's a bouncy little tune about flying to the Carribean for a weekend of sun, sex, and cocktails–nothing that would appeal to a proper Methodist gentleman.

It got so bad that my kids wouldn't let me hum a single bar of that song without putting their hands over their ears and singing "LALALALA."

I don't know what this all means, if it means anything. I hope I haven't told you more about myself than I intended. Chances are if you've read all the way to the bottom of this column, maybe you have a song stuck in your head too.

****

The Soundtrack of our Lives

In late 2002, former Beatle Paul McCartney released a new CD of songs from his twenty-city Driving USA tour which started in California and ended in Florida.

On May 10 of that year, I was in Seat 1, Row S, Section 128 of Dallas' Reunion Arena when Paul took the stage and sang thirty-eight songs in just under three hours.

The first time Paul mounted a Texas stage was Sept.18, 1964, when the curtain rose at Dallas' Memorial Coliseum, and the Fab Four played to a solid wall of screaming teens. Opening acts included The Righteous Brothers and Jackie DeShannon.

Absent at that event thirty-eight years ago was a certain thirteen-year-old Dallas native named Michele–one *L*–who, unable to afford tickets to the concert, somehow obtained the Beatles' phone number and, with typical thirteen-year-old girl logic, tried to arrange a meeting with the lads. Not surprisingly, she didn't get through.

Meanwhile, hundreds of miles away, I was lovesick over a different Michelle–two *L*'s–who sat in front of me in Mr. Hanson's algebra class. I would lie in my room and listen to Paul sing, "Michelle, ma belle, sons des mots qui vont tres bien ensemble." The lyrics mirrored how I felt toward my Michelle: I'll get to you somehow. With the skewed logic teenage boys enjoy, I knew the song meant that Fate would entwine her destiny with mine. I just knew it.

Decades later I ran into Michelle–two ells–at our 25th high school reunion. Two beautiful children had accompanied her from California. Though she was as charming as ever, arthritis had forced her retirement from dentistry.

As Paul sang the thirty-eight songs at Reunion Arena, initially I thought I'd scribble a play list on my hand with a pen. He started with "Hello, Goodbye," then went to "All My Loving" and "Getting Better." The person in the seat next to me suggested I use a piece of paper. The only paper I could find was my airline boarding pass receipt, so that's what I used.

Reunion Arena was packed to the rafters. Not all the fans were my age, either. A teenage girl in the next row danced and sang along with every song. There were old hippies, plenty of yuppies (one almost had to be a yuppie to afford a ticket), and lots of small children.

A few of the songs Paul played were unfamiliar to me, such as "Heather's Song," dedicated to his new wife, but most were old friends.

For some odd reason, many songs from my youth come with associations attached, and hearing the songs conjures vivid mental images: "Blackbird"–Surfside Beach near Freeport, Texas. I can smell the salt water. "Mother Nature's Son"–my apartment in Butchertown, Kentucky. I've just received a letter from a girl I knew in college. "The Weight"–the balcony at Park Cities Baptist Church in Dallas, during a Baptist Student Union convention.

"Here Today"–driving slowly south of San Antonio in the middle of the night, looking for snakes. "Maybe I'm Amazed"–in the car with my dad, on our way to buy tomato plants in the spring of some year. "Can't Buy Me Love"–the attic of my pal Dale Britton's house in Kansas. We would listen to Beatles songs and talk about girls. He knew about my thing for Michelle. "Yesterday"–the upstairs hall of my grandparents' home in St. Louis, Missouri. I first heard the song through a tiny radio there, and was spellbound.

When Paul sat at a psychedelic piano on the Reunion Arena stage and launched into "Hey Jude," I pulled out my cell phone and punched my home number, hoping my kids would answer and share the moment. Paul was so loud I couldn't tell if my phone was ringing or not, let alone whether anyone answered. Later I found out they had.

We all sang along with "Hey Jude." Quite a few people wiped away tears. This was, after all, the soundtrack to our lives, performed by the man who wrote it, that guy down there in the red knit shirt and jeans. Thunderous applause followed, then a six-song encore:

"The Long and Winding Road"–driving along 21st Street in Wichita, Kansas, near the stockyards, in the summertime, with the windows rolled down; "Lady Madonna"–sailing down the highway in a 1958 Chevy; "I Saw Her Standing There"–Glorieta, N.M., snow everywhere; "Yesterday;" "Sgt. Pepper's Lonely Heart Club Band"– a humid June afternoon in Kansas; "The End"–my dorm room in Gordon Hall, Lubbock.

Afterwards, walking out of Reunion Arena into the spring night, I thought about the thirteen-year-old girl who tried to call the

Beatles in 1964. That girl became the girl who wrote letters to me in Kentucky, then became my wife and the woman sitting in Seat 2, Row S, Section 128.

So in a way, Fate was right about our destinies being entwined. I just had the spelling wrong.

Cats and Dogs

Wanted: Dead or Alive

Our neighborhood has been terrorized lately by a wily old tomcat I call Osama bin Laden.

This feline is one bad cat. He doesn't appear to belong to anyone but just roams the alleys and slips in and out of whatever yard he wishes, snacking on baby birds, garbage, or whatever else he can find or catch.

My two kitties are mortally afraid of Osama and rightfully so. He lives to fight. During the rare times my cats go outside–they get these urges to explore, and I occasionally relent and let them out into our fenced back yard—he invariably finds them and gives them a good pounding. He'll come right up to my back door, looking for a fight. Bold, yes.

Earlier this year, Osama made the mistake of clawing a neighbor's child. He's unpredictable that way. One minute he was sitting on their front porch, not letting anyone pet him but not acting like a danger either, and the next minute he dug his claws into the little girl's leg before bolting away.

We called the city's animal control people and had a trap set. I didn't want to hurt the old tom–just get rid of him. He was a menace to society. Feral cats have no business setting up shop in a residential neighborhood.

City workers brought a wire trap from which they said no cat had ever escaped. We baited it with a few kernels of dry cat food and waited.

Pretty soon here came Osama, sauntering along like he owned the joint. In his mind probably he did. He sniffed around the trap. Then he lay down next to it and pretended to doze.

His attitude seemed to say, "You're gonna have to do better than this if you want to catch me."

After a week or so of watching Osama toy with the trap, we called the city and told someone to come get it. From a secret hiding place, Osama laughed as the animal control officer put the trap in his truck and drove away. We were back to square one.

At times he'd let you walk right up to him. The thought did occur to me to merely reach out and wring his neck in one quick motion. I'm not a violent person, though, and besides, who knows what diseases that cat might be carrying? One bite and I might be sorry I ever got so close.

Of course a gun would do the trick, but that would be dangerous not to mention illegal. I didn't want to get arrested over this cat.

As the year wore on, Osama appeared and disappeared like a ghost. He could flow over a six-foot wooden fence like water. One day I saw him watching me from under a storage building–his alert, scarred face staring at me like the Sphinx. I grabbed the nearest object–a garden trowel–and threw it at him; rather, at the spot where he'd been.

Recently he attacked my neighbor's child again. This time the neighbor grabbed a baseball bat and chased him down the street, intent on braining that cat. Of course my neighbor didn't even get close. That was when I devised my plan to rid the world of Osama bin Laden.

No cat can resist tuna fish, I reasoned. I drove to the animal shelter and borrowed the city's cat trap again. Without opening the trap door, I set it in the alley and put a fresh can of tuna fish next to it. Things were about to get interesting.

The next day the tuna fish was gone. I repeated this several days in a row, just getting Osama accustomed to the taste of tuna and the presence of a harmless trap. He played right along with my plan.

Then I opened the trap door and set the tuna just inside the door where a cat could eat without getting caught. This he did for several days.

The final phase of my plan was to actually put the tuna all the way into the back of the trap, where Osama would step on the metal plate which springs the door shut. After liberally sprinkling the ground around the trap with yummy tuna juice, I set the can all the way in and went in the house to wait.

As it happened, I was looking out the back window at the exact moment when Osama came strolling down the alley for his daily snack. He noted that the tuna was in a different spot. Circling the trap, he appeared to calculate his odds. He sniffed the juice on the ground.

Ever so slowly, he stretched into the trap as far as he could go without stepping on the spring-loaded trigger. The tuna was still slightly out of reach.

He sat in the dust and pondered the situation. If he went in the trap, he would be caught and taken to the animal shelter where he would surely be put to death. If he stayed out of the trap, he could continue living his life of crime and freedom.

Osama turned and walked away.

****

A Few Words From Women Who Love Cats

It would be pretty easy to write off The Cat Women as a bunch of kooks.

After I wrote about a tomcat named Osama terrorizing my neighborhood, attacking children and beating up other cats (mine included), and after I fantasized about wringing its neck or shooting it (two things I never would actually do–but The Cat Women don't know that), I was deluged with mail from Women Who Love Cats.

For people who compassionately devote themselves to dumb animals, these cat people don't mind using their claws and drawing a little blood, exhibiting a dearth of compassion toward humans pestered by feral cats:

"Mr. Horsley, you are a horse's patoot," wrote one irate cat lover.

"What a total jerk you are," wrote another, "and I am so thankful that you live nowhere near our state. I hope your paper gets enough mail to cost you your job. I think that your name should be Osama."

"You, sir," wrote a third, "are what I consider a 'cat snob.' The only good cat is the one in your home. And naming a cat after a terrorist, a mass murderer? Oh, my, aren't you clever?"

Some tried to blame me for the feral cat loose in my neighborhood: "Do you realize it is cold-hearted, sick people like yourself who allow cats outside who are to blame for his situation?"

This same woman called the tomcat a "poor, defenseless cat" and further suggested that the children being attacked were themselves to blame: "You can't expect me to believe that the child did nothing or didn't try to do anything to the cat. . . . I have three kids and I have cats. . . . I know the truth about that situation."

Another blamed the parents of the child: "I find it interesting that after the first attack, they allowed the child to be outside when the cat reappeared, instead of getting the child into their house, then chasing the cat away."

The lady who called me a "horse's patoot" (I must say I like her style) admitted that she has eleven cats, down from twenty-three last year. Another suggested that society risks another Black Plague if we rid our neighborhoods of feral cats. Quite a few urged me to trap the cat, have it neutered and vaccinated (at my expense) then re-release it into my neighborhood and *feed it for the rest of its natural life.*

Like I said, it would be easy to write them off as a bunch of balmy eccentrics.

However.

A few of their comments made sense.

One woman suggested that a way for people like me to understand people like her is to read her letter and substitute the word *child* every time the word *cat* appears. Some cat lovers feel toward cats like the rest of us feel toward human children.

While I don't share this view, it does help me understand where she's coming from. I'm not going to argue with her, but just try to accept her for who she is.

Another woman wrote that she cried when she read my column. That made me stop and think.

There's so much meanness, violence, and cruelty in this world. Readers told stories of starving cats, drowned kittens, and felines roasted alive. Whatever else you can say about The Cat Women, they are tender-hearted individuals who extend love toward a reviled segment of the animal kingdom.

Something about that appeals to me.

I've learned that there are national and international organizations dedicated to the welfare of feral cats. One of the most popular is Alley Cat Allies (www.alleycat.org), which educates the public about spay/neuter programs and non-lethal ways to deal with the problem of wild cats.

Several women wrote level-headed letters detailing how to trap the cat and turn it over to an animal shelter. One woman on the East Coast arranged for me to get in touch with an animal rescue specialist in Amarillo and went so far as to call the specialist herself to arrange a meeting.

So now I've talked to the local animal rescue people. Together we're going to find a way to trap Osama humanely, have him doctored and neutered, and see if he calms down enough to be adopted.

If not, the notion of releasing Osama back into my neighborhood after he's been fixed is so certifiably nuts that I just might try it and see what happens.

* * *

Animal lovers everywhere might want to know how I finally trapped Osama, the wild tomcat terrorizing my neighborhood.

You recall that this tom was too smart to enter a standard live trap.

The capture involved a can of cat food, lots of patience, and a long piece of nylon twine.

After discovering that Osama was sleeping in an old storage shed behind my house, I started putting cat food in there every day. At first he'd disappear when he saw me coming. Eventually he became so tame that he'd merely slink into the alley until I set out his dinner, and immediately he would enter to eat.

Then I rigged up the string to close the door after he was inside dining on Friskees Prime Entree cat food.

I backed across the yard and lay on my stomach to watch when he entered the shed. He saw me lying there. He also saw the string stretching across the yard, probably due to its unfortunately bright yellow color. He stared at me for a full fifteen minutes.

As he had already demonstrated on numerous occasions, he was no dummy. He knew something was up but didn't know what.

Hunger finally got the best of him, and he hopped into the shed. I counted to a hundred and then yanked that string. The door closed with a solid *ker-clunk*. I had him.

A quick call to Judi Glidewell, cat rehabilitator par excellence, brought her Cat Rescue Squad to my house. In less time than it takes to say "cat scratch fever," Judi had a noose around Osama's midsection and was lifting him through the air.

She directed him to a cage, and that was that.

Now I'm told he's taking to captivity quite well. Neutering and doctoring seem to have agreed with him. The next step will be placing him up for adoption.

* * *

Critter Camp's Judi Glidewell sent along a recent photo of the Cat Formerly Known as Osama. He's looking fit and happy, a contented puss if ever there was one.

In the picture, poinsettias and greenery surround the supine feline, and a fire crackles in the background. His ears are only slightly lowered, as if maybe the photographer hadn't purchased the correct brand of kitty treats. Otherwise he's looking very relaxed. I could be mistaken, but I think his tail might be swishing. Other than that, he's a picture of holiday joy.

Neutering helped changed his marauding ways, so the letters of his former name have been rearranged to form his new name, Samoa, to reflect his new, satisfied self. Samoa is scheduled to be adopted soon.

I'm told there's an outside chance he might run away from his new owner and eventually find his way back to my yard, in which case I'll have to trap him again and take him back to Critter Camp for additional pacification.

It does my heart good to see this cat in a safe environment. He's a good-looking tom. If he and I didn't have all that history between us, I might consider adopting him myself.

****

Bad News is Better Than No News

That was me standing in the middle of the freeway, scooping a cat from the pavement with a shovel.

A person always tries to exercise caution in such enterprises. You don't want to cause an accident, or be on the receiving end of one either. Probably I was breaking a federal regulation or two, being a pedestrian on a government right of way. But I made sure no traffic was coming during the execution of my mission.

Which was to move the cat's remains from the pavement to the side of the highway where a person could safely identify them as possibly belonging to a certain family pet named Rascal, missing for more than three weeks.

As soon as I arrived at the site of the deceased cat, I regretted putting off this task as long as I had. Four days earlier I had spied the feline lying in the southbound lane. It seemed to match the description of Rascal, but I was traveling at a high rate of speed and couldn't be sure.

Every day thereafter I told myself to go check that cat, and maybe put some children's minds at ease. Or not.

You could say there are two kinds of people in the world. Some prefer to avoid unpleasant news if they can. Many owners of missing cats would doubtless go ahead and live their entire lives, privately regretting that Rascal never came home but not thinking too much more about it. They prefer not to go down the "what if" path.

Others can't seem to rest until they know as much as possible, even if the truth is uncomfortable. I seem to fit this latter category. I've sought to know things–anything, everything. If my lawnmower quits running, I'll use a wrench until it's nothing but a pile of parts on the garage floor. I might need help putting it back together, but I also might learn why it quit and be able to prevent the problem next time.

This tendency is not necessarily a virtue. It's gotten me into a few unhappy situations. But still, I'd rather know the truth and be temporarily miserable than be happily committed to a falsehood.

For four days I told myself to check that cat on the freeway, but I resisted for obvious reasons. Finally I realized that if I waited much longer, checking would be pointless.

Once I moved the remains to a safe location, what I discovered was that certain identifying marks were not present on the deceased. It was not Rascal.

Which brought me back to square one. Where could that darned cat be? I've thought of all the various ways a cat can disappear into thin air:

Though he wasn't a wanderer, he might have meandered into a cranky neighbor's yard and been hauled to cat jail on Osage Road. The city gives you seventy-two hours to claim lost cats and dogs, I've learned, so every other day we've driven there to stroll up and down the aisles, searching. Plenty of friendly lost pets are begging to be adopted, but not the one we most wanted to see.

He might have hopped into a Dumpster in the alley and been tipped into a city sanitation truck for transport to the landfill. I ruled out this possibility because he hated the sound of the dump truck and would flee at its approach.

Maybe he got the itchy foot and high-tailed it for parts unknown. One problem with this theory is his extreme fondness for the six o'clock hour, when a can of his favorite food is opened and placed before him.

Even if he wandered off, his stomach would send him home for supper. For seven hundred days in a row he was by the back door at suppertime, without fail. Then *POOF*, he was gone. Also, he's a neutered gentleman of sedentary persuasion, not given to perambulation. He's lazy as the dickens, not a fighter or a ladies' man. I can't see him heading for the hills. Just to be sure, we've combed the neighborhood. Nada.

It has crossed my mind that someone purloined the puss. This theory is held by his "technical" masters, i.e., the people who talked me into getting him in the first place by promising to perform all sorts of outrageous chores for "their" cat. For instance, feeding him (yeah right), cleaning out the litter box (don't make me laugh), etc.

It's hard to imagine anyone stealing a grown cat, though, when so many adorable kittens are free for the asking at the animal shelter. Don't think the adorable kittens have escaped the notice of certain children, either.

But I'm not ready to think about kittens. I want my cat back. I miss him. I dream about him coming home. I can't rest until I know.

* * *

Obituary: Miss Ashley the cat passed away Monday, July 17, 2000. She was born in rural Randall County and had lived most of her life in Potter County, Texas. She never married and is survived by her biological parents of Randall County, numerous brothers and sisters, and her adoptive family, of the home.

Miss Ashley came to Potter County at the age of two months in a carrying case made from a laundry basket with a cardboard lid. She acclimated easily to her new environment and excelled at litter box. She only had a few accidents.

She endeared herself to everyone she met, owing to her sweet disposition and gregarious personality. Her purr could be heard by anyone within a forty-foot radius. Area felines came to realize Ashley would rather play than fight. Her numerous human friends had various nicknames for her, including Puddin', Kitty, and Precious. At the time of death, she was up to date on all her shots and tags.

A brief graveside service was held at the home. Flower arrangements were provided by the family, and interment included her favorite toy. In addition to her adoptive family, she is survived by a special friend, Gus the dog, of the home. In lieu of flowers, motorists are urged to exercise caution when operating a vehicle in residential areas.

****

Saying Goodbye to Gus

Last week it became necessary to say goodbye to Gus the dog, our ten-year-old Lab mix. He had stopped eating, and when I felt around on his belly I discovered an ominous mass the size of a baseball. Gus has eaten lots of objects I considered inedible, but I was pretty sure a baseball wasn't one of them.

A quick trip to the vet brought the bad news. "Uh-oh," the doctor said when he massaged Gus' belly–a word you never want to hear your doctor say. "It feels like cancer, but the only way to know for sure would be to open him up and take a look around."

I didn't like the sound of that, either.

"If the disease is on the liver or lymph nodes, we just won't wake Gus from the anesthesia. He'd have no quality of life even if we tried to remove what we could. However, if it's on the spleen and can be excised, we can remove it without serious harm to Gus."

My intuition said this wasn't going to turn out well. Over the past few months, Gus had begun to run out of gas. Privately I began to mourn at that moment.

Gus came to us as a gift in 1990. His mama was a neighbor's Brittany spaniel named Miss Ellie. His daddy was a black Lab whose name we didn't catch. The pups were born on April Fool's Day.

His birthday seemed appropriate, because Gus was a walking fool. Not once in ten years of evening walks and hikes in the canyon

54

did he fail to throw his whole self into the task. I suppose the Brittany side of his genetic package made him a little hyper, because for every mile I walked, he'd walk three. Sometimes it wore me out just watching him.

The Lab side of him made him gentle and friendly. One time our house was burglarized while we were away. The thief came in through the back door, and I'm sure Gus gave him the same salivary greeting he bestowed upon all guests. He never met a burglar he didn't like.

In preparation for the exploratory procedure, I withheld food and water the evening prior. Doing without food didn't seem to bother Gus, since he wasn't eating anyway. We took one last walk around Memorial Park. Lately he'd been having difficulty keeping up, but that evening I detected a little more pep in his step. Maybe he, too, suspected that his end was near. Who can say how much a dog comprehends?

The next morning the family said its goodbyes. I had explained to the children that Gus might not come home alive from this trip to the vet. His tail thumped against the side of his doghouse as he received farewell pats on the head.

Although it was premature, I was thinking about where in the garden to dig the hole. I knew he wouldn't appreciate being planted too close to a cat, and there are several cats enjoying eternal rest among the tomato vines. Gus went to his empty water bowl, sniffed it, and looked at me.

I rattled his leash and said, "Let's go, boy."

I cried most of the way to the vet. I'd lost a human friend on Father's Day and wasn't sure which loss was the cause of my tears. The two deaths seemed connected. Gus sat in the back seat and looked out the window like always. Was he memorizing every last detail of this marvelous earth? Probably not. Probably he was wondering why his stupid master had dumped out his water and failed to refill it.

Next door to the vet's office is a large vacant lot with lots of fresh odors to investigate. I let Gus take his time. After once around, I wasn't quite ready so we went around again. He gave me a queer look but, opportunist that he is, didn't hesitate to freshen up the scents he'd just freshened.

Finally the dreaded moment came. I slipped off his chain and the vet slipped a nylon noose over his head. I squeezed his neck hard and wished him good luck. The people at the vet's office must have thought I was quite the crybaby.

I went home and went about my business, waiting for the call. Gus' life was full of love and plenty of ham bones. What more could a dog want? I wondered if the grocery would take back an unopened sack of dog food. On the off chance that Gus would make it through this surgery, I didn't begin the hole yet.

The phone rang.

"Well, it was cancer just like we thought," the vet said calmly. "The tumor was the size of a softball, connected to the spleen, and didn't seem to involve other organs. He lost a lot of blood so I want to keep him overnight. You can pick him up in the morning. He should be okay in a few days."

A paradox: Life is so fragile and yet so durable.

* * *

People have asked how Gus the dog is faring after his bout with surgery. I'm happy to report that Gus has regained his zest for life and seems to have twice the energy as before his malignant spleen was removed. He capers like a pup when it's time for the evening walk.

Funny thing: He has stopped limping too. He had developed a lame front paw and was taking expensive anti-arthritis tablets. After the surgery–which came nowhere near his front paw–the limp vanished. Explain that, Doctor.

L.J. of Amarillo responded to my Gus column by sending a copy of *The Canadian Record* newspaper. *The Record's* cover story concerns Tess, a Scottish terrier from Lipscomb County who spent a week inside a hollow cottonwood tree fifteen feet above ground before being liberated when the tree was cut down and sawed open.

Children named Caroline and Sam were pleased when the tree was cleaved and out popped their dog.

"They pulled her out," says the story, "to discover a skinnier pet than they remembered, covered with bites from carpenter ants, and . . . 'smelling like wet wood.' "

****

What More Could a Dog Want?

Gus the dog entered into rest Thursday, Nov. 29, 2001. He was eleven people years old.

Some might recall his close call last summer. Had it not been for the surgical skills of Dr. Darrell Yarbrough, we would have lost him then.

Instead, we got to enjoy Gus for six additional months, five of them good.

On his final trip to the vet last week, Gus looked out the window all the way. Then he turned to me, gazed up with those soft brown Lab eyes, and this is what he said:

"Hey, Dave, why is everyone crying today? I've had a fantastic life–all a dog could ever ask for and more. You shouldn't feel bad about this.

"Think about all those trips to the canyon. We tore up some trails together, didn't we? Remember how I'd blast through patches of prickly pear until my paws looked like pincushions, and then tiptoe back for sticker removal? Seems like you always carried tweezers.

"You didn't realize it at the time, but those hikes were precious to me. There was no place I'd rather be than out on the trails, drinking water out of your hat and taking in the scents.

"Of course, I could have done without that time you hoisted me up a cliff using belts knotted together. Otherwise, it was all a delight.

"The walks through the neighborhood were terrific too. Remember the time I mistook a plastic bag for a vicious monster? Thanks for not laughing too hard.

"What about the time the backyard fence bit me and wouldn't let go? I still don't know how that happened. Lucky for me you heard the commotion.

"Our dead-of-night walks were always fun. One thing about you, Dave: I never knew what time of day or night you'd feel like walking.

"I guess humans are funny that way. You take a dog–he'll run around in daylight, but come nightfall, all he wants is a warm place to hole up.

"Which reminds me–thanks a million for that electric heater. This short hair never was much account on a cold night. The homemade doghouse was a nice touch too.

"In fact, all my life was pretty grand. Whenever I needed anything, there it was. Someone always provided. When I got hungry, food appeared. When the algae in my water bowl got too green, you'd always scrub it out. When I'd tear a toenail, off we'd go to get it fixed.

"For some reason, people just seemed to love me. It's the darnedest thing. No matter where I went, everyone wanted to touch me. Children would want to pat my head. Women liked to feel of me. That friend of yours–what was his name?–would sit and read a book while he stroked my ears. I don't know how heaven could be much better than that.

"So cheer up, Dave. I have no regrets. Well, very few, anyway. I'm sorry about the wanting-in-wanting-out days. It's a dog thing, and I doubt you'd understand.

"I'm sorry I didn't have children. When I was young, I always figured it would happen eventually. But then, coincidental with a trip to the vet, I lost interest. I'm not sure what happened.

"Probably I should have made more effort to get to know the cats. You can give them my food bowl, since they were always trying to eat out of it.

"Give them whatever's left of my dog food, too, if they want it. If not, give it to the squirrels. I'm sorry I never did catch one of those rascals.

"Now I'm too old and worn down to think about catching squirrels. Walking has become a chore. I've lost my appetite–I'm not even thirsty. I can't seem to get comfortable. It's weird.

"You've been dreading this day, I know. Dogs are tops at reading body language, and you're not as good as you think at hiding your feelings. I can see your tension and sadness.

"Dave, you're doing the right thing. Like the song says, all things must pass. It's time for me to go. It's been one heckuva party, and I thank you for it.

"Don't worry about me now. I always find my way home."

Gus is survived by his family, by numerous friends and relatives, and by special friends Corkie and Little Guy.

A brief service was held at the home. Interment was in the family garden, between the tomatoes and the pole beans.

In lieu of flowers, memorials can be made to the S.P.C.A.

Faith

Feeling Like a Stranger in My Own Religion

When I first heard that Franklin Graham, son of the famous evangelist, was coming to town for a three-night event, I knew I wanted to hear him. His father is one of the few popular evangelists (Greek: "good news bringer") for whom I have much respect, but I didn't know anything about the younger Graham.

I've probably been to more revivals and evangelistic crusades than most people. I've witnessed the best and many others who weren't as gifted. I thought I could write fairly about Franklin Graham.

So on a breezy Sunday evening I joined a throng of believers at Dick Bivins Stadium who came seeking, perhaps, a reed blowing in the wind, a voice crying in the wilderness. I left feeling troubled in spirit.

Feeling troubled after worship is nothing new. I've had a lifetime of practice. You might say that one purpose of worship is to disquiet the spirit, to shake up complacency. The prophets of old made a career of pricking the conscience of people who considered themselves godly, and Jesus certainly had a gift for disturbing the self-satisfied.

But critiquing Franklin Graham is like critiquing the pope–there's no graceful way to do it without appearing anti-God to some. Even though the Lord liberally criticized the publicly religious of his day, too many Christians today are thin-skinned about criticism. We're quick to point out the errors of other faiths, however.

A lot of good people spent months getting ready for the Franklin Graham event. It was a well-planned, well-run show. But to me it had the look and feel of a party by Christians for Christians. Sure, Christians deserve to party, but where were the kids in gang attire, people with tongue studs and tattoos, angry drug addicts, prostitutes with AIDS, drunken transients, outcasts and outlaws? In other words, the unwanted misfits of society whom Jesus seemed to attract?

What I saw were 24,000 nicely dressed, mostly Caucasian Christians. Hispanics seemed noticeably absent, even though the featured singer was Jaci Velasquez. I counted six African-Americans, but I later realized that the same black man had gone past three times.

Maybe it shouldn't surprise me that a middle-aged man like Graham would draw a throng similar to himself, but I expected the crowd to be more representative not only of Amarillo, but of the target audience.

I also expected Graham to be different. He shares with his father the lanky frame and rugged good looks but lacks the orator's voice, timing, and charisma. That's not his fault–preachers' kids seldom measure up to their old men. He seems a decent fellow, runs a smooth festival, and eases much human misery through the relief organization Samaritan's Purse.

But a traveling evangelist invites comparison to other orators, and Graham seemed stiff, maybe even uncomfortable, in the pulpit. It made me wonder if his deeper gifts lay in other ministries and he'd been urged into the pulpit against his instincts.

His message wasn't what I expected either. Based loosely on the fifth chapter of Daniel–the "handwriting on the wall" story–it managed to slam homosexuals, abortion-rights advocates ("Some of you are guilty of murder–abortion is murder!"), sexually active teens, and other faiths ("There is no way you can come to a Holy God except through Jesus Christ").

Calling a young woman who's had an abortion a murderer doesn't seem like the best way to reach out to her. If any homosexuals were in the audience that night, they probably left feeling despised and rejected by the Lamb of God. And suggesting to people of other religions that their faith is false and ours is true requires an immodest degree of spiritual arrogance.

Some of what Graham said I found downright bizarre. He compared the unfortunate souls aboard the doomed Concorde flight with the drunken court of King Belshazzar in ancient Babylon. It seemed insensitive. He even managed to turn the tragedy aboard the submarine Kursk into a sermon point. To me, Christian charity might have us delay capitalizing on the deaths of fellow humans, at least until their families have a chance to get them home and bury them.

I wish Franklin Graham, knowing he had a stadium full of the faithful, had used his time to a better end. He might have spoken a prophetic message, challenging the hypocrisy and self-righteousness of which all believers have ample measure.

Or he might have nurtured the body of Christ, using his pastoral role to speak encouragement to the vast majority of his audience who weren't murderers, liars, adulterers, transmitters of sexual diseases, drunks, abortionists, or any of the rest of his list of the guilty. Most seemed like ordinary people trying to live the best way they know.

My feeling of disquiet remains. While my journalistic task is to immerse myself in experience and then write honestly, I don't expect many will share my lack of enthusiasm.

Sometimes I feel like a stranger in my own religion.

****

Plain and Simple, It's Not

When I was a child, I pretty much believed what people told me.

"Salamanders can live in hot coals without being burned."

"A fat elf in a red suit brings presents down the chimney."

Once I reached a certain age, however, I began to wonder about some of the things I'd been taught. I was always curious that way.

I didn't have to cook any amphibians to conclude that I'd been fed a line of hooey about salamanders. The depressing truth about Santa Claus almost ruined Christmas one year, but I felt myself grow up a little.

I grew up in a conservative Christian home. I gave my heart to Jesus at age nine and was baptized into the fellowship of the saints, but that didn't stop me from wondering about the things I'd been taught. Some of it seemed pretty far-fetched, and separating truth from falsehood was a ticklish business.

In school, for example, we applied the laws of science to understand how the physical world behaved. Scientific laws could be verified and repeated.

But in matters of faith there was no set of universal laws to apply. Each religion and denomination seemed sure its way was best. I grew skeptical of glib answers.

Luckily I had responsible spiritual guides through much of my youth, and I escaped the grosser manipulation and abuse which turn some people against the church. The church and the people in it blessed and enriched me in countless ways and continue to do so.

But I'm still not one-hundred percent comfortable with religion, mine or anyone else's. And the more certain someone is that his way is the only way, to the exclusion of other views, the more my skepticism kicks in.

After I left Kansas and began my solitary way in the world, I encountered people who didn't seem to fit the neat categories I'd been taught. My religion allowed for only two kinds of people–lost and saved. The lost included all non-Christians, including Catholics and Mormons; most other denominations (especially Church of Christ, who got baptism wrong); and quite a few Baptists, whom God would spit out–*PATOO*–for being lukewarm.

Heaven, I'd come to believe, would be populated mostly by Southern Baptists plus a few Methodists to keep us honest. But then I met people of other faiths whose lives exhibited all the classic signs of a Christian character: humility, patience, compassion, honesty, charity, devotion–traits to which, coincidentally, most religions aspire.

And many of the hell-raisers I met on Saturday night were in church the next morning. Some of the Christians seemed less Christian than the non-Christians. Distinctions began to blur.

Now, after more than forty years of wrestling with faith and skepticism and trying to discover the proper role of critical thinking in religion, I find myself at a curious place. I'm more convinced than ever of God's grace in the world, moving in all faiths. And I'm more aware of religious dishonesty than ever.

For example, I received letters in response to my Franklin Graham column suggesting that if only I would read the Bible, everything would become plain and simple. I've been reading the Bible for almost half a century. I have a theology degree from a top Baptist seminary. And I'm here to tell you that if there's anything the Bible is not, it's plain or simple.

Majestic, subtle, rich, eternal–yes. Plain and simple? Not to me. The more I study the Bible, the more I'm aware of my ignorance. While I understand the yearning for simple answers to life's questions, artificial simplicity isn't doing anybody a favor. If you want me to check my mind at the door of your church, I'll move along.

The Bible is a set of documents written over a period of hundreds of years, sometimes to known audiences for known purposes, sometimes not. Sometimes the author is apparent but other times obscure. Sometimes what the writer intends seems obvious, but other times it's anything but obvious.

People who quote the Bible in judgment of others conveniently overlook the fact that they've taken a complex, 1,500-page collection of religious writings and selected only the equivalent of half a dozen pages to use against people they consider sinners. This really gets my Irish up.

Jesus, we're told, directed his most stinging criticism against the religious know-it-alls of his day: the first-century Pharisees who were just as cocksure of their views as some of today's religious authorities.

God have mercy on us for seeing the splinter in the sinner's eye and ignoring the plank in our own.

* * *

I expected to get hammered because of what I said about the Franklin Graham event, but what I didn't expect was the volume of mail, phone calls, and personal comments in agreement. While a viewpoint's validity isn't determined by vote, it's gratifying to know I'm not alone.

Because of Franklin Graham, I've been thinking more about my beliefs and views. How we determine a viewpoint's validity is an important question. Are all viewpoints equally valid? If so, what's the point in wrestling with faith issues if any answer will suffice? Why not just believe whatever feels good?

And if all viewpoints aren't equally valid, what's the best way to choose between them? These questions lead back at least as far as Abraham, Moses, and Plato, and might provide grist for a column titled, "How Do You Know What You Think You Know?"

****

Trust and Obey

What's the proper role of critical thinking in religion? Should certain areas of thought be off limits to believers?

During earlier periods of our country's history–and even today in some nations–you could be jailed for asking the wrong religious questions. That's the trouble with thinking: It leads to questions. It often leads to answers, too, but not always.

The dichotomy between religious ways of thinking and what I'll call scientific ways of thinking has produced uncomfortable tensions in my life. These two views of reality don't reside easily in one soul.

Some believe that since faith deals with the spiritual realm and science with the physical, there's no conflict between faith and science. Trouble is, I've never been good at keeping them apart.

For example, we used to sing a hymn in church: "Trust and obey, for there's no other way to be happy in Jesus but to trust and obey."

The idea was to obey authority (the pastor, the Bible, God) and you'll be happy.

Blind obedience to authority, however, seemed contrary to what I was taught in school. The scientific method is to hypothesize and test. Science moves forward by questioning its assumptions. That's how we learned that the earth circles the sun instead of vice versa.

Singing that song put me in a bind. On the one hand, I wanted to be a good Christian. On the other hand, I wanted to be a good steward of my God-given intelligence. How could I trust and obey while questioning my assumptions?

My beliefs about the Bible provide an illustration. Many people think the Bible was written by God. I recall a preacher once saying that even the punctuation and the page numbers had God as their author. Should we, therefore, follow Scripture in everything we think, do, and say? Should we "trust and obey" since it's God himself who said it?

Some do claim to live this way. I once saw a bumper sticker: "God said it, I believe it, that settles it!"

My problem with this attitude is that it's dishonest. People who claim to live by every word of Scripture don't really try to. People who say God's Word is their ultimate authority actually mean they select parts of the Bible and minimize or ignore the rest.

Which is okay. We all do it. We have favorite verses, books, characters, and themes which move us. Some prefer the Psalms, some the parables of Jesus. Some spend their time studying the Revelation of John.

Nobody–but nobody–tries to live by every single word of Scripture. Women don't keep quiet in church like St. Paul recommends. We don't sacrifice bulls and shun pork as Jehovah commands. We recognize the legitimacy of divorce and remarriage although Jesus teaches something different. So where does that leave us?

It leaves me applying my critical thinking even to matters of faith. That's the only way I can be a Christian. Faith is too important to leave to "the authorities" even if they seem trustworthy. I have to probe and test for truth myself. In today's shrinking world of diverse views and traditions, testing for truth seems the only way to be a responsible steward.

When attempting to test for truth, I take many things into account. I listen to evidence, consult experts, examine tradition, and exercise reason. But in the end, it's little old me who decides what I think is true.

No priest or potentate, no cloistered scholar or TV preacher has the final word about what I will believe. No marks on a piece of paper–whether it's the Bible, the Koran, or the Book of Mormon– are the final authority in matters of faith and practice. Since I'm the interpreter of the marks, the final authority is me.

While I might approach the wisdom of the ages with hat in hand, I'm my own court of final appeals. Sometimes the wisdom of the ages is flat wrong. This might sound like a recipe for anarchy unless you believe in the Spirit within.

People who say they're Bible-believing Christians who look to God's Word for all life's answers really mean they look until they find an answer they can live with and pass over ones which don't seem to fit. Which is exactly what I'm saying too.

I'll listen to the testimony of the saints as well as the witness of sinners. If something makes sense, I'll believe it for as long as it seems true. If it doesn't make sense, wild horses can't force me to believe.

Most religious people, I suspect, harbor private doubts about whether every detail of what they've been taught is true. They keep quiet because they value certainty above honesty.

I'm the opposite. I'd rather face an uncomfortable truth than knowingly live an illusion.

Trust and obey? An informed conscience is what I trust and obey, so help me God.

****

David T. Horsley

Truth Should Have Room to Roam

Question: Should followers of various world religions be allowed to attempt the conversion of believers of other religions? Or put another way, would it be a good idea to prohibit certain kinds of proselytizing?

This question recently came to me as I read a newspaper article describing an Italian bishop's complaint that Islamic fundamentalists were trying to turn good Catholics into good Muslims. Under the headline, "Islam Aiming for Christian Conquest," Bishop Giuseppe Bernardini of Izmir, Turkey, warned fellow bishops of a resurgence of Muslim activity aimed at converting Christians to Islam.

"The 'domination' has already started," Bishop Bernardini said, "with petrodollars, used not to create jobs in poor countries . . . but to build mosques and cultural centers in Christian countries . . . including Rome, center of Christianity." He seems to be implying that someone ought to stop Islam from making inroads into traditionally Christian areas.

But his next statement is telling: "Who cannot see in this a clear program of expansion and *reconquest?*" (Italics mine).

Such a question strikes me as terribly ironic. The *re* in reconquest was made possible by centuries of invasion, brutality, slaughter, and repression by Christians against the "infidels" who inhabited the historic nations of the Middle East. In other words, Bishop Bernardini seems to think that since we Christians already conquered the Muslims once, they ought to have the decency to *stay* conquered, God bless 'em!

In case you think this issue is mostly confined to the other side of the globe, think again. In the early summer of each year, Jehovah's Witnesses go door to door on my street, trying to spread their own particular version of Christianity. I've had extended conversations with some of them, and I received the distinct impression that if I chose to abandon my Methodist way of looking at things and took up the Jehovah's Witnesses way, it would be perfectly all right with them. So in a sense you might say the Witnesses were out seeking converts.

Should this sort of thing be allowed?

Similarly, should we permit Mormon missionaries to pedal their bikes up and down our town, seeking people who might be open to the Mormon way? You've seen them with their black pants and white shirts and little backpacks. Is this what you would call acceptable behavior by Mormons in an area where Catholic and Baptist and Church of Christ and other "traditional" churches dominate?

Or take the example of something called the International Church of Christ. I admit my knowledge of the group is sketchy, but I do know that recently its members applied for a charter to become an authorized campus organization at West Texas A&M University. The WT campus newspaper editorialized against granting the charter.

Eventually the charter application was returned for technical reasons, but the question remains: Should "outside" groups such as the ICOC be permitted into the arena of public discussion? Should we allow our impressionable college students to have the truth of their ideas challenged by a variety of outside influences?

My answer: It depends on what we consider truth to be. If we see truth as a shining hilltop citadel, defended at all cost against outsiders, then maybe we should prohibit views contrary to our own. In this case, all we need to do is define exactly which of many versions of truth is the One Truth, develop a self-validating system of absolute certainty, and champion that cause at the expense of the rest.

If we decide, for instance, that the Methodist way is the One True Way, then we'll run those Mormons right off the porch with a broom.

If, on the other hand, we tend to see truth more like water, constantly moving through all of life, circulating through each living thing and giving some of itself to each, then we recognize the impossibility of trying to claim all the water in the world as our own personal possession. Water is hard to hoard. Viewing truth in this way, we'll learn to find pleasure in the sound of rain on our neighbor's roof as well as our own, or watching clouds, or peeling a juicy orange. We might invite those Mormons, Muslims, ICOC, and Jehovah's Witnesses to join us in dialogue on the porch swing, over a cold drink.

My favorite seventeenth-century poet and Christian apologist John Milton argued in *Areopagitica* that truth should be allowed to roam free: "She needs no policies, nor stratagems, nor licensing to make her victorious–those are the shifts and the defenses that error uses against her power. Give her but room, and do not bind her when she sleeps, for then she speaks not true . . . but then rather turns herself into all shapes except her own."

So to the good bishop of Izmir, I would recommend he allow the truth of Christianity to grapple unfettered with any and all challengers. Don't shrink from a contest between two mighty views of reality. If a mosque rises in the shadow of the cathedral, maybe the Almighty is trying to teach us something.

****

Angels in the Alley

There's a homeless guy sleeping behind my house. He arrives at dusk and is up and gone at dawn. Gone to where, I couldn't say.

A month or so ago someone discarded an old mattress in the alley in such a way that it lay in the path of traffic. Fearing the garbage truck might be deterred by such an obstacle, I dragged the mattress to one side and folded it in half so it wouldn't take up so much space.

As it happened, the folded half didn't stay down. It raised itself up against the fence, creating a pretty nice little sleeping area or padded bench. It was a queen-size mattress with a few stains.

Next thing I knew, empty beer cans and soft drink cups began to appear beside the mattress. It was awhile before I put two and two together.

Then one morning I went early to the Dumpster and saw the guy sleeping. He had long scraggly hair and a ragged beard. He looked comfortable there on the queen-size mattress, sleeping as if God's in his heaven and all's right with the world. Still, part of me was outraged that a man would be sleeping in my alley. I thought maybe I should call the police.

Another part of me thought: What harm is he doing?

A week passed and I began to smell a slight urine odor in the alley. It stood to reason that if the guy was drinking beer and sleeping among the trumpet vines and nightshades, he wasn't hiking to the Amarillo Club to use the facilities.

The conservative side of me disapproved of a stranger urinating in my alley and wanted something done about the problem.

My liberal side reminded me that it wasn't too long ago that I used to whiz in the woods. As usual, my liberal side won out.

The woods whizzing happened during a period in my life when I supported my family as a carpenter. A man hired me to help build a house in the woods and, as soon as the septic system was installed, asked me not to use the toilet unless absolutely necessary. In other words, please whiz in the woods–that was his message.

It took awhile for a city boy like myself to grow accustomed to that. But eventually I did, and soon it felt weird to use indoor plumbing when there were so many thirsty bushes outside.

So, contemplating the stranger urinating in my alley, I had to remind myself that there's nothing intrinsically evil about that. He wasn't exposing himself to children. He wasn't creating a nuisance. He wasn't stealing anything or asking for a handout. He had simply found a comfort in what surely was an otherwise sorrowful life and was taking advantage of it.

Still, my conservative side wanted to call the cops or at least phone the city's heavy trash people and ask them to remove that mattress. No mattress, no homeless guy–end of story.

My liberal side said hold the phone. It began to quote Scripture, something my liberal side is fond of doing. "For when I was hungry, you gave me food; when thirsty, you gave me drink; when I was a stranger you took me into your home, when naked you clothed me. When I was ill you came to my help, when in prison you visited me."

This, according to Matthew, was Christ himself talking.

Was it possible, I wondered, that this homeless guy urinating in the alley was Christ in disguise? What did men do along the shores of Galilee when they needed to relieve themselves? Was I entertaining an angel unawares?

Looking at the situation with somewhat different eyes, I imagined that the advent of this bearded stranger was Christ's arrival in our city. He roamed the alleys and shelters of our town, sleeping on sand burrs and eating out of Dumpsters. He was mostly invisible.

Then one happy day he found a decent mattress on which to lay his weary head. It wasn't new, but it was a sight better than what he'd had and plenty good enough for a vagabond. As he had done long ago, he quietly made his home in an unexpected place.

And what did I want to do? Have the mattress removed by the proper authorities, sending Christ back to the thorns.

Instead, I took a cup of coffee to the alley one morning. I really didn't think the homeless guy was Christ, but why take a chance?

"Anything you did for one of my brothers here, however humble, you did for me."

He politely declined the coffee, saying that he was on his way to a place where he would receive breakfast.

"I have food that you know not of," whispered my Bible-quoting side.

This evening before writing these words, I took two bottles of imported beer to the alley, resolved to sit with the stranger and listen to his story.

The alley was silent and dark. The mattress was empty.

****

We Have Much to be Thankful For

Dear God,

I give you thanks for the variety of seasons, especially for this one now with its colorful endings, Indian summers, the sound of leaves underfoot each morning, the smell of air growing colder, long and longer shadows every afternoon, early darkness with ancient Orion wheeling high and proud again across his frozen domain. It is a wonder-full world.

I give you thanks for making a life in which people receive such an unlimited variety of choices. You must have known this would result in a constant state of near-anarchy, but you went ahead with it. Awesome.

Thanks, too, for making humans capable of eating three moderate meals a day or one big one and for all the resultant pleasures of ritual, sensation and taste, conversation, and rhythms of hunger and satisfaction. It's a good system.

Thanks for the curious ability you gave the earth to heal itself, to generate life from death, without which we'd be afloat in poisoned seas of our own making or sitting atop a smouldering mound of history's rubbish, but with which even our folly and ignorance of your Creation aren't fatal to us unless we persist in them.

Thanks for the simple daily spectacles of sky and cloud and color which, if I can learn to appreciate them, provide even greater drama than prime time TV.

Thanks for providing a spirit of tolerance in people, which lets Republican sit down to supper with Democrat, pro- and anti-everything chat respectfully with each other, adversaries kneel together at the Communion rail, antagonists with scant warmth congratulate each other when a child is born, old enemies pause to consider if just for a moment the tiniest impulse of reconciliation.

Thanks for making our minds naturally curious. We might just as easily have been as mentally inert as cows or starfish. Instead our minds rove the universe, seeking to understand. That was a nice touch.

Thanks for hard-wiring us for adaptability and change. Grief, for example, might kill us if we couldn't grow through it. Ecstasy might have a similar outcome. Instead we assimilate, modify, learn to like things we once didn't, or at the very least cover our wounds with scars and our pain with pearl.

Thanks not only for the love we feel we deserve and ought to receive, but also for undeserved love, unlooked-for regard, the unexpected kindness of strangers and friendliness of acquaintances. In an indifferent dog-eat-dog universe, we might expect to find only selfishness and greed; instead we find fondness, affinity, self-sacrifice. I don't understand this but I thank you for it.

Thanks for constructing the human heart with such interesting combinations of infantile urges and hatreds on the one hand, and mature wisdom on the other hand. It does seem at times that the infantile urges and hatreds have the upper hand. But you've made it possible for even those twin demons to be transformed by kindness into something like eccentric uncles, bereft of their former destructive power.

Thanks for visionaries like the Pilgrims and Mozart and Frank Lloyd Wright, who transform the world by the scale of their vision, and for normal people like my postal carrier who transforms my mailbox every day into a zone of modest anticipation.

Thanks for all the millions of ordinary gracious moments occurring constantly throughout the earth: parents caring for children, children playing and exploring, teachers showing patient dedication to a task, minimum-wage nursing home employees being kind merely because they prefer to be, people making music for its own sake, craftsmen doing good work when inferior work would suffice.

Thanks for the furious fertility of almost every square inch of our planet: the blooming life of oceans, the teeming soil, the air chock-full of spores and pollen and winged seed and other soaring life, sidewalk cracks jammed with sprouts, city landfills swarming with white gulls.

Thanks for filling life with enough mystery–hiding things from the wise, you might say–for a lifetime of wondering. And for the marvelous paradoxes lying hidden behind ordinary things: how a fire in the hearth warms the soul but fire out of control is the devil's tool, how a glass of wine is so good with dinner but too much wine leads to grief, how sex at the right time with the right person is a taste of heaven but the same gift, abused, is pure hell.

And thanks for making the complicated and expensive pleasures of life less accessible than the immediate and simple ones: coffee at sunrise, poetry, pumpkin pie. Amen.

Sports, Health, and Fitness

My New Favorite Sport

I became a soccer fan on Saturday, July 10, 1999 at about 3:00 p.m. Central Time, at least half an hour before Brandi Chastain took off her shirt in front of millions–maybe billions–of television viewers. In case you were in a distant galaxy that day, that's when the U.S. Women's Soccer team won the World Cup, the big kahuna championship of soccer.

Before that day, I'd never given soccer much thought. I hope this doesn't sound bigoted, but soccer always has seemed sort of a Third-World sport, vaguely foreign and unfamiliar. We already have the uniquely American spectator sport of football that I don't watch, so I've never needed another game not to watch.

It's true I observed several years of kids' soccer games from the sidelines. But somehow I never saw the virtues of soccer before that Saturday Brandi "temporarily lost her mind" (her words) and disrobed on international TV and in front of 90,185 fans at the Rose Bowl.

Now I've done a one-eighty about soccer. It seems vastly superior to any other sport you can watch on television, especially football, for reasons I will now enumerate:

Commercials. Ever put a stopwatch on an NFL football game to see how many minutes of actual play occur during a regular game? Don't do it–it will depress you to learn you're so mentally challenged that you'd endure that many commercials for so little sport. With soccer (I didn't know this until the Saturday Brandi stripped), there are two forty-fve-minute halves. No commercials until halftime. None, nada, zip. That's because there's no *time* for commercials, on account of the:

Nonstop Action. You want action? Soccer gives you plenty. In fact, soccer gives you *too* much action. With soccer, there's something happening *every second* of the first period. No time for bathroom breaks or trips to the fridge. Ditto the second period, and the same goes for:

Overtime. Soccer overtime is different from football overtime. With football, overtime can be just as drawn out and ad-choked as regular play. Only the NFL could make something called "Sudden Death" seem boring. With soccer the overtime continues, commercial-free just like regulation time, then at the end a woman takes off her shirt. How you gonna improve on that? Especially since in soccer there's no:

Hot-dogging. You've seen NFL players score and then strut around like roosters on Viagra, spike the ball feverishly, inciting the crowd to worship. As sickening a display of self-congratulatory posturing and egomania as you'll see this side of MTV. You won't see much of that in soccer because, well, not much *happens* in soccer worth crowing about. Even when something does happen, the players are too exhausted to strut.

NFL running backs could take a lesson here. The most exciting moment in Saturday's match wasn't Brandi Chastain's final penalty goal or even her tearing off her clothes to reveal a black sports bra.

No, the most exciting moment was goalkeeper Briana Scurry's block of China's third penalty kick. In my book, Scurry was the real hero of the game, and she modestly celebrated for maybe thirty seconds before play resumed. Sometimes less is more, especially when you're up against:

The Rules of Soccer. Of course, no one really understands what's happening in soccer, because the game was invented in Third-World countries where rules depend on which military junta is in power at the moment. With no rules to confuse viewers, there's no jumping up from the sofa and screaming, "OFF SIDES! OFF

SIDES!" because you wouldn't know off sides from OFF! Insect Repellent.

You don't even know how many players are supposed to be on the field. They seemed to start with five, then more and more kept appearing until I think each team had twenty-three players active on the field at the end. With so many players to keep in uniforms, you'd think equipment would be a problem, but it's really not, because in soccer:

There's No Equipment to Speak of! No shoulder pads. No helmets to hurl against the ground during temper tantrums. No annoying measuring chains because the ball never holds still enough to measure. Besides, there are no hash marks, so there's nothing to measure *from* or *to*.

No down markers because in soccer it's always fourth down and goal. No expensive uniforms, just ordinary shirts and shorts and black underwear, which we later learned was a Nike Inner Actives sports bra, available at your better athletic stores for around $40.

So from now on, that will be me in front of the TV, hanging on every head shot and bicycle kick, just as soon as I figure out when soccer season starts, or ends, or if there *is* a season. And next time Brandi Chastain kicks a goal, the eerie silence you'll hear will be men everywhere holding their breath.

****

Running In Circles

Notwithstanding its numerous benefits to body and soul, jogging always has been a peculiar bane of my existence.

In high school all the really desirable girls–meaning those who never would consider dating guys in my group–were attracted to the athletes. So I became an athlete in training. I tried tennis first but spent so much time running after errant balls that the coach suggested I forget about balls and rackets and just concentrate on the running.

That sounded good to me. A kid from our school had recently broken the four-minute mile, and our track and field program still basked in Jim Ryun's glory.

I decided to become the next Jim Ryun. Defying known laws of physics, at the crack of dawn I'd rise, suit up, and tackle a long hill near my house. With a tailwind I could usually make it back down again.

Such training was probably good for me, but it didn't land me a spot on the track team like I'd hoped. Instead, I was invited to join the cross-country team.

If there's anything worse than running a mile over flat country, it's running two miles over rolling country. The coveted letter jacket remained elusive.

Later Jim Ryun stumbled in Mexico City and faded into oblivion, and with him faded my Olympian dream.

Still later, after a decade of on-and-off running, I realized what was missing from my life: the exhilaration of completing a marathon. I trained like crazy for a month, and on marathon day learned the true meaning of the phrase, *waves of nausea.* I crossed the finish line just as two giggling teenage girls sprinted past.

Finally, teenage girls were chasing me!

Since then I've scaled back my training program to a few lethargic jogs each week. I've never experienced that endorphin high some runners feel. Running isn't fun or glamorous. Concrete surfaces jar the joints, the Panhandle's dry air cracks lips and hands, and our wind seems to tilt the landscape uphill both ways.

The cinder path at Ellwood Park, I learned, is easier on the knees, so I began jogging there amid occasional catcalls from transients huddled around hobo fires.

"Hey Buddy, got the time?" they'd call as I lumbered past.

One time a wino leaped from his shade and flew past me, arms and legs flailing, to the cheers of his companions. I had to admire his style. I would have asked him for the time if I'd been able to catch my breath.

Another time I tripped over my own feet and went down hard, smashing my Walkman to smithereens and skinning my knees and elbows. Luckily it was a cold day, and no one was around to see my encounter with gravity.

During the past few months, I've noticed a new guy working out at the park. His circuit runs counter to mine, so we pass, facing each other, several times. Etiquette demands a greeting the first time we cross, and then we ignore each other.

He's hard to ignore, however. One arm hangs useless at his side, its wrist and hand curled, claw-like. One leg doesn't work right, either. In his good arm he clutches an aluminum walking aid. His unsteady gait works up a pretty good sweat.

I don't know what happened to create his disability. The first time I saw him, I figured it was a head injury, maybe a car wreck. I felt sad to see him struggling so.

But he kept after it. Week after week he'd hobble big loops around the park. My attitude toward him began to change. Whereas at first I noticed how different we were–he with his infirmity and me relatively intact–gradually I began to see our similarities.

We both were trying to get the most from our limited capacity. We shared a solitary urge that drew us to the park even on days when he and I were the only humans to be seen.

Whatever our differences, come late afternoon, when the elm trees threw long shadows, and weak orange light glowed from nearby church towers, we'd both start pulling on our running shoes.

Both of us were committed to resisting the inevitable as long as possible.

In the end, of course, time, gravity, and Newtonian physics will have their way with us all. Bodies at rest will tend to remain at rest whether we like it or not.

In the meantime, Sir Isaac Newton can eat my dust.

****

Brain Relieved of Command by Lower Power

Scene One–The Jogging Track At Ellwood Park

Brain: Okay, people, listen up! Begin jogging on my mark! 3,2,1! COMmence . . . JOG! Left! Right! Left! Right!

Ankles: Ow, ow, ow, ow! That really hurts. I told you we should have warmed up first.

Hips: I think I've got a pointer going here. Yes, it's definitely a pointer. Extremely painful now. I'm dropping back.

Brain: Keep moving, people. That's it, nice and slow. Hut, hut! Looking good.

Spine: You call this looking good? We look like Lurch on *The Addams Family*!

Knees: Hey, what's that sound? We've never made that sound before! Something popping. Did somebody fire a weapon?

Brain: That's just nitrogen pockets. Nothing to worry about.

Knees: Nitrogen pockets? That stuff's flammable! We're gonna blow!

Thighs: Would you shut your face? We're the ones doing all the work.

Lungs: My left foot! We're burning up in here. I smell smoke.

Stomach: That's just me. Major acid reflux starting. Oh, why didn't we get a Pepcid before we left HQ?

Brain: Get ahold of yourselves. No one ever died from a little stomach acid.

Stomach: You call this a little? Does the term *Atlantic Ocean* mean anything to you?

Glutes: Quit your whining, fat boy. You're a wuss.

Knees: Lay off him. Just because your last name's Maximus doesn't make you better than us.

Brain: Okay, people, let's pick up the pace.

Lungs: Somebody call 911!

Scene Two–Twenty Minutes Later

Ears: Hear that? Those hobos want to know if we've got the time.

Mouth: Tell 'em to save their wine money and buy a clock!

Stomach: My my, aren't we hospitable today!

Knees: We're at a hospital? Oh, thank God!

Brain: Stretch it out, people. Let's get a little oxygen debt going now!

Lungs: Sir! Oxygen-wise, we're already in arrears, Sir!

Glutes: Leave us out of this! Permission to expel methane?

Mouth: M-E-T-H-A-N-E.

Glutes: EXPEL, you moron!

Brain: Wait till we pass that jogger ahead.

Eyes: Hey, check her out! Nice outfit!

Knees: While you're expelling, how about taking some of this nitrogen off my hands?

Thighs: All of a sudden we don't feel so good. What's this funny feeling?

Brain: Just lactic acid. Nothing to worry about. Keep moving!

Stomach: Oh great! More acid! My pH is already off the scale!

Mouth: I'm drying out up here. Onset of dehydration! Major cotton mouth!

Knees: He's not a major–he's just a sergeant.

Scene Three–Ten Minutes Later

Thighs: How much farther, Chief?

Knees: Yeah, we're turning to water here. Might buckle at any minute!

Lungs: Can't . . . hold . . . out . . . much . . . longer!!!!

Ankles: The recruiter never mentioned being pounded on concrete!

Brain: See that park bench up ahead? Let's sprint to it and call it a day.

Stomach: Sprint? He's gotta be kidding!

Eyes: Park bench? I see two of 'em. Everything's getting fuzzy!

Brain: Then aim in between them.

Lower Brain: Sir, I'm respectfully relieving you of command, Sir!

Brain: By whose authority, soldier?

Lower Brain: Don't ask me–I'm just a reptile.

Knees: We're with the reptile!

Stomach: Me, too! All in favor of joining the reptile say 'aye'!

All: AYE!!

Brain: You'll pay for this. I'm going back to HQ and writing an incident report. You'll all be sorry you were ever born!

All: We're already sorry! Throw him in the brig! Yea!

Lower Brain: Company . . . HALT!

****

Watching the Moon Rise

After living half a century, men attain the age at which the healing sciences recommend a medical procedure involving a garden hose, a tiny camera, a doctor to steer the garden hose, and the patient lying in what is, since a man can't have babies, the most undignified position of his life.

But I get ahead of myself. Prior to assuming the undignified position, the patient must first undergo a series of preparatory procedures designed to gradually work up through ever-increasing degrees of humiliation to total annihilation of modesty, decency, and common sense.

It all starts when one is handed a powerful purgative liquid and instructed carefully how to drink it the night before. To visualize this purgative liquid, think of a solution comprised of the salty effluent that seeps out the little hole in your ice cream freezer, mixed with warm pickle juice and topped off with antifreeze. Now you're in the ballpark.

By itself, the powerful purgative liquid is no more effective than ordinary pickle juice. However, the instructions command the patient to drink approximately fifty-five gallons of water within one minute of swallowing the purgative. The instructions also warn the patient to remain within twenty-four inches of a commode or similar object for the next twelve hours or until death, whichever comes first.

If men didn't have symptoms "down there" before drinking the solution–and most of us don't or we would have been forced into this position years ago–they will afterward. To visualize the effect of this powerful purgative on one's gastrointestinal system . . . on second thought, let's not. Suffice it to say that the letters in "one's gastrointestinal system" can be rearranged to spell "intense nitroglycerine gas."

The next morning, what's left of the patient is hooked up to an intravenous tube, otherwise known as an "IV." This accomplishes three things. First, it reinflates the patient who by now resembles a deflated air mattress with feet.

Second, it enables the doctor to administer powerful sedative drugs so the patient will go through with the procedure and not run screaming into the street.

But more importantly, it mechanically fetters the patient to a cumbersome electronic apparatus, rendering him disinclined–in his drug-induced euphoria–to flee the premises. Studies have shown that ninety-nine percent of all patients who are not thus restrained pose a flight risk

Incidentally, this is the same flight risk percentage as normal heterosexual males about to undergo accidental sex-change surgery.

Once the patient is reduced by powerful drugs to a serene, blithering idiot, the fun part begins. Three doctors in clown suits grab one end of the hose and run 100 yards down the hall while singing, "Fire on the mountain, run boys run." It's possible that is a hallucination caused by the drugs.

It's no hallucination, however, when one of the doctors spikes a bag of IV solution on the floor and the other two yell, "Touchdown!" and hold their arms up.

Next, nurses in bunny suits waving pom-poms swirl a rag mop in a kettle of axle grease while singing, "Then came the day at the bottom of the mine when a timber cracked and men started cryin'."

An alien from Roswell, N.M., directs the nurses as they swab down the fire hose along its one-hundred-yard length, and Ansel Adams inexplicably strolls into the operating room and attaches a large-format camera to one end of the hose.

"This is the same camera I used," he says, "to take my most famous photograph–'Moonrise over Hernandez.'"

The patient feels only a slight pressure in the nether reaches, similar to the sensation one might expect from backing into the device used to tunnel under the English Channel.

The patient's mind wanders languidly from one narcotic rhapsody to the next. He observes that the term *IV* is indistinguishable from the Roman numeral IV and ponders possible hidden implications of this fact. He recalls a PBS documentary on the machines–yes! there were two!–used to dig under the English Channel: one from the French side and one from the English. The French served champagne when the two augers met.

Next thing the patient knows, Ansel Adams is thrusting photographs of his–the patient's–nether reaches into his–the patient's–face. One photo resembles a close-up of the inside of a seedless watermelon. Another looks like a Georgia O'Keeffe poppy. A third bears an uncanny resemblance to a clock face.

"That's my wristwatch, you idiot," Ansel Adams says.

Then the patient wakes up at home, having dreamed the whole ordeal.

Mind you, I myself have not undergone this important medical procedure.

But I know people who have, and I know my turn is coming.

****

The End of the Line for Big John

Doctors tell us that of all the types of cancer known to feed on human flesh, colon cancer is among the most treatable if caught early enough.

The trick is discovering you have colon cancer before it gets out of hand. Since early cancer sometimes does its dirty work with little or no symptoms, the only way to tell it's there is to "visualize" it, medical jargon meaning to "look" at it.

Currently there are two ways to visualize a person's colon: find a very, very small doctor and dip him in Vaseline, or have a procedure known as a colonoscopy.

Last year a friend underwent colonoscopy and discovered he had early-stage colon cancer. Doctors removed the involved parts and my friend is fine. I promised myself I'd have one of those and write about it. This is my report.

7:00 p.m. The instructions say to drink this Phospho-Soda tonight and again in the morning before my procedure. How bad can it be? Just mix it with Sprite and down the hatch she goes. Hmmm, tastes like a really bad margarita. Way too much salt.

8:00 p.m. Is something supposed to be happening? Only a few rumblings down in the mine. For some reason the Jimmy Dean song "Big John" keeps going through my head.

9:00 p.m. What would you call this feeling? Pressure maybe. I just noticed on the instructions that I'm supposed to drink three glasses of clear liquids. Wonder if beer is considered a clear liquid?

11:00 p.m. Without getting too graphic here, a line from "Big John": "There came a day way down in the mine when a timber cracked and men started cryin'."

1:00 a.m. Another line from the song: "The smoke and gas belched out of that mine, and everybody knew it was the end of the line for Big John."

2:00 a.m. What was I thinking?

3:30 a.m. I'm supposed to take more Phospho-Soda in half an hour, but let's do it now and get this over with.

6:00 a.m. Just a guess, but that's about as clean as it's possible for a colon to be. Now a quick trip to the hospital.

7:00 a.m. A nice male nurse helps me into what he calls "moon pants," medical jargon for paper pants with a big flap on the back. I check the label—it actually says Moon Pants. The nurse takes my vital signs and starts an IV.

8:00 a.m. The doctor arrives and I'm wheeled into the treatment room. It's like a refrigerator in here. Two nice female nurses fetch additional blankets, take my pulse and blood pressure, and instruct me to lie on my left side. I see a TV monitor hanging from the ceiling. "A miner yelled out, 'There's a light up above!' and twenty men scrambled from a would-be grave."

8:–something. The doctor instructs the nurse to start part of the Demerol, a powerful pain-killing drug. Funny thing is, I'm in no pain whatsoever. As the Demerol goes in, a deep sense of relaxation washes over me. Wahoo, this is some good stuff.

Then she injects the Versed, a drug which induces amnesia, medical jargon for total memory loss. She explains that most people sleep through the procedure and don't remember a thing. I explain that I'm a working columnist and must stay awake to get this story. She smiles knowingly and pushes the rest of the Demerol.

13:00 o'clock   The most interesting TV program just came on. They're exploring this big cave, maybe in Mexico. Weird formations line the cave's pink walls. Stalactites, stalagmites–is that bat guano? Must be a bat colony here. Would you look at that calcite flow! The nurse is watching the program with me. I know she's talking because I can see her mouth move, but no sound comes out. Or is it the other way around? Man this Demerol is great. When are we going to start that procedure, Doc? Just say the word, Doc, and I'll take a deep breath or whatever.

Can you hear me, Doc? My lips are moving but no sound is coming out. What say we tape this show and watch it later? Whoa–check out that sinkhole!

14:00 o'clock. I'm back in the holding area, dressed, my moon pants gone. I have no memory whatsoever of getting dressed. Then I'm in the car, wife at the wheel, speeding east on I-40. I don't remember walking to the car. I tell her I can drive; she gives me one of her looks. Then I'm home. Hey, who took these neat pictures of a bat cave? Nice color. Somehow I get upstairs and into bed. Man that Demerol is something. I could sleep forever.

From the medical report: "The endoscope was passed without difficulty by manual insertion to the secum confirmed by appendiceal orifice and ileocecal valve. Retroflexion was performed. The quality of the preparation was good. [Thanks, Shiner Bock!] . . . There were no masses or polyps found. . . . There was no evidence of colonic carcinoma in the colon. The colonoscopy was otherwise normal."

What does it mean, MANUAL INSERTION?

Take a Hike!

Trek Toward Tower Through Two-Toro Territory

In autumn, men's thoughts turn naturally to the outdoors. For weeks I'd been waiting for a morning cool enough to hike, and on a crisp Saturday I finally got my wish.

Landowners had given me permission to hike their ranch, provided I didn't start any fires or leave any litter. A telecommunications tower on the distant horizon would be the landmark toward which I'd walk.

"Try not to get lost," the owner had warned. What a kidder. As long as I could see that tower, how could I possibly get lost?

8:15 a.m. A strong tailwind whips the new wheat shoots. By day's end I might be thankful for a tailwind, but it will carry my scent to any critters in my path and hurt my chance of seeing a coyote or turkey and maybe a bobcat.

9:00 a.m. My route takes me across cultivated fields into broken, sloping country. Crossing electric fences always makes me nervous–you never know if they're turned on. I've seen cowhands touch them to find out, but I'm not a cowhand–a fact which will become obvious soon enough.

9:15 a.m. I've hiked for an hour now, and that tower doesn't look a bit closer. In fact, where did it go? Here's an unusual object: a half-size steel hat, lying atop the prairie soil. It looks like it might be an old hub cap, except it's galvanized instead of chromed. A little hole has been drilled into the brim. I try to imagine what antique purpose this rusty thing might have served.

9:27 a.m. A tiny, desiccated box turtle stares at me from hollow eye sockets. Its shell is still egg-shaped. What calamity might have befallen it so early in life? I hang its little shell on a mesquite thorn.

10:00 a.m. This pasture is mixed grasses and an occasional cholla. The turf is deep and springy, with clumps of sweet sage here and there. I pull a sage stem and crush the leaves between my fingers, releasing a heavenly scent. I spy another one of those steel hubcaps.

10:31 a.m. The only way around this thicket of mesquite is through, so in I plunge. I curse the mesquite as it tears at my clothes. Smelling lots of bovine odor now. Up ahead I see a black barn, toward which edifice I walk.

10:32 a.m. Dang, that isn't a black barn–it's merely a black bull the SIZE of a barn. I'm maybe twenty feet away when he turns his head to give me the evil eye. The mesquite between him and me suddenly seems wispy and insubstantial. The bull's testicles hang nearly to the ground, but mine are heading the opposite direction. I've never been stomped by a bull, but I've seen it on TV, so I carefully climb over the nearest five-strand to safety. The bull never moves.

11:14 a.m. A bovine crime scene–cow bones littering the prairie. I turn them over: pelvis, femur, vertebrae. The skull grins beside a clump of grama grass, its bifurcated jawbones yards apart. Beetles scurry when I flip a shoulder blade.

12:39 p.m. This is some beautiful country. Recent rains have caused wildflowers to burst forth, even this late in the year. Puddles dot the otherwise dry stream beds. I round a hill and startle a hawk dozing in a stunted hackberry tree. He fusses as he rides the wind.

The sound of rap music comes from the brush ahead. Cautiously I advance through the catclaw and cholla. The bass part of the music becomes louder–a muffled, rhythmic chuffing. Suddenly the source comes into view: another huge bull. How many bulls does one ranch need? This one has caught my scent and isn't happy. He paws the dirt and snorts like a cartoon bull. I make a wide circle around him.

12:56 p.m.   The land opens to rolling prairie cut by looping stream beds.   In the distance, something shiny reflects the sun. Toward this I march until I arrive at a massive Coca-Cola cooler lying on its side.   The rusted name plate reads, "Cork Insulated. Progress Refrigeration Co., Louisville, Ky."   No road or sign of human activity exist for miles.   I think of the various ways a half-ton cooler might have gotten here.

1:30 p.m.   In a dry creek bed lie hundreds of flint shards.   Here's a delicate red arrowhead, its tip broken.   I have permission to hike but not to collect arrowheads, so I leave it where it is.   The tower is getting a tiny bit closer.

1:45 p.m.   I stop for lunch in the shade of a pitiful mesquite. From a Ziplock bag I pull a PBJ sandwich.   Syrup from the jelly has soaked through the bread.   I've eaten at some of the finest restaurants in the country, but I can't recall anything so tasty as this sandwich. The flies seem to like it too.

3:00 p.m.   The tower gets closer.   I'm on autopilot now.   Features of the landscape which might have interested me earlier don't warrant a glance.   This is one long-ass hike.

4:30 p.m.   Finally I reach the infernal tower and sprawl in the grass to make a cell phone call.   While I wait for my ride, I see that the tower's aircraft warning light is burned out, so I call the 800 number printed on the tower.

A man answers: "We already have a repair order on file. Thank you for calling."   After I hang up, I realize I forgot to mention the gigantic eagle nest, high up in the tower's cross-members.

I don't envy the guy who has to climb up there with a lightbulb in one hand and tear apart that bird's nest.

Nothing Better

I had almost decided autumn wasn't coming this year. Usually October is my favorite month, but this one was starting to annoy me. Ninety-nine degrees last Tuesday? Fuggeddaboutit.

Due to the heat and drought, I'd lost my appetite. There's nothing like hot weather to sap your desire for food. Lack of appetite, however, never deters a dedicated eater, so all my pants were getting snug in the waistband. Who wants to exercise when it's ninety-nine degrees? Sheesh.

I'd also been getting heat aches. Maybe there's a better medical term, but I call them heat aches: a cross between headaches and heartaches, and they're brought on by excessive, interminable, unseasonable heat combined with yearning for cool weather. You walk around in a cranky mood. You cuss your September electric bill.

Heat aches also make you toss and turn at night, so I'd been sleeping poorly. After a few weeks of poor sleep, a body gets some negative energy going.

Then something happened. It started with a funny smell in the air. I noticed the finches were attacking the sunflower seeds with unusual vigor. Around noon the wind shifted to the north, and low, hazy clouds scuttled over the city. Soon a white, gauzy sky obscured the sun. Within two hours fall had arrived.

Now everything has changed. Mornings are deliciously cool. Afternoons are the right kind of warm. And the nights–yeehaa, that's some good sleeping weather. All my neighbors have fires in their fireplaces, and the smell of wood smoke at night is better than a sleeping pill.

Brisk autumn days always give me the itchy foot. I feel like driving to an isolated spot in the middle of nowhere and striking off on foot toward the horizon. So instead of writing a column for today, I'm heading for the hills. No thinking will be permitted.

First order of business: pack a lunch. I'll splurge and get a fresh kaiser roll at the bakery, slice it in half, and pile on the deli ham and Swiss cheese. Maybe a little hot mustard too. Add some crisp lettuce and wrap 'er up.

Chips are next. For hiking purposes it's hard to beat Pringles in a crush-proof tube. The store carries the half-size tube, but this is my day off and I intend to burn some calories. I'm getting the big tube, twelve solid inches of hydrogenated vegetable oil, salt, and molded potato puree, all nesting in saturated glory. This is my reward for losing my appetite during August and September.

Cool weather gets me thinking about all that candy my kids will be bringing home in a few weeks. For dessert let's pack some candy bars. It's been awhile since I had a Snickers–probably last Halloween–but I'm partial to Almond Joy as well. What say we toss in two of each?

You don't want to hit the trail dehydrated, so I'm packing plenty of water: two half-gallon jugs. That's probably too much, but what if I sprain an ankle and have to spend the night alone under the stars?

I don't want to be one of those guys you read about, located by the search-and-rescue team "dehydrated and suffering from exposure." I want that helicopter to make a restroom break halfway to the hospital because I've been drinking plenty of water.

Now let's look at the maps. Here's a good map of the Rita Blanca National Grassland north of Dalhart. Bound to be some good hiking up there. I've been hearing occasional reports of cougars in our northern counties. Maybe I'll find a dry wash and follow it for a day, just to see if I can scare up a panther or two. That would make me a happy person.

But Rita Blanca is two hours from here. Eastern New Mexico is a little closer and also contains some lonely landscape. Trouble is, I don't know whose land it is. Some land owners are touchy about trespassers. Because I prefer not to get shot on my day off, I'll skip New Mexico this time.

Hey, look here. A topographical map of the Wayside Quadrant showing some places in our own Palo Duro State Park I've not yet visited. There are parts of the park where no one ever goes, and, since I prefer to keep it that way, I'll not say exactly where those parts are. But they'd sure make a splendid hike on a chilly fall morning.

Yes, that's what I'll do. I'll oil my hiking boots, stuff my pockets with Kleenex and aspirin and Chapstick, shoulder my pack, and disappear into the Palo Duro. Maybe I'll just sit and listen to the music of running water or watch beavers mend a dam. Or take a nap in the shade of an ancient juniper or kick up an arrowhead.

If I'm not back in a few days, send in the dogs. They can find me at the end of the trail of Pringles crumbs.

* * *

Last year while our state park was closed for road repairs, I asked readers to suggest other picturesque places to hike. Several mentioned Buffalo Lake, a wildlife refuge near Umbarger.

It took me a year to finally get to Buffalo Lake, but I wasn't disappointed on a recent Saturday when a friend and I spent the day there.

Horrified, appalled, amused, revolted, intrigued–yes. Disappointed, no.

Buffalo Lake is haunted. Haunted by the ghosts of vanity, greed, carelessness, and bad planning. It's a wrecked monument to hubris. I loved it.

As best I could piece together the history of the place–difficult to do since the ranger station was closed and the brochure racks empty of everything except dirt dauber nests–Umbarger Dam was built in the 1930s and declared fatally flawed just three years later. The lake probably never should have been allowed to fill with water. Mistake number one.

According to plaques posted around the lake, runoff from nearby cattle feeding operations gradually turned the water into nitrogen soup, otherwise known as algae heaven, killing fish and creating unhealthy sediment on the bottom. Mistake number two.

Several decades of debate about what to do with the polluted lake and its unsafe dam failed to produce an action plan. Mistake number three. It took a flood in the late 1970s to scare everyone badly enough to force the draining of the lake. The plug was pulled, and the former lake bottom became a "wildlife refuge," a place where row crops were planted in hopes of pulling excess nitrogen from the soil.

We've been pulling out nitrogen for twenty-five years now. There was no one to ask whether we've pulled enough. Judging from the millions of rotting fish carcasses lining what's left of the shoreline, I'd say the answer is no. The odor was suffocating.

What little shallow water remained near the dam was a garish shade of green. The most common bird present on the day I visited was the turkey vulture. There must have been hundreds feeding on the dead fish.

And yet Buffalo Lake has a strange sort of charm. Maybe it's the crumbling concrete slabs where cabins once stood. One can almost hear the echo of children's laughter, the bleat of outboard motors, the whisper of a rod and reel. Ghosts.

I hope some old-timer will contact me and tell me about the old days before Buffalo Lake became The Lake That Isn't.

****

Pass the French's

Question of the day: How long will mustard keep? Does it need to be refrigerated? What if it's tightly sealed in a glass jar and buried in Palo Duro Canyon for thirty-one years?

This question was on my mind one warm morning as I shouldered a light pack and hiked toward a certain canyon rock formation.

When I was in college, a buddy and I spent the night at the base of that rock, about halfway up the canyon wall. As far as we knew, the rock didn't have a name although it was a distinctive boulder. We gave it a name which I am unable, in a family newspaper, to divulge.

I don't recall taking hot dogs up there or cooking them over a fire, but we must have–otherwise why would we need a jar of French's mustard?

Mind you, I don't recommend spending the night in Palo Duro Canyon unless it's at one of the designated campsites. Just hiking off and sleeping under the stars is frowned upon by the authorities, and for good reason.

And I shake my head at the thought of starting an illegal ground fire all those years ago. Even if it wasn't against the law then–which it probably was–it was not smart. Ground fires have ways of getting loose and causing problems, and usually the problems are catastrophically out-of-proportion to the original fire.

Today, if I were to discover college boys starting a ground fire in the canyon, I'd call a ranger and have them kicked out, pronto.

Three decades ago, however, nobody kicked us out. After spending the night in the shadow of that mighty rock, we loaded gear for the hike back to our car. I decided against carrying that almost-full jar of mustard, so I buried it. Never imaging thirty-one years would pass, I vowed to return someday, dig it up, and report on its condition.

Last week it took me awhile to decide which rock was the right rock. All rocks start to look alike, and in our canyon there are plenty to choose from, each one first cousin to the others.

I selected a promising-looking boulder and began hiking. Forty-five minutes later I was at the scene of our old camp. I was happy to see that time had been kind to it.

But other nitwits like us hadn't.

Beer bottles were scattered about, their labels long since vanished. Half-buried shards of broken glass littered the ground along with coals from numerous campfires.

Most shockingly, the smooth face of the rock where we'd scratched a message to time–SJ, DH, 10/18/71–was completely covered with other graffiti.

Perusing the initials and dates, I noted that ours were the earliest. Initial pride changed to chagrin as I imagined that someone coming along after us had possibly seen our initials and realized that "our" rock might make a good spot for sleeping. Had our little *delicto flagrante* started an unfortunate precedent?

With a stick I poked around the spot where I remember burying the mustard jar. Nada. I enlarged the search area, but still found nothing. Maybe some rascal had absconded with the French's. Or better yet, maybe some lonely camper had prayed fervently for condiments to flavor his hot dogs, looked down, and seen that mustard lid sticking up through the dust.

Before I turned to hike back down, I collected as many beer bottles as my pack would hold. I felt responsible.

There were plenty of beer cans, too, but somehow these didn't seem as offensive as the shiny glass bottles. After a hundred years, a beer bottle will look pretty much like it did on day one.

However, time burnishes aluminum beer cans to a nice dull patina. The painted-on labels evaporate. They almost look like cylindrical stones.

There were other, older cans at the base of our rock too, tin cans which might have predated our 1971 escapade. Who knows? Cowboys from the old JA Ranch might have tossed them down. After a certain period of years, such cans achieve the status of historical artifact.

Their flaky, rusty surface already was returning to dust. I left them in place.

On the way down I took a different route. At a spot where water pours off the caprock during rain, I found a lovely little water-carved channel. Its fluted sides were chiseled and polished by water from a thousand thunderstorms.

Even more interesting to me were several sets of scratch marks on the smooth sides of the dark rock, made not by two-legged creatures but four-legged. Each set of scratches showed tracks corresponding to four claws. Bobcat? Coyote? What else could have made those scratch marks?

Maybe a coyote climbed out of the canyon with a jar of French's in its jaws.

This Writing Life

Just Do It

Such a curious business, this writing life.

You can be any color you want, tall or short, fat, thin, frizzy hair, straight hair, no hair–it makes no difference. Your readers won't care.

You can have pierced ears and a ponytail or not. Crooked teeth, yellow teeth, no teeth. Bad breath, bad credit, bad dreams. Write the dreams.

You can be straight or bent. In a wheelchair, typing with braced wrists or a pencil in your teeth. You will sound as if you're healthy and whole. Look at Stephen Hawking.

It makes no difference if you're attractive. Beautiful people have no advantage whatsoever. A big nose, big pores, one big eyebrow, hairy moles, ugly as sin. Thick glasses, a bad eye, one eye, no eyes, or two gorgeous baby blues. Jumpin' Jack Flash's toothless bearded hag writes just as well as Julia Roberts, who someday might become toothless and bearded. She can still write up a storm then.

You can be fit as a fiddle, churning through the pages, get up, go jog ten miles, come back, drink orange juice, rip off twenty more pages. Or not. Maybe you're sick as a dog, diseased, riddled with cancer, bedridden. People with cancer sometimes write the most beautiful stories. Take *Cold Sassy Tree*.

If you went to college and majored in English, minored in journalism, have all sorts of initials after your name, good for you.

If you skipped school and got kicked out of tenth grade for truancy or delinquency or burglary, you might still be able to write if you have the grit and desire.

Maybe you have a problem with substance abuse. Maybe you'd rather have a "bottle in front of me than a frontal lobotomy." You look into the heart of the beast and it takes more than you have to stand against it. You can still write. Look at Hemingway, Faulkner, a jillion others. Of course tee-totalers write just as well, and without the morning terrors.

Pregnant women make good writers. So do former roughnecks, strippers, gentlemen ranchers, waitresses, attorneys, carhops. Prisoners make especially good writers. Look at Paul of Tarsus. All you need is pen and paper and a little light coming through the prison window.

Kids with nothing to say sometimes find something and say it with writing. People who've never really lived a life write characters who do. These characters become more real than the person who wrote them.

Politicians and people with mental disorders sometimes make whopping good writers. People who've been used, misused, abused, maligned, broken or damaged write some achingly good stuff. Depressed people make good writers if writing doesn't cure their depression. Or even if it does.

Women, housewives, Junior Leaguers or by-junior-beleaguered, all have been published. Dog-lovers and dogcatchers, small fries and big fish in little ponds, little honchos and big enchiladas, muckety-mucks and muck-ups, all have found pleasure and profit in writing.

Left-wingers and right-wingers, people who just wing it, night owls and early birds, all have been known to put feather to paper.

You don't need a fancy computer or typewriter. You don't need a home or a car. You don't need much of anything. You don't even need much of a life or a future. Look at Anne Frank.

Don't worry about talent, either. That doesn't stop many notorious writers from releasing their gaseous creations into the world. Talent is fine if you have it; if you don't, try to get it. If you fail to get it, write about failure.

People with great ideas sometimes become great writers. People with ordinary ideas may also become great writers. People with no ideas can write about the state of idealessness.

Writers with writer's block, blocked bowels, blocked arteries, blockheads, people who've been around the block, many have written blockbusters.

So stop saying you're going to write. Begin writing now.

****

Why Writers Don't Give Speeches

Every once in a while, columnists get asked to give public speeches. Call it a hazard of the trade. People seem to assume that since a writer can put together words on a page, he should be able to put together words before a live audience. This is usually a dangerous assumption.

The first factor preventing writers from becoming effective public speakers is an innate tendency to procrastinate. Having six months to write a piece doesn't really help a congenital procrastinator. He's going to wait until five months and twenty-nine days have passed before beginning.

I've often pondered why this is so. Perhaps it's because most of us have busy lives even before the new work assignment, so the new stuff must go to the end of the line and wait its turn alongside thank-you notes and storm windows. Or perhaps it's just that we're lazy and don't wish to work until we can't put it off any longer. Or maybe some people work best under pressure, and having six months to complete a task is no pressure.

Science has recently discovered a procrastinating gene in the human chromosome which might further explain why writers are the way they are. Scientists nicknamed the gene "Mañana 321." People born with this gene can't do anything before the last possible moment. It is suspected that most writers have the Mañana 321 gene in their DNA. You can't fight Mother Nature.

Whatever the underlying reasons for it, procrastination isn't a good thing where speeches are concerned. Speeches need to simmer. Their flavors need time to blend. This can't happen overnight, but overnight is all a writer has because he waited until the last minute.

So rather than a speech, what the live audience gets is a rough draft of a speech. I've lost count of how many times I've given rough drafts of speeches. The audience response is about what you'd expect–something between courteous perplexity and stunned silence.

For example, the last speech I gave was to a group of ministers. During the preparation phase of the speech I had several possible themes, ample supporting material for each, and some effective visual aids. I couldn't decide from among the themes, so I ended up using them all.

Given enough time and enough fear, I easily could have developed any one of the themes into a strong essay. But since neither time nor fear were on my side, the speech wandered from point to point with no logic that I could discern. An outline of my remarks would have resembled the tributary system of the Canadian River, without the Canadian River.

A second reason writers make poor public speakers has to do with the rhetorician's art. Nobody wants to hear someone stand up and read from a manuscript. That's about as exciting as watching paint dry. So writers are doubly cursed: We couldn't write a good speech if we wanted to because we wait too late to begin, but we really don't want to write a good speech because we know the audience won't suffer us doing what we do best–reading from a manuscript.

The best public speakers work from notes, glancing down occasionally to see where they are and what's coming. But to a writer, *notes* is synonymous with *rough draft*, and we've already seen what happens when a writer stands before an audience with a rough draft in his hand. It isn't pretty.

So writers try to prepare only a minimal outline of their remarks, knowing that details can be added during the speech itself. Another big mistake. (Did I mention that writers are slow learners?) No writer fills in details from a standing position. Sitting, kneeling, reclining– yes. Especially sitting and reclining. But never standing.

No, writers like to try out words and phrases. We're born experimenters. A word has to not only sound good and convey the right sense, but look good next to its neighbor words on the page. In the privacy of our own homes, writers add and delete, add and delete, endlessly. There's no reason live audiences should be subjected to anything as recursive as writing. They want a few uplifting anecdotes and a closing thought.

Picture, then, the writer giving a speech. He's a fish out of water, standing there with a rough draft of an outline detailing some half-baked ideas, looking out at expectant faces, knowing he's about to disappoint most and baffle the rest of them. The audience will likely be so traumatized by the experience that they'll never read his work again. But does that stop him from delivering the speech?

No. Which is why I just accepted an invitation to address a group of middle-school students three months from now.. For once, I've got plenty of time to prepare something really good.

****

Success as Elusive as Coronado's Golden Cities

Readers have been asking when my novel will be available. It's hard to give a short answer.

Several years ago I wrote a novel set in Palo Duro Canyon. The Spanish conquistadors have always fascinated me, so my novel wove two storylines–sixteenth-century and twenty-first–into one tale set in the canyon.

José Felipe, a fictitious member of Coronado's expedition, narrates the first storyline. He's a homesick teenager. Eleanor Grissom, a fictitious rancher, is the protagonist of the modern storyline. She's been around the block a few times and has some sharp edges.

It took almost two years to plow to the end, but when I finally finished and showed it to a literary agency, they liked it. They suggested revisions which improved the story, and they agreed to represent me.

For two more years the agency peddled my novel to New York publishers. During that time I entered it in a writing contest with the Southwest Writers Workshop. Much to my surprise, it won first place in the Mainstream Fiction category.

My protagonist, in the words of one judge, was "drawn extremely well–her acerbic wit and self-deprecating sense of humor are compelling. Conflict is set up beautifully and certainly creates tension. Dialogue is very natural and well-balanced with the narrative."

While in Albuquerque to collect the prize, I met several New York editors. They seemed cordial but said such a novel would be hard to market to urban readers.

Pardon my breaking into the story here to say that in the novel, a group of investors seeks to build a western heritage theme park in Palo Duro Canyon. The New York editors considered this idea far-fetched.

Eventually the literary agency gave up. I was back to square one.

Then I saw a newspaper article about a new editor at Texas Tech University Press. Since Tech is my alma mater, I thought TTU Press might be sympathetic. They took the novel "under consideration."

TTU Press sent it to several professional readers for evaluation. The editor called one day with good news: The first reader loved it. "Horsley's *Conquistador*," the reader said, "is the best work of fiction I've seen from Tech Press. I am confident in saying that you must publish it."

I was on cloud nine. Then the second reader sent his report: "Publication not recommended. Significant revision needed. . . . I think it is the verbose letters from Pedro. [sic] . . . The story line is too long." Tech Press decided to pass.

Since the novel had no luck finding a publisher but plenty of luck winning prizes, I entered another contest. The Austin Writers' League awarded it first place in Western Fiction.

Okay, I thought, I have a novel that wins prizes but not publishing contracts. Oh, well. I chucked it in a drawer and forgot about it.

A few years passed before a friend mentioned that a press in Houston was launching a Southwest fiction series. With more cynicism than hope, I dusted off *Conquistador* and sent it to Houston. They loved it and sent a contract.

The Houston publisher sent it to yet another professional reader who suggested revisions. The revisions made sense, so I did a total rewrite. I hauled two buffalo skulls to the canyon and spent an afternoon shooting a cover photo.

Original publication date was supposed to be Labor Day, 2003. Then the publisher told me it might be October 1.

I could live with that, I said, as long as we had the book in stores in time for Christmas. Soon I was informed it would be "after the first of the year."

What the heck. It was out of my hands.

Finally the long-awaited galley proofs arrived, camera-ready pages laid out exactly like they'll appear in the finished book. Galley correction is an author's final chance to spot tiny flaws before the book goes to print.

But what I spotted weren't tiny flaws. My novel had been rewritten by a person or persons unfamiliar with Panhandle culture or people. My characters had been cleaned up, buffed down, sanitized. Grammatical errors had been inserted. My "baby" had become an incoherent stranger.

"Whoa!" I said.

Now *Conquistador* sits in the drawer again. A contract remains as elusive as Coronado's cities of gold. Like him, I've journeyed across the literary landscape and come home empty-handed.

****

Crazy Pale Face

Conquistador's long, circuitous journey is finally coming to an end, thanks to print-on-demand (POD) technology in which everything about the book–text, fonts, format, paper type, and cover– is stored in a computer in Philadelphia, PA, and when anyone in the world places an order, the computer prints and ships one book.

What sounds like a relatively simple plan actually involves a whale of a lot of work for the author, because each design decision rests solely on yours truly. Take the book's cover, for example.

This novel is set in Palo Duro Canyon, and I always envisioned a wide photo of the canyon for the cover. My thoughts turned naturally to Louise Daniel, who owned and operated several special cameras capable of taking dramatic horizontal photos of startling effect.

Louise was happy to let me use one of her photos. That was the easy part.

The hard part involved buffalo bones. For reasons I can't describe too much without giving away the plot, I needed some bison bones and an old crucifix for a separate photo to be superimposed on the back cover. I had a picture in my mind which guided me.

By asking around, I found two people who owned old buffalo bones and didn't mind loaning them for a photo. I even found an antique Spanish crucifix perfect for my needs. All these items I loaded into my car along with a shovel, bucket, and camera, and headed to the canyon to search for the perfect sand bar along the Prairie Dog Town Fork of the Red River.

I had a spiel prepared in case park rangers asked me what the heck I was doing.

Ranger: "Sir, why are you digging up that buffalo skull?"

Writer: "I'm not digging it up, Officer. I'm burying it."

Ranger: "Okay, why are you burying a buffalo skull?"

Writer: "So I can take a picture of it and *then* dig it up."

Ranger: "Sir, you have the right to remain silent . . ."

On a warm Saturday morning I drove to Water Crossing No. 2 and parked. The smart thing would have been to bring several assistants to carry equipment and bones, but my two photographic aids were busy doing what they do best on Saturday mornings–sawing logs.

Hiking awhile along a dry branch of the creek, I finally located a sand bar I thought would work. I had to work fast, because the angle of the sun would soon be wrong and I'd have to wait until late afternoon. Deer flies and mosquitos hounded me as I lugged everything to the site and began digging.

You'd think the soil along a creek would be easy digging, and you'd be correct until you hit a submerged boulder. Digging a hole big enough to hold a buffalo skull involved several false starts before I found a spot free of rocks. Into the hole went the skull and loose bones and enough backfill until just one horn, an eye socket, and a rib were peeking out.

Next I had to fetch water in the bucket and douse the whole area. The flowing part of the creek was several hundred feet away, and five gallons of water gets to be pretty heavy over that distance. I stuck the crucifix in the soil next to the skull and let fly the water. Not enough. Back to the creek for more. Still not enough.

You see, this skull needed to look like a flash flood had uncovered it after it had been buried for 462 years. I snapped a roll of film even though I didn't like the composition. What the picture needed was roots, tree roots entwined through the skull and maybe one snaking through the skull's eye socket.

I dug up everything and relocated to another spot where the sun's angle was better. Quickly I dug another hole and found some roots to add, then repeated the interment process, the water lugging and flinging process, and the photo shoot. I only quit when I ran out of film.

On the way back to the car it occurred to me how curious this bone business was.

Imagine an old buffalo on the prairie two hundred years ago, munching grass and minding its own business. This would have been before there was a Texas.

The buffalo is herded off a cliff by Comanches, and its bones are buried by nature for two centuries, then uncovered by a white man, then buried twenty years later by another white man, only to be doused, uncovered, reburied, redoused, etc. What would the Comanches think, watching from a distance?

"Mmm. These white people are crazy."

Politics

My Guy

Presidential elections are difficult for columnists. No matter what we say, half the readers won't like it.

But it's hard to stay on the sidelines while the battle rages. A close race hangs in the balance. After watching the televised debates, I've decided to take a public stand. I'm giving the full weight of my endorsement to the ticket every thinking person should support.

During the first debate I thought my guy looked fabulous. The blue suit, the white shirt, the red tie–the effect was presidential and more than a little patriotic. It brought to mind the stars and bars of Old Glory.

I thought he handled himself well too. He didn't get rattled by his opponent's biased remarks. Afterward, he exuded confidence while hugging family and well-wishers. That's the kind of man we need in the White House: one who'll go toe to toe with an adversary and have energy left for schmoozing a crowd.

The other guy looked sort of tired. I didn't like the way he smiled or how he blinked. His pronunciation of certain words annoyed me. Afterward, I thought he looked whipped, as if the polls might show a tie but deep in his heart he knew he'd lost.

He tried to keep up with my guy in post-debate hugs and kisses, but I noticed a distinct cynicism in his kissing. Is this the man whose finger we want on the nuclear button? Not hardly.

The vice-presidential debates were revealing as well. I thought my guy looked relaxed and in control. That's important for a man who'll be a heartbeat away from the presidency. His opponent was trying a little too hard to look relaxed. I'll bet his insides were churning.

My guy faced the questions head on, even the tough ones, and reflected honor on the name at the top of the ticket. The other guy was too nice to suit me. I think he held back, fearing the reaction if the American people knew his true views.

The second presidential debate cemented my feelings for my ticket. My guy conducted himself with dignity and aplomb. He showed a firm grasp of the complex issues every president must face. He engendered my trust and respect.

His opponent showed that, while he might be able to debate his way out of a wet paper bag, he couldn't answer the tough questions to my satisfaction. And I didn't much care for certain comments he made either.

Issues? My guys are rock-solid on the issues. They've shown leadership and ability time and time again. The other guys seem clueless half the time. I guess that comes from having few real credentials of their own, but relying on the record and accomplishments of powerful men who preceded them.

On gun control: The American people aren't going to sit by and watch the ideas of those other two clowns become law. It just isn't going to happen. This great nation won't tolerate being taken down that path.

Or education: If there's one issue my candidate can be proud of, it's his record on education. He knows the minds of our young people are our greatest national treasure, and our system of education is the envy of the world. To squander a chance to expand opportunities for the education of tomorrow's leaders would be nothing short of criminal.

Military readiness is another hot topic in this election. My guys have shown by their actions and words that they're committed to a strong national defense. The only reason our democracy has remained strong while other systems of government have come and gone is our dedication to supporting the proud men and women of our armed forces.

My friends in the military tell me that if that bozo from the other ticket is elected commander in chief, our military readiness and morale will suffer. America cannot afford to make such a costly mistake.

Fiscal policy? You don't need a PhD in economics to know that my guy has a commonsense approach based on sound economic principles, fairness, and the best interest of the country as a whole.

If you want my advice, go with the serious candidate whose record speaks for itself. Those other two guys can go suck an egg.

* * *

Response to last week's political column was strong in support of both sides. I received mail both from Democrats and Republicans alike, saying, "Attaboy! Give 'em heck!"

It was supposed to be a satirical piece. By discussing the issues and candidates in hackneyed yet vague terms, I hoped to demonstrate the vapidity of most political discourse, which doesn't educate or enlighten–it just puffs up the speaker and demeans the opposition. The labels and accusations are interchangeable.

We're all sure our side's right, and people on the other side are mutton-heads. But what if we can't tell on which side the mutton-heads lie? We're pretty sure they're out there. But where?

Anyway, I enjoyed the mail. Rest assured that I'm in total agreement with you all, and I know our side will win in November. In fact, I guarantee it.

****

The Square Peg Party

Elections sometimes leave me feeling like a square peg in a round hole. You'd think I'd get used to this feeling, but I haven't.

It's not that I mind being in a minority. I was taught to hold fast to my convictions, try to keep an open mind, and let the chips fall where they may. If one ends up outside the majority, so be it.

Right now a little voice is telling me I ought to become a Republican like everyone else.

I'm giving this some thought. Trouble is, I fear the Republicans don't want the likes of me, on account of my political views don't line up with the traditional Republican ideas of helping the strong get stronger while hoping the weak find a way to benefit, shoveling money at our military while hoping it gets spent wisely, and despoiling the environment while calling one's self an environmentalist.

I could go on, but you get the idea.

What's especially awkward for the likes of me is that some of my ideas *do* seem to mesh with the Republicans. I believe in tax reform, a balanced budget, and I'm against late-term abortion. So maybe I'm a latent Republican.

The situation is complicated further by the fact that I don't agree with half the Democratic Party objectives, either. I think the traditional liberal ideas of gun control, however well-intended, benefit criminals to the detriment of the rest of us; I suspect many labor unions are about as corrupt as it's possible to get; and I disagree with shoveling money at social problems and hoping it gets spent wisely.

So actually I don't fit in with either party too well, and the election underscored this fact.

I've never voted for a Bush, father or son. That makes me a Democrat, right?

But I haven't dwelled on the squirrelly way our current Bush got elected. I accept him as my president. That makes me a Republican.

I celebrated on election night, 1992, when Bill Clinton got elected. That makes me a Democrat.

Clinton's shenanigans, however, mortified me, and it was a relief when his smirking face finally left the White House, so I guess I'm a Republican.

However, I believe, like Barry Goldwater (another odd duck), that the question of a person's sexual orientation is of absolutely no consequence in the military or elsewhere. That's a firm Democratic Party plank. But Goldwater was a Republican.

And so is the notion of being "pro-life," meaning anti-abortion. My views on abortion don't line up with either party: As long as the fetus looks like a lizard, you're free to abort it. When it starts to look like a person, then you can't. I never said my view was logical.

Speaking of illogical, Republicans like to cozy up to the so-called "religious right," meaning the Bible-thumpers, fundamentalists, and Moral Majority Christians. Having grown up a fundamentalist, I know their mind-set. They'd like to turn our pluralistic society into a theocracy, with themselves in command. I'm agin' it, so I guess I'm a Democrat.

But hold the phone. What about affirmative action, one of the foundational planks of the Democrats? It seems unfair to me, so I'd have to be against it, although by so doing, I go against noted Republican Colin Powell, who has gone on record as an advocate of affirmative action. So this makes me a Republican.

School vouchers? I'm against them. I believe in public education, and vouchers will weaken our public schools. I suppose that makes me a Democrat.

But my ideas about capital punishment make me a Republican. George Bush and his party don't seem to mind putting criminals to death if their crimes are heinous enough, and neither do I as long as wealthy murderers are put to death along with all the others.

It seems apparent that I don't really fit into either party. This is the trouble with only having two viable political parties: If you're not A, then you have no choice but to be B.

Maybe one result of the Republican landslide of 2002 ago will be the total disappearance of the Democratic Party. This could be a good thing in the long run.

With only Republicans left standing on the political landscape in a decade or two, voters would need to reorganize along some other ideological grounds besides simply A or B.

But by then, I might be too old to get to the polls.

****

Randall County Rattles with Bones of Contention

The list of things I don't understand just keeps getting longer. Seems like the older I get, the fewer things I know much about. I always thought it would work the other way around.

Take Randall County, Texas, for example. Here we have a perfect rectangle of Panhandle countryside which includes one of the most beautiful and best-run state parks in Texas. The people in Randall County are prosperous, enjoy excellent schools, watch cable TV, and don't miss many meals.

Their four-year university is part of the renowned A&M system, they have an interstate highway, and they're competently represented in Austin. I imagine most expect to go to heaven when they die.

And yet it's hard to pick up a newspaper without hearing someone in Randall county mad as rattlesnakes at someone else in Randall County. There's no such thing as a controversy too small for public spleen-venting. Either the elected officials are angry at the people who elected them or angry at each other or both, and vice versa. If they can't tear each other down, any old courthouse will do. In this age of plenty, with a booming economy and our governor about to assume the presidency, Randall County still practices tag-team government. They seem determined to be unhappy, come hell or high sewage.

One Controversy of the Week was a spill of some raw sewage in an alley in Randall County. If this had happened in Potter County, what do you bet somebody would have dispatched a maintenance guy to fix the problem within twelve hours? Yet in Randall County, nothing rolls downhill faster than civic goodwill. Are the citizens of Randall County watching too much Jerry Springer? Here's a tip: Try Mother Love's philosophy of Forgive and Forget.

I don't mean disrespect to my neighbors to the south, because many are my friends. I just can't understand why everything has to be such a cat fight all the time. It seems the sensible and sane voice of reason is drowned out by the bickering, libelous, litigious voice of recrimination, thin skin, and hurt feelings. I'll bet I could list twenty high-profile public controversies in Randall County within the past five years. Don't worry–I'm not going to do it. Seeing the list might get people mad all over again, like maybe they'd forgotten something they're supposed to be mad about.

Here in Potter County, we have a huge renovation project involving public funds. The old Santa Fe Railroad building soon will be home to county government, at a cost of several million local, state, and federal dollars. Imagine the free-for-all if this project had been situated in Randall County. There'd be a line of lawyers two blocks long, waiting to file lawsuits against everybody and anybody connected with the project: Potter County Judge Arthur Ware and the county commissioners; the architects, contractors, and assorted passers-by; the Texas Department of Transportation, the Occupational Safety and Health Administration, and the Environmental Protections Agency.

Assuming, that is, the citizens hadn't already razed the building and put up a parking lot.

Instead, the project seems to be going smoothly. I say *seems* because I haven't been following it too closely. I trust the people in charge are doing their jobs. Sure, costs have overshot the original estimates, like we knew they would, but still, nobody has his drawers in a wad.

Why is it the people of Potter County can roll with the punches and find common ground, while the people of Randall County are always on the ground, rolling and punching?

I have a theory. Notice that the county line between Potter and Randall counties roughly coincides with the watershed boundaries between the Canadian and Red rivers. Rainwater in my street gutter runs north to the Canadian River, while just a few blocks away in

Randall County it runs south to the Red. Are you thinking what I'm thinking?

Those of us in the Canadian watershed have dispositions more like Canadians, eh? We're a tolerant bunch, slow to anger, deficient in the pugilistic arts. Canada hasn't declared war on anybody since . . . well, centuries ago. The game of ice hockey, you recall, was invented by Canadians in an attempt to maintain a pulse in our northern neighbors. Our philosophy of government is to elect people, then forget about them.

Our neighbors in Randall County, however, live in the Red River watershed. What comes to mind when you think of the word *red*? Blood, anger, fire, hot coals, danger, bullfights, disaster. "Seeing red" isn't just an expression for being angry; it means, "I'm a resident of Randall County and I'm not going to take it anymore!" Their philosophy of government is to elect people, then watch closely until they make a wrong move.

Like I said at the beginning, I'm not sure I understand the slow-motion donnybrook of Randall County. I'm sticking to my theory until someone gives me a better explanation.

****

Let Us Pray

As a Christian, I'm a strong believer in prayer. Every morning for the past few decades, I've begun the day with prayer. It seems to get me started on the right foot. *This is the day that the Lord has made; let us rejoice and be glad in it.*

During the day, I've practiced what St. Paul advised the Thessalonians: Pray without ceasing. Prayer can be formal or informal, and most of mine are the latter–nonverbal, unrehearsed, intimate expressions of concern, joy, or thanks.

Such prayers don't necessarily begin with "Our Father who art in heaven" and don't end with "Amen." In fact, formal prayer is just a fraction of the prayer picture. Spontaneous prayer that erupts unbidden, such as a simple "Oh, thank God," might be closer to the heart than one beginning, "Our dear Heavenly Father."

Sometimes prayer and work blend in such a way that it's hard to tell one from the other. Have you ever become so connected to an activity that time disappears and your work seems to flow from the deepest part of yourself? I consider that a kind of prayer too.

At bedtime I no longer recite the prayer I learned as a child, "Now I lay me down to sleep." But I do like to take a moment and thank God for the blessings of the day, which, when I pause to think about them, are always more numerous than I thought.

Since September 11, 2001, I've received quite a few e-mails about prayer–some from friends and some from strangers. A common theme seems to be that now is the time for Christians to seize the moment and restore prayer to our public schools. This one is typical:

"Please take a moment to call Governor Perry's office at 800-252-9600 to voice your support for public prayer and legalizing school prayer. We just did and they really appreciated it.

"After Governor Perry openly supported public prayer, including ending that prayer with the words, '. . . in Jesus' Name, Amen,' and making legalizing school prayer an issue, he was attacked by an Austin newspaper which stated that 'people would be offended.' His office was then hit with scores of negative phone calls. Let Governor Perry know that REAL Texans are very much behind him on this!

"Please make that toll-free phone call today and forward this to others who will do so also. Thanks! His office hours are 8-6 and you can leave a message on the recorder."

I seem to be in the minority on this issue. While many thoughtful Christians push to "restore" prayer in schools, I am adamantly opposed to "legalizing school prayer." I believe this phrase is code for imposing a particular version of spirituality onto our children.

Advocates of "legalizing school prayer" can't quite admit that school prayer is already legal. Students can start praying the moment they set foot on school property. They may gather around the flagpole to pray, as many do. They pray at their lockers, on the way to class, during class, between classes, at lunch, and after school.

However, people who wish to "legalize school prayer" aren't satisfied that school prayer is already legal. They want to go one step further and create a society in which "every knee shall bow and every tongue shall confess that Jesus Christ is Lord."

To some Christians, the idea that we'll someday force everyone to believe in Jesus is a spiritual aphrodisiac. It stirs them into a righteous frenzy.

To me, the notion of making America a Christian nation through subtle coercion of schoolchildren is ghastly. It goes against everything I believe about faith. It's not much different from what the Taliban did in Afghanistan: create a culture based on a particular view of spiritual reality, and demand compliance.

Ever since the emperor Constantine converted the known world at the point of a sword, some Christians have been in love with the idea of forcing others to believe like we do. Other religions have done it, too, but I'm not a member of other religions, so I'll let others deal with other religions.

What interests me as a Christian is to ensure, as our courts have wisely done, that no employee or agent of government at any level be allowed to use his or her position to promote religion.

It doesn't matter whether it's Hindus, Muslims, or Presbyterians who wish to speak to their Creator over a school's pubic announcement system. I don't want any of them leading my child in public prayer. That's what churches are for.

And that's what I told Gov. Rick Perry.

Parenting

Just Doing Their Jobs

Being the parent of a teenager can take a person to some unusual places. One day my teen announced that "all his friends" were meeting at Millennium, Potter County's new teen dance club, and he hoped to be with them.

Having read the newspaper reports about Millennium and how Randall County authorities had run it out of their county, I said, "No way, absolutely not, forget it, it's not gonna happen, no child of mine, blah blah blah."

You know the drill. Sometimes parents have to put their foot down.

Then a few days of intensive persuasion simply wore his mother and me down. I staved off the total collapse of parental authority by adopting the "savvy negotiator" stance. I laid out my conditions:

1) Yes, he could go but ONLY if I went with him
2) At the FIRST sight of alcohol consumption, we're outta there and he'll never return
3) Ditto the first whiff of marijuana
4) Ditto the first fight

We parents, remembering our own childhoods, naturally want kids to be kids while they can, to have a life of their own, and hang out with their friends. I recall once asking my parents, "Mom, Dad, can I spend the night fishing on the river with my pals?" and the animated discussion which followed. They finally let me go, but only after laying down some pretty stiff conditions. Of course, the one they neglected to mention was, "Do not throw a handful of .22 cartridges into the campfire while your pals are sleeping."

Anyway, my teen wasn't keen on my accompanying him to Millennium, but he sensed we'd reached the stall point, so he agreed to my conditions. To avoid being mistaken for a teen that night, I wore my "parental" clothes: plaid LL Bean shirt, gimme cap, old jeans. My teen, commenting on my attire, tactfully noted that I'd gone "way past parental" into "geezer."

Outside the Millennium Club, three uniformed security officers patted us down while loud music vibrated the walls. Once inside, my teen quickly disappeared into the blacklit semi-darkness.

I wandered around for a look-see. Against the east wall were two pool tables with a few kids playing eight ball. At the north end was a soft drink concession and a breakdance area. I watched a few skinny boys in baggy clothes spin like dervishes on the slick vinyl floor. It was something I might have tried several decades ago.

On a stool outside the girls' bathroom sat a security guard. She told me her job was to monitor the bathroom for signs of trouble. What kind of trouble? Fights, smoking, stuff like that. So has there been any trouble? None that she knew of. What would she do if she smelled pot? Go get the manager.

At the south end was a large-screen TV area with sofas. Although I'd been assured by a friend of my teen that Millennium prohibited "making out," I could see that this was a place where making out could occur. All I saw was a few kids watching TV wrestlers posture and strut while fake blood glistened on their steroid biceps.

A large dance area dominated the center of Millennium. Several raised platforms afforded showoffs a place to get attention. While I watched, two young ladies stepped up on the platform to bump and grind. One of them, young though she seemed, showed some pretty mature moves. I recalled that Randall County authorities had named suggestive dancing as one reason they'd kicked Millennium out of their territory.

There's no denying that teenagers are sexual beings. I wondered: Is society helping kids by providing a relatively safe place for them to display their sexuality? Or do places like Millennium simply encourage harmful acting out?

Another thing on my mind as I strolled around the club was a statement by Randall County District Attorney James Farren concerning cockroaches. Depending on how you interpret Farren's remark, he was either drawing an analogy between teens and cockroaches–which Farren denies–or between the Millennium staff and cockroaches.

Either way, I imagine he'd like to take that unfortunate statement back. I didn't see any cockroaches during my time in Millennium, just a bunch of self-conscious adolescents of various sizes, shapes, and colors, wearing outrageous costumes and listening to incomprehensible music.

In other words, doing what American teens have been doing for at least four decades. You tell me whether it's good or bad.

After I'd seen enough, I went outside and sat in my car to write some notes. Through my side window I had a good view of youngsters queuing up for the pat-down. One boy showed up wearing a jacket thirteen sizes too big, and pants with the crotch at his knees. What do you suppose he was hoping for? I imagine he hoped, deep inside, to be affirmed, to fit in, to feel the esteem of his friends. Maybe to taste life, his own life, apart from Mom and Dad.

Of course, he wouldn't have said it that way. On the way home I asked my son for his opinion of the club.

"It was fun."

* * *

My column about Potter County's newest teen dance club, Millennium, brought some response from readers.

N.A. wrote: "As a parent of two fourteen-year-olds, I've been nagged to death to allow them to go to the club. I finally gave in and let them go, but was afraid I was being overly permissive and giving them free rein to go to a den of dope-smoking, alcohol-consuming despoilers of fourteen-year-old innocents.

"I gave your column to one of my boys and he confirmed that your description of the club was entirely accurate. . . . The club sounds no worse than (and very much like) the Borger Youth Center of my teen days–back when most of our dancing was considered suggestive by adults. I've always thought that if we parents could share our insider information, we'd be way ahead of the game."

Whether Millennium is or is not a den of iniquity might depend on your definition of iniquity. If Millennium breaks the law by allowing teens to use alcohol or drugs on the premises, then we've got a problem which should not be ignored. But if teens are just hanging out and *looking* suspicious, for pete's sake that's their JOB.

It says so right here in the Teen Handbook: "Teens must wear absurd clothes, listen to trashy music, and always must appear to be contemplating mischief, harboring improper motives, or entertaining impure thoughts."

I have a feeling that if, instead of dropping teens off at the door, parents would take a minute to go inside the Millennium Club and check it out, we'd have fewer misunderstandings as well as fewer occurrences of illegal activity.

****

Let Me Tell You About the Birds and Bees

Sex education has come a long way since I got mine. Back in the early '60s we learned about the birds and the bees from two primary sources. The first was school "film strips" in "hygiene" class.

Try explaining to kids today what "hygiene" classes were about:

"No, kids, it wasn't exactly about hand washing."

"But it was about something dirty, right Dad?"

"Who said anything about dirty? Sex isn't dirty."

"Hygiene class was about SEX?"

"Um, yeah, but we learned effective teeth-brushing, too."

"Whoopie."

Harder still is trying to explain what a "film strip" was:

"Well, kids, it was sort of like a movie, only slower."

"You mean like a video, don't you, Dad?"

"Not exactly. Videos hadn't been invented. The picture didn't move–it was more like a slide show, with all the slides on one piece of film."

"Oooo, bet that was exciting. How could you stand to watch something that didn't move?"

"Well, actually it did move, but only when Mrs. Confer pushed a button to advance the film to the next picture."

"What were the pictures OF, Dad?"

"The usual–you know–the parts of a flower, human development, a cross section of a vagi–"

"GROSS!"

The second source of sex education was the Boy Scouts. Put half a dozen adolescent boys in a tent for several nights running, and eventually a rudimentary picture of human sexuality will emerge. Maybe not an *accurate* picture, but what we lacked in facts we made up for in imagination.

Scout 1: "Okay, here's what we know for sure: Babies grow inside the mommy because the daddy's sperms swim around and around the egg until one of them pokes a hole in it. Does anyone know how the sperm got there in the first place?"

Scout 2: "I think they–you know–DID it."

Scout 3: "Yeah, the *S*-word."

Scout 4: "You said '*S*-word'! I'm telling!"

Scout 1: "Sit down, Horsley. What about the *S*-word makes sperm? The film strip only said that the sperm 'are deposited' by the male. Does the male KNOW he's depositing? Or does it just, like, happen?"

Scout 2: "Yeah, like you might be depositing right now."

Scout 1: "Am not!"

Scout 2: "Are too!"

Scout 4: "I think if we knew more about that depositing business, we'd be onto something."

Scout 5: "Maybe it's like when my dad gasses up the car. The longer he leaves the nozzle in, the more gas he gets."

Scout 6: "Speaking of gas, who did that?"

Thankfully, here in the new millennium, things have improved vastly. We now have sex on the front page of the newspaper, sex on TV, and sex on the Internet. Our culture is saturated with sex, but that's not necessarily a good thing. One problem is a lot of bad information getting passed around.

Which is why I thought last week's Kids in the Know program, sponsored by Planned Parenthood, would be such a terrific thing for my kids. You know–get the straight facts from experts in the field, doctors and nurses and such, and leave me out of it.

"Hey kids! It's time for a good wholesome conference on the *S*-word!"

"No way, Dad. We went last year!"

"Yeah, but this is different. All new stuff, like games and people dressed up as testicles." (I made up the testicle part.)

"Forget it, 'cause we're not going."

In the end I managed to prevail by pulling rank and putting my foot down, but it wasn't a pretty picture. How different from the old days when kids begged their parents for sex information, only to hear the standard answer: "Go ask your mother."

Now it's, "You're going to receive sex education, young lady, whether you like it or not!"

After the conference, I asked how they enjoyed it, and received the standard answer: "It was boring."

Sex might be different things to different people, but *boring* isn't one of them. I've learned that *boring* is a deflection term, used to divert attention from hot issues.

So I know that if I'm patient and approach them on a good day in the right way and cross my fingers and toes, I *might* get them to say eight consecutive words about the conference. Which, after all, was one purpose of the Kids in the Know conference–to increase communication between parents and kids.

I'm glad we had this little talk.

****

Bliss in the Back Seat

Late spring always feels like transition time. In the chain of life's endings and beginnings, the shift from May to June feels especially strong.

May is a month of saying goodbye, boxing up your stuff, cleaning out your locker, and hitting the road. May is finality, ceremony, graduation.

June is a month of beginnings, fresh relationships, a clean slate, endless possibilities. June is travel, water, romance, music.

People with children go through this shift each time school ends, but this year it's more pronounced for me because my youngest is ending her middle school career. A few years ago I wrote a piece here about her first day of kindergarten, or rather, about how her mother and I felt on the evening before her first day. That was what—nine years ago? My, my.

Now here I sit, waiting for her to exit the school for the last time. Of the myriad chores of parenthood, picking up kids after school is one of the more pleasant rituals. I've grown so accustomed to its circadian rhythms that no matter where I am at 3:30 p.m., my thoughts naturally turn toward school.

At my house we are fortunate that one parent always has been available to do the after-school pick-up, and I'm glad that parent has been me. Next year, however, my son the new driver will be hauling his sister home, so this marks the official end of my duty as after-school picker-upper. I'm not quite ready for this chore to cease.

Multiplying eleven years since my oldest started school times 165 school days per year shows that 1,815 times I've pulled up outside a school, switched off the engine, tipped back the seat, and waited for the raucous, joyful stream of young life to spill out of the school.

It was here that I once observed a woman beating a young child with a stick. I wrote a column about it which still generates mail. It was here I once got into a shouting match with a man who parked his car in what I considered a socially irresponsible manner. Don't know what I was thinking, really. It was here a hailstorm once hit just as school was letting out, and children ran for the cover of whichever car was closest, including mine.

Besides the obvious bonding that occurs when a child learns to trust in a parent's punctuality, I've discovered that this picking-up chore comes with a nice little perk: the afternoon nap.

When my kids were small, I'd often listen to music while I waited. Sometimes the music was conducive to dozing off. Happy the man whose seat fully reclines. Then I started carrying a pillow in the car. One day I crawled into the back seat and fell dead asleep until little fingernails tapped on the window.

Strangely enough, some of the best sleeping I do is in the back seat of this car. I began arriving twenty minutes early just so I could get some sleep. I can sleep just fine with the radio blasting, whereas at home it must be quiet, and even then I sometimes sleep fitfully. Explain that if you can, Doctor.

Computers

Anchors Aweigh!

Because of certain personal idiosyncracies, I waited longer than most before joining the computer age. I was still pecking away on a manual Royal typewriter when my friends were storing data on five and a quarter-inch floppy diskettes, back when diskettes were literally floppy. I could see that if I waited much longer, I'd soon get left in the dust on a remote dirt road off the Information Highway.

So I bought my first computer for $2,600. That seemed like an obscene amount of money in 1990, and even today it seems fairly risque. I hesitate to say the computer was slow, but it was made by a company called Molasses in January. Because of a set of odd circumstances, I still have that computer, and I'll tell you in a minute how much it's worth in today's market.

A of couple years after I bought my first computer, my wife bought one for her work. Since we'd already spent our savings on my computer, she paid hers off through payroll deductions, and the total cost was around $2,400. I hesitate to say her computer went obsolete quickly, but it was made by a company called Bananas, and in about the time it takes a green banana to turn black, we were faced with expensive upgrades.

Are you with me so far? My family's two computers cost us $5,000 in the early '90s.

If we'd invested that same $5,000 in the stock market in 1992–oh, never mind that. I don't want to think about it. What I want to think about is what to do with these two ancient computers. I tried advertising in the paper, but no one wants a technological dinosaur. I tried donating them to charity, but charity said thanks but no thanks.

I thought I had the problem solved when we held a garage sale and someone paid $100 for both computers and all attachments. Free at last! But soon the buyer brought them back, saying he didn't know it was possible for so little memory to reside in such big computer cases. To get rid of him, I gave his money back and have come up with some nifty uses for my old computers:

1) My old computer I carry around in the back of my car. This not only gives me better traction in snow, but if I wedge a five-gallon water jug refill against the computer, it keeps the jug from tipping over. Without something to lean against, the jug falls over and spills reverse-osmosis water onto my floor mats. For $2,600, I can keep from wasting three cents' worth of water per week which, if you do the math, means the computer will pay for itself in about 1,667 years. Of course, a concrete block would serve the same purpose, but who wants to carry a concrete block in his car?

2) The second old computer I now employ as a decoy against theft. On a yellow sticky note I wrote a message saying, "Dad's New Computer–Very Expensive–Please Don't Touch" and attached it to the old computer (which still looks brand new). Then I put the computer smack-dab in front of the most likely point of entry if thieves ever break into my house again. They'll see the old computer and steal it instead of the one I use to write these columns. Assuming, of course, they don't read the newspaper or have an ounce of sense, which most thieves don't.

3) I came up with a pretty ingenious use for the old monitor, too. I drilled a big hole in the case and inserted a long piece of nylon rope. If I ever get invited to go bass fishing, I'll bring along the monitor for an anchor. If the knot accidentally comes loose and I end up losing the monitor on the bottom of Lake Meredith, oh well!

4) All the power cords and electronic cables for my old computers are different from the new cables and cords. New cables are "USB" type, which they say stands for Universal Serial Bus, but which I know really stands for User is Sure a Boob. Between the two old

computers, I had about twelve different cables. But I've discovered a use for them. I've knotted them all together and keep them in the trunk of my car to use as a tow chain if I ever need a tow. You wouldn't believe how strong those things are, and the rubber coating will prevent scratches on my bumper.

5) My old dot-matrix printer was top-rated when I bought it, but I've thought up a use for it, too, assuming the Smithsonian Museum doesn't get back to me. I'm selling it to MENSA, the international organization of geniuses, to use as the supreme intelligence test.

Here's how it will work: MENSA could put a genius candidate in a room with my old printer and the instruction manual. Using a stopwatch or—more likely—a calendar, they'll time the candidate to see how long it takes him to perform the simplest command, function, or procedure with the printer. Even loading paper requires six pages of small-print instructions. Every button and knob performs eight different functions, depending on which of five modes it's in.

It doesn't take a genius to see that anyone who can figure out how to make that printer work is off the chart, intelligence-wise, and automatically qualifies for MENSA.

****

New FI from ISP Sparks E-Mail SNAFU

If your computer was a little slow last week, it might have been my fault. I accidentally jammed up the airwaves or bandwidth or whatever.

Earlier, my Internet Service Provider had sent an urgent e-mail saying I had to change my e-mail address right away in order to accommodate the ISP's new fabulator interface. I hadn't been with this company long, and it surprised me that its old fabulator was no longer good.

But I did as I was told: called the Support Guy and let him walk me through the change. This took longer than I expected, because my computer's settings had to be recalibrated while we had the patient under anesthesia. The old settings were from last year, so they were WAY out of date. My ear kept getting hot under the light pressure of the phone receiver, and I had to keep switching from ear to ear to avoid spontaneous combustion of the ear lobe.

Finally the settings were rectified, and Support told me to notify my address book about the change. I hesitated. I knew there was a way to do this, but I couldn't recall it. The Support Guy said I could contact each person individually, or I could highlight the whole list and send notice to everyone.

"Remind me how to highlight the whole list," I said.

He said to put the cursor on the first name, scroll to the bottom, and press "Ctrl Alt Home" all at the same time. Either that, or "Ctrl Shift Pg Dn." Seems like there was a "Alt" in there somewhere too. It didn't matter, because I didn't have enough fingers anyway.

I called my secretary, Bernadette, over to help me. She pressed some of the keys and I pressed the others, and *voila!* My entire e-mail address book was highlighted. The computer screen cast a blue glow into the room, which highlighted the violets in Bernadette's tattoo.

A word here about newspaper columnists' e-mail address books. We get lots of e-mail from readers. When we reply to an e-mail, the computer automatically stores that person's address in the address book.

So my address book is very, very long, dating all the way back to the first Bush administration. Probably half the people in it are dead now. Someday I'll go through it and remove the entries I don't recognize, but that will require staying on the phone all day with Support Guy and risking ear lobe flameout.

Anyway, I pushed "Send," my computer groaned and lurched, and off went the change of address notice to everyone on the list. That's when the fun began.

Within seconds, return mail began to pour in. Most of it was from "System Admin." or "Delivery Failure" or "Undeliverable" or "Recipient Deceased Since First Clinton Term."

Deceased recipients was the least of my worries, however. I had inadvertently (a term too often associated with my Internet use) e-mailed my entire address list to everyone on the list. Some of the replies were none too kind: "You F____g Idiot!" was in the

"Subject" line of more than a few. Several of these I recognized as blood relatives.

There is, I know, a way to send e-mails to large groups without including the names of everyone in the group. I even know the term for this: "Blind Mailings." But, sadly, I don't recall how this is done.

Here is a verbatim reply from a friend: "I got an e-mail with HUNDREDS of addresses in it. Do you know anything about this?" I detected an accusatory tone.

That wasn't the worst part.

An equally inept friend of mine—let's call him "Sal"—was apparently inspired by my change-of-address notice to issue his own notice. Rather than highlighting just his whole address book and turning his secretary blue like I did, he sent his notice to *my* address book as well as his.

Don't ask me how he did this. If you held a gun to Sal's head and asked him how he did this, he couldn't tell you either. It's obvious that he borrowed my moves, though, because his e-mail had all his addresses plus all of mine. Sal was as ignorant as I about "Blind Mailing."

A new round of e-mails started pouring in: "You F___g Moron!" and "I don't know you—take me off your list" and "Who the hell are you?" Plus, all the dead guys on Sal's list were replying to me about his change of address.

I had to spray water on my hard drive to cool it off. Things have finally settled down now. One thing is obvious: This was the sort of mistake possible only in the age of new, improved, fabulator interfaces.

****

Kak Attack

Until a few weeks ago, I'd never heard of a "kakworm." It's an ugly word, and conjures an image of something I'd expect to find in an apple.

But a kakworm doesn't eat fruit. It's a computer virus that eats data, and my computer has one.

It might sound strange, but I was excited when I learned my computer had a virus. The experts tell me kakworms are relatively benign. They don't cause massive system failures and loss of data like some of the big-name viruses such as Melissa or the Love Bug.

Instead, kakworms are content to slowly nibble through one's software, occasionally rendering this program or that one inoperable. I rushed out and bought the latest anti-virus program I could find.

When I ran the anti-virus software, it "captured" several kakworms and put them in a safe area called a "quarantine."

This is endlessly fascinating to me. As a kid I loved to roam the neighborhood and collect creatures. I'd bring them home and put them in jars.

There was an art to this sort of thing–not just any old jar would do. The glass had to be clear with no ripples or ridges which might distort my view of the prisoner. Mayonnaise jars seemed to work best.

There was a right way and a wrong way to punch holes in the lid so the prisoner could breathe. The wrong way was to screw the lid on the jar and stab it a few times with a pocket knife. I learned the hard way that a snake will rub his nose to a bloody nub against such a lid.

The right way was to invert the lid and punch holes from the underside, so the sharp edges faced away from the prisoner. When he was released a week later, he'd be none the worse.

When I think of the kakworms imprisoned inside my computer's quarantine area, I envision a shelf full of mayonnaise jars. Inside the jars are my kakworms. They know they're trapped, so they just sit and brood.

Maybe I should feed them something. Years ago I would drop unlucky crickets into jars containing tarantulas or toads and watch the crickets become lunches. But what does a kakworm eat? Would a pet shop stock it?

It's possible that kakworms don't need to be fed. Maybe they remain virulent indefinitely.

I could delete the infected files, but you never know when science will discover a cure. Maybe someday I'll kill these worms and repair the damaged files.

Or maybe I'll just turn the kakworms loose in the alley.

****

Streaming Tech

Today I've come to say goodbye to my old computer. This will be the last column I write for the newspaper using Old Betsy the Battle Axe. She has served me–if not well, at least adequately (on most days anyway) since the first Clinton term, but in computer years that makes her Methuselah.

I should have replaced her before now, except I'm too technologically challenged to do so without losing half my files. No doubt transferring files from one computer to another is like breathing to some people, but it's a nail-biter for me. The longer I waited to replace her, the harder it got while the necessity for doing so increased.

On impulse I finally bought a new computer, sight unseen, over the telephone. I can't give brand names here, but it might rhyme with "Bell." This new computer is a native Texan.

If you think it strange to buy on impulse something as important to a writer as his computer, let me say it was the only way I could manage to do the deed. For years I'd been saying I ought to, but looking at the catalogue gave me the cold sweats. I had to take a running leap in order to make myself jump.

The new machine arrived in three business days. It sat in its box for another three. I was too chicken to open it. I knew that heartache lay ahead.

When I worked up the courage to unbox it and plug it in, several surprises were in store. First, the new computer has sound. I suppose Old Betsy had sound once, too, but her voice died a long time ago and I couldn't do without her long enough to take her to the shop.

Sound on a computer is a good thing. As I type these words, classical music floods my office, courtesy of the new computer. I don't understand how a computer can be a radio too, but do know it involves "streaming technology," which means (I think) it plucks the radio signal from the airwaves and delivers it to my ears in a steady "stream" of notes. That's the best way to listen to music–in streams of notes.

Old Betsy sits here glumly, listening to the music with me. The only time she makes a sound is when I tell her to find something on the A drive, when there's no disk in that drive. She has a fit then, grunting and clicking and coughing. Though she's voiceless, she gets her point across.

An even bigger shock occurred when I plugged in the new monitor. Old Betsy's monitor was top of the line in its day, meaning it resembles a 1950s television set. I honestly hadn't noticed that the picture was getting dimmer and dimmer until I turned on the new flat-screen monitor. It was like seeing color for the first time after watching black and white. I had to reach for the Ray-Bans.

Hues that vivid seem unnatural, but the screen itself seems almost *too* natural. It's soft to the touch and a little squishy. The spot you touch makes a funny ripple, like you've touched something alive. You don't just spray Windex on this screen like I did Old Betsy–it comes with a cleaning tool to make sure human hands never contact it.

This new machine is quiet too. I can't even tell if it's running. Old Betsy made sort of a growling noise all the time to let people know her brain was spinning. I guess I'd tuned it out, but the new one is so silent that I wonder if I'm merely dreaming of a computer. Even the keyboard is quiet–no more clacking keys.

The only sound this new machine makes occurs at odd moments. The first time I heard it, I thought a chorus of tiny trumpeters was warming up inside a tin can. It only happens when the computer is idle for a half-hour or so.

Another surprise was the speed of this new machine. I don't know all the technical lingo for it, but I think Old Betsy had four bytes of mega-ROM or something like that. This new device has 800 RAMS of GIG at 90 Hertz, or maybe Avis. Anyway, it's FAST.

What formerly took three or four minutes now happens in the blink of an eye. Calling up the home page, for example. With Betsy I had developed a system of rituals to perform while waiting on a task. Breathe in, breathe out, repeat. Make a few phone calls. Comb my hair. Clean the computer screen. Clip my nails. Stretch my Achilles tendons.

Now I don't have time for any of that. When you tell this new machine to do something, it's over with before you finish telling. From now on I'll be easy to spot in a crowd. Just look for the guy in sunglasses, with uncombed hair, long fingernails, limping because his Achilles tendons need stretching.

It's all this new computer's fault.

****

This Might Be Goodbye

Recently my new printer went on the fritz. Every time I tried to print, an error message flashed, "Unable to open file print.exe." Weird.

Then I started getting e-mails returned to my box as "undeliverable"even though I had never tried to deliver them in the first place.

I suspected hackers or a virus. The virus program that came with my computer wasn't doing the job, so I went to the Norton Antivirus Web site, paid $80 for a virus/spam/firewall package, and downloaded the files.

Norton began scanning. Sure enough, it found a virus and couldn't repair the file. Recalling how Sigourney Weaver burned herself up in order to destroy the alien DNA she harbored in one of those alien movies, I told Norton to delete the file.

Then Norton found another virus, then another and another. Pretty soon I was up to twenty infected files, which might explain why my printer wouldn't work. I deleted them and told Norton to remove all files it couldn't fix. In hindsight, that might have been a mistake.

When Norton had deleted one hundred infected files, I considered stopping the scan. At two hundred, I began to sweat bullets. At three hundred, I chewed off my fingernails. At four hundred, I was having muscle spasms. How, I wondered, could my computer continue working with four hundred files missing from the hard drive?

Answer: It couldn't. Windows wouldn't open or close. Commands wouldn't execute. The machine wouldn't even let me turn it off. It barely had a pulse, but my heart was pounding. I called Dell support.

I'll just hit the high points of what happened next. First, when you call tech support of any company on earth, you get put on hold for "between eight and fifteen minutes." About halfway through your fifteen minutes, you get another recorded message: "Due to unexpectedly heavy demand, we regret . . ."

Finally, "Jesse" at Dell answered. I was so grateful to have a human on the phone that I wanted to kiss the receiver. Figuring this might result in being placed on hold again, I instead explained what had happened as "Jesse" listened patiently (no doubt thinking, *Moron!*) and suggested we try restarting the computer in "safe mode."

This reminded me of the movie where Jodi Foster locked herself into the safe room of her mansion to escape killers. It didn't work for her either.

After about an hour of failed attempts to resuscitate my Dell, "Jesse" said I should contact Norton, since it was their virus program which had ruined it in the first place.

The Norton hold time was the same as Dell's, except every few minutes I had to suffer through royally annoying ads for Norton products. Finally "Isaac" came on the line and heard my complaint.

"You deleted *how many* infected files?"

"Isaac" said it was standard procedure to reformat the hard drive after half a dozen files had been deleted. He said four hundred was the highest number he'd ever heard.

I asked what he meant by "reformat the hard drive."

"Basically, you back up everything you want to keep in safe mode, erase your entire hard drive, reformat it, then reinstall your operating system, update and install all Norton products, scan everything, then reinstall your files."

I wanted to ask if he'd seen the movie *Total Recall* starring Arnold Schwarzenegger, because in that film Arnold has his memory erased just like "Isaac" proposed doing to my hard drive.

Instead, I asked, "Assuming I can even open my files using this black hole of a computer, what do I save them to?"

"Don't you have a CD burner? Oh, no! You don't have a CD burner? Well, I suppose you could save them onto floppies, if you had a big pile of floppies. You really ought to call Dell and let them walk you through this."

Translation: Someone as ignorant as you has no business attempting this operation.

I thanked him and called Dell back. After the perfunctory fifteen minutes holding, "Benita" came on the line and heard me out.

"I'm transferring you to Sammy," she said. I wish I could report what "Sammy" had to say, but my notes reflect only one cryptic word: "Tina."

"Tina" was either the code word for "take your computer to the Dumpster this minute!" or else she was a tekkie for Norton or Dell–I couldn't say which. Finally I got "Sharon," who instructed me how to save everything to an external zip drive and prepare the patient for brain surgery.

As soon as I finish typing this column, I intend to wipe my hard drive clean and attempt to perform a brain transplant.

If you never hear from me again, you'll know it didn't work.

Highways and Byways

Playing Dead Badly

While driving the highways and byways of our state recently, I spied something on the pavement. It was moving.

My history of stopping for objects in the road is well-documented, so no need to cover that ground now. As I executed a U-turn, the people in the back seat perked up.

"What did you see?" one asked.

"A turtle?" asked the other.

I pulled a safe distance off the roadway next to the slithering creature. No cars were in sight in either direction. As I approached, the snake saw me and coiled. Then it did something surprising: It doubled in size.

Maybe you've heard of puff adders. This particular adder was only two feet long, but when it puffed itself up, it somehow seemed more dangerous, maybe even deadly. At least that's what the snake seemed to want me to think.

Not to be deterred by its theatrics, I walked to within a foot of the thing. It then displayed another defensive behavior: It struck at my pant leg.

I've been struck at and bitten by snakes three times the size of this one, so its little feigns didn't affect me much. But I challenge any herpetologist to continue advancing when a snake strikes. I suspect it's in our genes to halt, and halt I did.

But that wasn't good enough for Mr. Snake. He then did an extraordinary thing: He up and died right there in the southbound lane of Highway 83.

When I say died, I mean he rolled onto his back, struck a death-like pose, opened his mouth, and stuck out his tongue.

I've heard of people being scared to death by snakes, but this was the first time I witnessed a snake being scared to death by people. I felt sort of bad. I have nothing against snakes, and it didn't seem polite for a visitor like myself to hurt a snake on its home turf when it was minding its own business.

With the toe of my shoe I flipped the dead snake over onto its belly, and lo! a miracle occurred: The dead snake flipped itself over onto its back. Again I righted the serpent, and again it unrighted itself, as if to say, "Hey! Can't you see I'm dead here?"

I picked up the dead snake and carried it to the car. When I put it in the trunk right-side up, it flipped to its dead position. The passengers were impressed.

"Cool! Can we keep it?"

We unslipped a pillowcase and dropped in the dead snake, knotting the top so it couldn't escape if it came back to life. Then we went merrily on our way.

That snake had a few more tricks up its sleeve, however. It wasn't long before we were met by an olfactory assault.

"EEEEWWWW! What's that SMELL?"

A powerful, skunk-like odor filled the car as the adder emptied its scent glands into my pillowcase.

"Dad, get that thing out of here!"

The next town was Menard, county seat of Menard County and home of some of the best venison jerky on the planet. We found a convenient city park near the highway, on the banks of the San Saba River, and into that river went Mr. Snake.

Although the water was only a few inches deep, it was sufficient to cause the snake to remember that he was, in fact, alive after all. The last thing we saw was the snake heading east at a determined pace, going with the current.

My pillowcase seemed ruined and had to be tied to the luggage rack for the rest of the trip. Multiple washings have removed almost all the snake smell.

Here's what the book says about *Heterodon contortrix contortrix*:

"The hog-nosed snake . . . holds its ground if cornered, flattening and spreading the head and fore part of the body to twice their normal width. . . . [O]ccasional individuals will strike. . . . If further annoyed, the mouth is opened and rubbed on the ground and the body is contorted as if the snake were in the final stages of a death agony. . . ."

"The snake then rolls onto its back and lies perfectly still. If picked up it is limp and lifeless. . . . It can easily be induced to betray itself, however, if placed on its belly, since it invariably promptly rolls onto its back!"

****

Moneybags

Well, it's gone and happened again. Last week in Iowa the back doors of an armored truck flew open, and $320,000 in bills and change fell out onto the highway. There is something extremely fishy going on here.

Let's think a minute. Forget about armored trucks–let's think about *any* vehicle with a back doors that open. According to my research (which consisted of pursing my lips, staring out the window, and pulling a number from thin air), there are approximately 26.7 million such vehicles on the roads of this nation. Chances are you drive such a vehicle, as do I.

Of those 26.7 million vehicles, how many times do we hear about the back doors flying open suddenly and spilling out onto the highway any cargo *other than* cash?

Right–never.

For instance, many people shop at Sam's Warehouse and come home with lots of bulky, heavy items in the back of their sport utility vehicles, Suburbans, or minivans. You go to Sam's for a sack of dogfood and come home with two bales of nifty red shop rags, twelve rolls of shrink-wrapped duct tape; a keeno screwdriver set with forty-eight different interchangeable tips including Torx, hex, phillips and slot in both metric and English; a dozen XXX-Large pocket tee shirts in last year's colors; four gallons of hair conditioner; a ten-year supply of vitamins; a twenty-pound bag of grapefruit; plus your sack of dogfood.

Have you ever once heard of anyone's back doors flying open en route from Sam's Warehouse and spilling hair conditioner or duct tape or vitamins or grapefruits onto the roadway? No. It simply doesn't happen.

According to my research (which consisted of lightly tapping on the *I* and *F* keys with my index fingers for thirty seconds while staring out the window and humming "That Boy," which used to be Ringo's theme song but which apparently has been replaced by "Yellow Submarine"), there never has been a documented case of vitamins or grapefruit or screwdriver sets falling onto the road from the back of a moving vehicle.

Or take drugs. Here in the Panhandle, we're on the major supply route for drugs moving up from Mexico to the drug-users east and north of here. Hardly a day goes by without our police or state troopers pulling over a rental truck full of drugs. These delivery trucks are driven by loyal employees of the drug cartels who are under STRICT INSTRUCTIONS not to wear their seat belts, no matter what.

This makes them easy for our police to spot: rental trucks with out-of-state tags, weaving all over the road, and no seat belts in sight. It's a no-brainer. ("Sir, do you know why I pulled you over?" "Is this a trick question, Officer?" "No–you weren't wearing your seat belt." "S**T, NOT AGAIN!!" "Mind if I search the back of your van?" "Not at all, Officer. You wouldn't happen to have a beach towel handy, would you? It seems I'm beginning to sweat.")

But how many times do the back doors of these drug delivery trucks or vans fly suddenly open, spilling crack or smack or maryjane onto the highway? Right–never. It simply never happens. Even the addled brains of drug delivery truck drivers have sense enough to

LATCH THE BACK DOORS so their cargo doesn't fall out. It's the first thing they teach in drug-runner school: "Keep the friggin' back doors latched, and don't ever put on that friggin' seat belt."

So if millions and millions of housewives and ranchers can make it home from Sam's Club without spilling their cargo, and an equal number of drug runners can get from the rich opium fields of Oaxaca without spilling theirs, and countless millions of other step-vans, bobtail trucks, and government vehicles can deliver umpteen thousand different products, crisscrossing the nation 24/7, including giant tractor-trailers hauling steer bones from the slaughterhouse to the dogfood plant in open-top trucks against a strong headwind without ever losing so much as a rib bone, *why does money continue to fall out the back of armored vehicles?*

Here's my theory (arrived at while trying to move a toothpick from tooth to tooth without using my hands at all–just lip and tongue manipulation, although the word *manipulation* does imply the use of a hand):

It takes three guys. One guy files down the door latch so that a slight breeze will cause it to fly open suddenly. This takes awhile, but he stays on task until it's done. Another guy stacks the loose sacks of money right inside the back door. This is important, because throwing the money sacks too far forward will result in no spill when the doors fly open.

Once the money bags are in the truck, a third guy pushes the bags up against the back door, so they're leaning on the door in such a way as to fall out once the doors are opened.

If my theory is not correct, I want to hear from armored truck employees about how it's really done.

****

O Brother!

On the way home from an errand east of town, I put in the soundtrack CD to the movie *O Brother Where Art Thou?* It's a fine film and my new favorite movie of all time, and the soundtrack is equally excellent—full of old gospel and blues music and some which defies description.

As I drove along, the song "Down By the River to Pray" came on and altered my consciousness a wee bit.

Music does that to me. Normally I don't pick up hitchhikers. But anyone who's spent even five minutes by the side of the road with his thumb out can't help feeling a tug of sympathy for hitchhikers, even hairy, wild-looking ones.

That tug, combined with the music I was playing, caused me to hit the brakes when I saw a clean-shaven man standing near FM 1912 with his thumb in the air. I stopped.

"How you doing, Partner?" I asked.

Normally I don't call strangers *Partner.* I guess I was feeling a little like George Clooney in the above-mentioned movie, which is a modern retelling of *The Odyssey* in which Clooney plays a hyperactive Odysseus.

As he fastened his seat belt, the hitchhiker said he was a career military man on a brief leave from his base in Sacramento, CA. He needed to be back tomorrow morning or they might come looking for him. He said he'd gotten a ride to that spot from the airport.

Wasn't California west of our airport, not east?

Yes, he said, but he'd hitched a ride with a hotel shuttle and it happened to be going east. He was a military doctor and was on "unscheduled leave" from his base. He had three surgeries scheduled in the morning: a total hip replacement and two ACLs.

I wondered if "unscheduled leave" was the same as AWOL. Was I harboring a military fugitive?

I asked what an ACL was, and he explained it—anterior cruciate ligament. He ran his finger down his knee to show the ligament's location. The hip replacements weren't too hard, but the ACLs were tricky. If he wasn't back by in the morning, he said, he could be in hot water with his base commander. They might even haul him before a military court. He didn't know how in the world he could make it back in time. If only he could get to Albuquerque, he might catch a flight for Sacramento and make it on time.

I started to say that our airport used to offer flights to Albuquerque.

He couldn't believe his bad luck at being stranded in Amarillo. Here he was, a doctor with money in the bank but hardly a cent on him. He'd tried to go to a local bank and get some cash. There was some mix-up with the wire transfer. He had $324,000 in CDs in the bank back home, but a lot of good it was doing him now. Even his Gucci shoes, he said, weren't helping him out now.

I looked at his shoes. They were nice shoes, but I'm no judge of Gucci.

Ever since his wife died, he continued, his daughter has been going wild. That's why he had to come to Amarillo–to see about his daughter. She's fourteen and dating a man twenty-nine. It's giving him fits.

No fourteen-year-old should be having anything to do with a twenty-nine-year-old man, he said. The very thought was a scandal, and a hardship on him. In a way it was a good thing his wife wasn't alive to see it. He tried to talk sense into his daughter but you know how it is talking to teenagers.

Yes, I know.

He wished he was back among his friends in the refugee camp in Bosnia. That was where he really belonged. When he signed on to treat those poor refugees, he knew he'd found his life's calling. The other doctors in Bosnia were the only true friends he had.

It must be tough being away from people who care about you, I said.

Yes. Those Bosnians have suffered beyond description. He served sixteen years in that refugee camp. The things his eyes have seen. Now he has to get back to Sacramento and scrub for surgery in the morning. The caseload will be staring him in the face. He put his head in his hands. He just was so grateful for the ride, even if it was going the wrong way.

I mentioned that Sacramento was straight ahead–just stay on I-40 and eventually you'll be darned close.

He reiterated his gratitude. We talked about hitch hiking, and how people won't stop for a person like they used to, on account of all the meanness in the world. I told him that he didn't look like a serial killer to me, and we laughed.

He quoted a proverb about entertaining angels unaware. He said that I was his angel.

When I let him out I gave him ten bucks. I thought his story was worth that much, maybe more.

****

Bear Country

In my lifetime I've accidentally run over one dog and one cat. The dog, which I thought sure I had killed, was okay after it regained consciousness. The cat wasn't so fortunate. I also ran over a snake once, though I tried to avoid it. (Snakes are my friends. Hey– another plank in the Square Peg party platform: Be Kind to Snakes). I've come close to hitting deer, armadillos, possums, rabbits, and raccoons.

One creature I never thought about hitting with an automobile is a black bear. But that's exactly what a motorist on I-40 did.

When I saw the story in the paper, I got on the phone and tried to track down the unlucky driver. Turns out the accident was a hit-and-run. Perhaps the driver thought he'd hit a large dog. A Department of Public Safety trooper out of the Borger office found the deceased bear near Conway.

Something about this incident tickles my fancy. I happen to be fond of bears, and, in a weird way, it pleases me to learn that bears are making forays into the Texas Panhandle. There are people, no doubt, who wish bears would just stay in New Mexico, thank you, but there are probably an equal number who wouldn't mind coexisting with *Ursus americanus*. I'm sorry the bear got hit, but its presence suggests there are other still around. I like that.

Black bears, unlike their grizzly cousins, usually retreat from human contact. They are timid souls more inclined toward grubs, insects, and vegetable matter–including garbage if they can find it– than bringing down large game. An adult female will fight to protect her cubs, but black bears keep mostly to themselves.

Although people in other states live alongside black bears, I wouldn't think bears' odds of establishing a permanent Panhandle presence are strong. Judging from all the bullet holes in roadside signs, historical markers, rural mailboxes, and windmill vanes, I imagine irresponsible gun owners roam our state in sufficient numbers to make a bear comeback unlikely.

But still I like to think of bears living in the wilder parts of our region. I like to think landowners might give bears the benefit of the doubt and leave them be as long as they don't bother livestock. Is this too idealistic?

We almost wiped out the buffalo, then regretted it and brought them back. Some area ranchers have reintroduced elk to the Panhandle. Maybe bears would add a little western romance to the Top of Texas.

****

Bra Story Titillates Readers

The other day I was stopped at a red light when something lying on the pavement caught my eye. I looked closer and saw that it was a black brassiere.

My first impulse, upon seeing objects lying in the street, always has been to hop out and retrieve them. I voiced this intent to the people in the car with me, and their unanimous reply was instantaneous:

"Dad, please don't!"

All right, all right–I left that bra alone. It seemed in perfectly good condition, though. Nobody had run over it yet, like maybe it had been recently tossed.

I'm no expert, but it looked to be maybe a 32-C or so. Even though I had no use for it, it pained me to drive off and leave a brassiere in the street. I would have felt the same way about a socket wrench or a trailer ball. One just doesn't leave useful objects lying in streets.

As I drove away, I wondered out loud how an article of underwear had come to be lying on the pavement. I thought it might make a pretty good story.

Then a better thought occurred to me: Why not invite the readers of this column to make up stories about how that bra got there? Such an exercise might provide some interesting reading.

So here's the deal. I want you, readers of this newspaper, to use your imagination in describing how that bra got in the street. Keep your story under one hundred words, so we can fit seven or eight in a future column. I'll edit as necessary. Remember this is a family newspaper, but have fun. You've always wanted to write a short story–now's your chance.

* * *

Two weeks ago I invited readers to make up stories pertaining to the black bra I found lying in the street. Within hours my inbox was bustin' with mail. Apparently a lot of people are sitting around daydreaming about breasts and bras, and eager to talk about it. And I thought only newspaper columnists did this!

Anyway, here, in no particular order of literary merit, is a sampling of the stories, using authors' initials only:

"It was a dark and stormy night. She drove down the quiet street, seething. Unlike the staffers of the Globe-News, she could not afford a personal trainer at a tony fitness center. Her weight loss effort was a private affair, her only incentive a lacy, undersized black bra she kept in her handbag. Now, it only mocked her futile dieting efforts. Raging, she hurled it out her car window. Moments later, through tear-stained eyes, she saw the green-and-red sign that offered solace: Krispy Kreme." – D.S.

" 'I hate these things!' my wife said. 'They are hot and scratchy. Why would society make us wear something as uncomfortable as a bra?' We were returning home from a gathering with friends.

" 'Well, if it bothers you so much, then just take it off and pitch it,' I said.

"We had just enjoyed several glasses of wine, and the effects were still with us. The next thing I knew, she had shucked that lace monster off–if you can call a 32-A a monster–and thrown it out the window. Good wine provides the courage to do the unthinkable. The party was just beginning." – M. R.

"On a hot summer day, thirty years after I had awaited the blossoming of 'them,' I'm sitting at a stoplight. My bra is pinching the dog out of me. Moms don't spend money on new bras; they make do with two sizes too small. I finally decide that I can't take it anymore. I pull the ol' 'unfasten, slip it off the arms and out of the blouse' trick, and before I know it–out the window it went! I couldn't wait for the light to change so that anyone I knew would think that I had dropped it by accident. 'Oops, did you see that? A bra just fell out of her car!' Suddenly I remember that I have to go to the store on my way home. Oh, well, no one will notice that I don't have that bra on anymore. I'll just tuck 'them' into my pants." – D.D.

"G-Man: 'Okay, Victoria, you're 32, see? Your secret days in the underworld are over, see? Come clean or you're out to dry.'

"Victoria: 'You've got the touch, G-Man. I'll snap. I held up a teller at the bank–well, me and Socks Varicose and Frenchy La Girdle. We hung out, then blew town fast. Ended up in Amarillo where we split up. Hung out at a strip club. Got close to the girls till I got loaded and went bust and they got too big for me. Tossed me out like a cheap knockoff. You got lucky, G-Man.'

"G-Man: 'Just my job, ma'am.'" – P.S.

"Three girls driving one evening had passed some good looking young men and then the young men passed them, etc. The girl riding shotgun decided to give them a thrill and took off her bra, leaving her shirt on. The next time the girls passed the young men, she bared all and then slung her bra at them." – M.W.

"She unhooked it the second she got in her car. The final hearing was concluded, and she was finally divorced. She rolled down the windows, cranked the stereo, and, as she sped away from the courthouse, flung the despised garment to the West Texas winds.

" 'Free at last,' she yelled to no one in particular. Just saying it was exhilarating. He had always insisted she wear one. After all, he had a reputation in this town." – J.B.

"I feel sure the lost black bra belongs to my friend Lou. She has to have been in town recently if brassieres are appearing in strange places. She's the only woman I've ever known who can hold you mesmerized with her funny tales, never break eye contact, never take off her clothing, but can remove her despised and hated bra in about five seconds, and then ask where she can dispose of it! Obviously this time she just threw it out of the car window! I'm just sorry she didn't call when she was here–we could have had a wonderful visit." – M.G.

"That bra belongs to my wife! Unaware of that when I found it in my car, I tucked it between the seats, planning to get back at my 'practical joke friends' whom I assumed had placed it there. My wife unexpectedly dropped by the office for lunch, and while opening the car door for her, I spotted the bra strap sticking out between the seats. Rushing around, I managed to extricate the item unnoticed, and you know the rest of the story." – D.B.

My sincere thanks to everyone who wrote, including those who sent poetry, which, unfortunately, takes up too much space to reproduce lucidly, and those who sent long stories which, unfortunately, are difficult to edit into a single coherent paragraph. Bra stories are still coming in, so I might have to devote another column just to stay abreast of the volume.

****

Breasts On the Bayou

Dateline–New Orleans This is an old, old town. When the Texas Panhandle was nothing but a wind-scoured prairie full of buffalo grass and grasshoppers, residents of New Orleans were preparing to celebrate their city's bicentennial. Since nobody thought to ask them to stop, they kept right on partying.

Celebration has become a way of life here. The casual visitor should understand that locals toast the pale morning sun. Then they lift the cup against the noonday heat. They toast the afternoon shadows. And the evenings–oo la la, *mon cher*. One is never more than a minute away from something loud and passionate in New Orleans.

Here in the French Quarter, for example, the original site of Spanish and later French colonial power, tourists visit museums to learn how Thomas Jefferson's upstart government virtually stole the Louisiana territory–vaguely defined as all lands drained by the Mississippi–from Napoleon for a price approaching four cents an acre. But to learn how to steal a peek, revelers find their way to Bourbon Street, the site of what might be conservatively termed *drunken pandemonium* when the sun goes down.

Visitors needn't wait until Mardi Gras to taste pandemonium. Apparently *les bons temps* are in a constant state of *roulez*. Crowds of mostly young would-be players jam the streets after dark, making walking difficult for anyone with a destination. The odor of sweat and cigars and beer, the thump of clashing musical genres, the dizzying strobes of technicolor neon combine to disorient and confuse. One takes care that the mount of an equestrian constable doesn't step on one's foot.

Walking comes to a grinding halt when the tourist encounters a spontaneous eruption of testosterone. Young men in the crowd– either milling in the street or leaning cross-eyed from the ubiquitous balconies–spy a strolling damsel of ample bosom. The rowdies erupt into boisterous chant and continue until the damsel either hurries from the scene or lifts her shirt to reveal, to the utter delight of the crowd, her naked breasts. The oglers express gratitude by tossing a string of cheap plastic beads to the blushing exhibitionist.

Never one to be mistaken for a prude, the author has seen plenty of breasts. Perhaps not plenty as in "lots and lots" but more than a few. Probably somewhere between a few and plenty. Closer to a few, actually, but enough to grasp the subtleties and possibilities of the matter. And yet it never occurred to him that a lady might be persuaded, by cheering and stomping and chanting, to rip open her shirt and expose her breasts to public scrutiny.

This method of courtship seems to be an institution in the French Quarter. One easily imagines the French themselves inventing it. A female member of the author's party attempts without the prerequisite exhibitionism to solicit beads from a randy gang of balcony-hangers, and is roundly jeered off the street. For a town nicknamed The Big Easy, New Orleans enforces strictly its social conventions.

Another inescapable convention is live music. There is more music here per square foot than any other city in the Louisiana Purchase. Rock 'n' roll, rhythm and blues, redneck, and country music vie for attention with the famous sound of New Orleans jazz.

People in the author's party, wishing to hear authentic old-time jazz, are directed to an unassuming storefront named Preservation Hall, surely one of the most poorly-preserved structures in Louisiana. Its most recent paint job appears to have been done during the Spanish occupation. For five dollars, one gains entrance to the most unlikely of music venues: a dark, claustrophobic room jam-packed with warm, damp music aficionados.

Seven old men of various races and degrees of decrepitude saunter onto the stage. By way of introduction, the band leader toots a brief trumpet riff, and, to some imperceptible signal, the music begins. Like sweet chicory coffee, it's hot but smooth. The arthritic keyboard man tickles his way up and down a battered, open-face piano. The drummer barely touches his snare with the brush. To polite applause, the horn section rises to its feet one at a time as solos come round.

Toward the end of the set the band leader glances at his watch. A fat white cat sleeping in a corner stretches, arches its back, and leaves the room. The band leader checks his watch again. The author wonders if the musicians are bored. Is this authentic Crescent City jazz, the joyful heartbeat of tenacious old Dixie, or just a sad imitation served in regulation shabbiness?

Cherie, it's hard to tell the *la difference*.

****

Two Outlaws on the Lam

One day I was driving down the Canyon Expressway, minding my own business, when something impacted my new car with a sharp *CLACK.* The sound was similar to a rock hitting the windshield, only louder.

Thinking maybe I'd been shot or perhaps a meteorite had struck my car, I looked around for damage but found none. Very strange.

Several weeks later I got in the car one morning and discovered a small crack snaking up from the lower edge of the windshield. What the–? Inspection revealed a large starburst, way down low on the black part of the glass beneath the wiper blades, visible only from outside the car. That explained the noise I'd heard.

Small windshield cracks, I've observed, don't always grow into big cracks. Sometimes they'll grow awhile and then seem to lose interest. No use replacing a windshield just for one little crack which might amount to nothing. I named it Clyde, as in Clyde Barrow the outlaw, and kept a close eye on it.

Clyde grew straight up about three-eighths of an inch every day, much like a wheat sprout. He almost seemed alive that way. Each new part would be slightly curved, so that, overall, Clyde had a squiggly shape, although his general direction was up. Obviously Clyde had ambitions.

In my experience, little problems sometimes turn into big problems if left alone. You can have a tiny blade of Johnson grass in your garden and think nothing of it, but next year that blade will be a clump, and the year after that, a patch. Soon you'll have no garden at all–just a lush field of Johnson grass. Dozens of examples of this sort of thing come to mind.

On the other hand, sometimes little problems don't grow. Sometimes they stay the same or go away. We've all had mysterious pains that came, stayed awhile, and vanished with no discernible effect.

Clyde didn't look to be vanishing, however. I recalled that several years ago a guy at the carwash had offered to fix a ding in my windshield. He said it wouldn't cost me a dime because insurance would cover it.

Suspecting a con, I called my agent and discovered that yes, State Farm would pay the cost of injecting the ding with resin to stop it from turning into a bona fide crack, thereby saving the company the cost of replacing the windshield.

So Clyde and I visited the windshield ding-fixer guy at the carwash. He took a tiny drill and bored a hole through the outer layer of the glass–windshields are two layers of glass, and cracks and chips are almost always in the outside layer–right at Clyde's growth end. Into this hole, the ding-fixer injected special glue.

The idea is to freeze the stresses within the glass that cause the crack to grow. To exert enough pressure to force the resin into the crack, the ding-fixer attached suction cups to the glass and positioned a tiny pump on top of Clyde before throwing the switch and filling Clyde full of hot glue.

True to his word, he didn't charge me a dime. Clyde seemed frustrated, butting his little head into that hole full of glue and being stopped cold. It looked like the end of the line for Mr. Barrow.

When cool weather arrived, I got in the car one day and discovered that Clyde had company–a second crack was coming up from the original starburst, growing parallel to the first. I had no choice but to name this new crack Bonnie.

In a few days, as if aware of his moll, Clyde broke out and went on the lam again.

Watching those cracks was like watching two snails race. They were neck and neck for a while, with Bonnie curving gently toward Clyde. It looked like they might merge. I guessed that if Bonnie ran into Clyde, she would disappear and only Clyde would remain.

But who really understands the mind of a woman? Bonnie, acting on primordial urges unknown perhaps even to her, suddenly veered right, away from her partner in crime, and leaped across the glass. In an astounding display of feminine wiles, she shot two feet from her old pal in a single day and angled toward oblivion at the edge of the windshield.

Clyde seemed poleaxed by this. Bonnie's departure stopped him dead in his tracks, and he hasn't moved a millimeter since she left. It just sucked the life out of him.

Bonnie, on the other hand, is sprinting for the windshield's edge, which I think of as sort of an international border. If she crosses that border, no one can touch her.

She'll be free as a bird.

****

An Unexpected Affinity

I've never wanted to visit New York. But my family decided to vacation on Manhattan Island, and that's how I ended up wandering around one of the hottest, nastiest, most astoundingly beautiful cities on the planet.

In the process, I had to unthink most of the things I've always thought about the Big Apple. For example, I've always heard New Yorkers were ferociously unfriendly. Untrue. We were rescued many times by the kindness of strangers on subway trains, on the street, and in taxis. After hearing David Letterman joke about New York taxi drivers, we were expecting them to bite our heads off. They were pussycats. Most seemed lonely for company, and were eager to show courtesy to a bevy of obvious out-of-towners.

The lone exception to this rule, and the only grouch we encountered all week, was a guard at the Empire State Building.

Me: "I'm looking for the ticket line for the observation deck."

Guard: "Right against the wall."

Me: "This wall here?"

Guard: "You see any other wall?"

Me (against my better judgment): "Actually yes. There's one there, one there, another there and one there."

Another misconception I had to shed is that Texans invented big. We don't know big. Amarillo's prized Santa Fe Building, for instance, would fit in the lobby of many Manhattan public buildings. The buildings there are simply gargantuan, a landscape of titanic scale, mile after mile of them. Any one of hundreds, plucked from New York and flown to Amarillo, would become the biggest building within a day's drive in any direction.

The wealth implied by so many grand buildings is hard to grasp. Most were constructed during the '20s and '30s, when our nation was chiseling out its self-concept in granite and limestone. We simply have nothing in Texas–I've looked–to compare with Grand Central Station, the Empire State Building, the Waldorf Astoria Hotel, St. Patrick's Cathedral, or the Statue of Liberty. We couldn't build structures like those now, even if we wanted to. The age of imagination for them has come and gone.

I was nervous about going to New York without my car, but that proved to be yet another fallacy. In New York, a car is a liability– you'll spend all day looking for a parking space which a New Yorker will beat you to. A person can get around with surprising speed using nothing but his feet. If you ride the subway, one $1.50 token will get you anywhere much faster than you could drive. And finally, if all else fails and you must cross town in a hurry, five people can taxi east to west in minutes for a dollar or two a head.

I even had an epiphany of sorts about the theater. I'd never enjoyed live theater, until last week when I saw plays on Broadway. Then it occurred to me that maybe the reason I've never liked theater is that I've never seen really good theater. After all the high school plays, college productions, and community theater events I've been party to, Broadway is in a different league. This isn't a criticism of community theater. It's just that when you spend two years getting a play ready, hire the best actors and production crews in the business, and charge eighty dollars a ticket, you can reach into the rarified air.

And speaking of theater, culture itself is larger than life in New York. Imagine going into a museum, turning a corner, and standing face to face with *Starry Night* by Vincent Van Gogh. It's a sobering experience. So was seeing Roy Lichtenstein's *Girl With Ball* hanging serenely in a corner.

Don't think my unexpected affinity for New York was total, however. My biggest gripe is that it stinks to high heaven, literally. Whoever plotted the city forgot that most essential element of civilized society: the alley. Mountains of ripe garbage block the sidewalks, leaking disgusting slime and causing an infernal stench. Street people tear the bags open and scatter debris to hell and back.

It's a serious problem, not to mention health hazard and a pox on tourism, which I'm surprised New Yorkers haven't yet solved.

Much as I liked New York, I was never so glad to see the clean air and wide open spaces of home. After breathing rancid smog and wandering around in a tourist's stupor in the mightiest city on earth, stepping off that American Eagle after midnight and sucking in deep lung-fulls of sweet, cool prairie air confirmed what I already knew: Here on the range I belong. But at least now I've begun to understand the bumper sticker, "I (heart) NY."

****

The Mighty Magnetron

It was a sleepy summer afternoon, and I was having trouble staying awake. Maybe I should pull over, I thought, and take a nap.

While I was stopped at a red light, I heard the rumble of distant thunder behind me. Funny thing was, there wasn't a cloud in the sky. Then the thunder rumbled again, closer, in quick succession, and a small sports car pulled alongside me. It wasn't thunder I was hearing–it was the deep bass from the car's sound system.

The music from my own car's radio was obliterated. Even though my windows were rolled up and the air conditioner was running, I might as well have been inside the other car. The noise vibrated my chest wall. I had to make a choice.

Inside the other car was a young man of about eighteen. I'm almost positive he was a decent sort, though he was trying hard to look and act like a bad boy. Everything about him, from the backward upside-down hat, to the shaved skull, to the tattoos and pierced eyebrows and fashionable cigarette dangling from his lips, screamed, "Look at me! I'm bad!"

I understand that young men his age have an obligation to behave in ways offensive to adult culture. I don't argue with that. He was showing his individuality by looking and acting like the regulation bad boy, a Platonic ideal existing in another plane.

Still, I draw the line when other people force me to listen to their music while I'm in the privacy of my vehicle or home. So I did what I had to do.

Reaching for a little dial on the dashboard of my car, I turned the directional indicator until it pointed at the young man's car. Then I depressed the "pulse activator" switch. There was a faint hum, barely audible over the noise of the young man's bass, as the Magnetron located in the trunk of my car emitted a powerful burst of electromagnetic energy.

The Magnetron is a device of my own design, made with parts readily available over the Internet or from the local salvage yard. Its energy source is a bank of twelve tractor batteries, connected serially, which is why the rear end of my car drags the ground. There is nothing illegal, so far as I know, in manufacturing or possessing such a device.

However, when I depressed the pulse activator switch and bathed the young man's car with an invisible electromagnetic burst, *that* was probably illegal. But then again, so was his forcing me to listen to his music, so we were even.

Maybe I was slightly more even. The powerful electromagnetic burst totally fried the electronics of his car. Instantly the engine died. The music stopped. His car's ignition system was toast. His expensive stereo system was junk. Even his wristwatch had stopped at precisely 3:42 p.m.

This all happened in the blink of an eye, while we waited for the light to turn green. I could see him staring at his instrument panel. I knew he was grinding the starter, but nothing was happening. Next he popped the hood, opened the door, and stepped out. Now that the music had stopped, he seemed smaller, younger. He lifted the hood and wiggled the battery wires. I rolled down my passenger side window.

"Got a problem?" I called.

"Nah," he replied. He pulled his cell phone from the clip at his belt and began punching in numbers. Then he frowned and looked at the phone. He shook it, thumped it with the heel of his other hand the way you might thump a faulty flashlight. He uttered an expletive and flipped his half-smoked cigarette into the gutter.

What he didn't know was that all electronic circuitry within the cone-shaped target area of my Magnetron was zapped. Even the garage door opener in his glove box was history. The only way to start his car now would be to replace the entire ignition system: all new wiring harness, onboard computer, alternator, coil, spark plug wires, and fuse box. Presumably, that would come before replacing the sound system.

"Need a lift?" I asked. He didn't seem a bad sort, and I'm in favor of helping out young people. In fact, he might have been your son or mine.

"I don't know what happened," he said. "All of a sudden, everything just, like, stopped."

My Mozart wafted out of the open window.

"Want me to call a tow truck?"

"I can fix it, no problem," he insisted.

I nodded. Dream on, I thought.

"Okay. Good luck."

The light turned green, and as I drove away I glanced in the mirror and saw him pacing around his car with his hands on his hips.

* * *

Requests poured in for my "Magentron," an imaginary device for zapping super-loud car stereos with an invisible pulse of electromagnetic energy, paralyzing permanently the electronic circuitry.

"I know where a lot of those 'radio-vibrators' flock," B.S. wrote. "We might work out a deal where I could borrow your car for a day and improve the noise of Amarillo immensely. However, I may want to borrow your car this summer. I would volunteer to hunt down the ice cream man and 'Magnetron' (can I use that as a verb?) his place of business. . . . I can't hear the cicadas for the noise of the ice cream man's loud speaker. That's a crime!"

J.H. had similar sentiments: "I wish it were true and everyone over fifty had one in their trunk. It might make driving a pleasure again."

Then there was this from O.G.: "Just read your article about the boom box noise and how you fried the young man's radio/disk/casette player. I want one. Just name your price. I will get a lien on my house, if needed to pay for it. . . . I promise that I will not tell the FBI, ATF, City, County or State Police. It will be cash up front. No questions asked. Just hurry."

I even heard from people as far away as Petaluma, California: "How many orders have you got for that thing? It would be a real money-maker in my town."

War

Dies Irae – September 11, 2001

Dear God, help us. Help us, we pray. Help us in our struggle with disbelief and grief and rage.

Our minds stumble over what our eyes behold. The hallucination of a jet disappearing into a tower like a stone thrown through a looking glass. The impossible image of office workers tumbling through space. Hollywood slo-mo sequences of towers collapsing into themselves. We know it can't be real. Help us awaken from this nightmare.

Kyrie eleison. Lord have mercy.

Help our minds wrap around this new reality. We can't take it in. It's a different sort of beast whose stinking breath washes over us. Its slow thighs raise clouds of indignant birds and poisonous dust. We can't breathe. It's breached our nursery door and peers with flat eyes into the cradle. Help us comprehend.

Christe eleison. Christ have mercy.

We might have withstood four hijackings, terrible as they were. We read about that sort of thing. We might have managed to shield our minds from the horror of four suicide crashes. It might even have been possible to repair damaged towers–spray out the fires, board up the gaping holes, bury the dead, hunt down the perpetrators–all theoretically doable, however agonizing.

But watching those towers explode to earth changed us. The skyline of our world is forever altered. Gone are the twin symbols of our culture's prowess. We bleed like a cut yearling.

Lacrimosa dies illa. Oh this day full of tears.

We pray that if by a miracle some poor souls lie pinned beneath doom's mountain of cinders, help them as only Thou can. Surround their darkness with bands of angels. Let them hear the shouts of their saviors, the roar of diesel, the groan of lifted concrete. Light their loneliness with Thy heavenly light.

Lux aeterna luceat eis, Domine. Light eternal shine upon them, Lord.

For families of the dead we pray. What scalding grief they bear we cannot know. Surround them with Thy loving kindness. May their departed loved ones find eternal rest in Thee.

Requiem aeternam. Grant them eternal rest.

Now our souls pant to loose the red tide of violence against our enemies. Blindly we would flail their cities into heaps of ash, their homes into smoking ruins, their bones into charcoal. It lies within our power to fuse their nation into a glowing plain of nuclear glass, with a sewage lagoon in the center where Osama bin Laden's tent once stood. The hot soot of anger burns our throats. Our thirst to avenge our dead contorts our faces into grimaces of death.

Quench our blood lust with your grace.

Salva me, fons pietatis. Save me, fount of pity.

Help us not become like our enemies who strike down the innocent with the sword of hatred. Instead of anarchy's writhing sea of vengeance, let justice roll down like waters. Help us know the difference between retribution and justice. Let the guilty be brought to justice, where every secret shall be revealed.

Judex ergo cum sedebit. When the judge takes his seat, all that is hidden shall appear.

We pray for our leaders during these dark days. Give them wise counsel and patience. Bless them with deep understanding and restraint. Give them ears to hear the legions of hell amassed at our gates, chanting War! War! Grant them eyes to see the battalions of darkness, row upon row under a black sun, spears glinting in shadow light, blood hot for a fight.

Dies irae, dies illa solvet saeculum in favilla. This day of wrath shall consume the world in ashes.

Help us show the world that even a wounded America is still a nation of law. Help us retain our best instincts and restrain our worst. Help us hold fast to our principles of liberty and justice for all.

We hear your clear voice above the tumult of jeering mobs who rejoice as their enemies perish: "Love your enemies and pray for your persecutors."

There must be some mistake. We know it's not possible that our enemies are also your children.

"Do not set yourself against the man who wrongs you." We'll pretend we didn't hear that.

Confutatis maledictis, when the damned are cast away
Flammis acribus addictis, and consigned to the flames
Voca me cum benedictis.
Call me to be with the blessed.
Amen.

****

A Father Contemplates Sending His Only Son Off to War

One evening after prayers, as I readied myself for bed, he came to me and said that in light of recent events, he wanted to join the army. He wondered what his mother and I would think.

I almost laughed but managed to catch myself. He had that tone he uses occasionally, casual on the surface and serious beneath.

"I want to do something for my country," he said.

Translation: My friends and I have been talking, and we think it would be fun to join together. Oh, I know them.

I started to say he could start by cleaning his room–that would help not only his country but also his mother. But it didn't seem like a joking moment and I didn't want to ruin it. What I said instead was, "I'm proud of you."

Truly, I was never so proud of him. He's only a boy, but now he wants to become a soldier and fight. I thank God he's not old enough to legally do it, but people have lied about their age before. He's tall for his age and might get away with it.

Seeing him standing there in the doorway, saying he wanted to fight, was one of those moments that comes with a whole set of mental images. One image was of some steely instructor handing him a weapon, a real weapon with real bullets. He'll be surprised how heavy a loaded weapon is. I know him–he won't feel like carrying it all day and sleeping with it at night. As soon as he hefts that loaded gun, he'll think to himself, "Uh oh."

Another image was of him in training. He's not much of a fighter. In fact, he's no fighter at all. Mock hand-to-hand combat will not go well for him. Other trainees will wish to be paired with him, because he looks threatening but would be an easy takedown.

I remember the first and only time he came home from school with a bloody nose. He was vague about the scuffle and acted like it was no big deal, but his mother and I could tell he was proud. Weeks later we found out from the teacher that it was only a nosebleed. No fighting was involved.

I also got a flashing image in my mind's eye of a nighttime fire fight. This is something he doesn't know about, but I do. Up close, a chorus of automatic weapons sounds like the end of the world. And is for some. Streams of tracer bullets coming at you, slapping into the dirt, make you pray the very earth will swallow you. And some it does.

When I asked him if he was sure about this decision, he said he was. He said he'd been praying about it and he felt God's direction.

How can I argue with that? That's the way we raised him. In all things seek God's will, then do what he commands. Without people willing to make hard choices when God urges it, what good would our faith be?

But I must tell you, privately, that all this God talk puts me in two minds. I know that, officially, we are a godly nation, and only by God's grace have we survived this long. Without God's help, today our country would be run by godless communists. I thank God for his victory over them every time I pray.

Deep inside, however, in my heart of hearts, I have doubts about God willing his children to war against each other. It doesn't seem like a good plan. No matter which side wins, some of his children will suffer and die. Such a scheme seems hatched by the devil.

I can't talk publicly about this, of course. I don't even discuss it with my wife. She might wonder about my faith.

If this war drags out too long, they might call up boys his age, and we'll be forced to send him into the war machine. On the outside, we will support this and pray for his safety. He is very brave to make such a choice.

Inside, we will be deathly afraid every day he is gone. She especially will be sick with fear. She lost a brother in combat. They never even found his body. Nothing of him to bury, nothing to hold close and remember.

That's another image that came to me as my son stood in the door and said he wanted to fight: his funeral procession. Another thing I would never mention to his mother. His flag-draped coffin shouldered by his friends. I don't know how life could continue.

I wonder if those who call for jihad know what it costs us parents. Surely they must. They are God's chosen servants. Still, the Taliban hides underground and sends my boy to face the enemy with trembling hands.

I pray Allah will make him strong. Allah is great. Allah's will be done.

* * *

A column that was probably too subtle for its own good was the story about the father contemplating his son going off to war.

Sometimes an idea pops to mind and clamors to be written down. All the writer has to do is sit down and let it write itself. An hour later, it's finished and sent to the paper.

However, the son-going-to-war column wasn't that way. I wrote and wrote. Then I showed it to people and asked for feedback. When they didn't get the intended point, I went back to the drawing board. I changed things and made it less subtle.

Or so I thought.

After the column appeared, I received an e-mail from a serviceman overseas:

"I just read your article," C. R. wrote, "and may I say it warms my heart to see America's youth today actually caring about their freedoms and wanting to do something about it."

Several other readers stopped me that week to say they enjoyed reading about my son's desire to join the military.

I couldn't think of a graceful way to say that the column wasn't about my son. I was not the speaker in the story. My son wasn't the son in question.

I fear the column strayed from its intended target and produced only collateral damage.

****

What Larger Mosaic?

More than in any previous war, images of this one flood into our homes. Which ones tell the true story?

A little boy runs alongside a massive head of Saddam as it's dragged through the streets of Baghdad by a crowd. He slaps the statue's face with his shoes and laughs. The reporter says that touching someone with the soles of one's shoes is an insult in the Arab world.

Another little boy, this one with no arms, cries in a hospital bed. Gauze wraps his bleeding stumps. The reporter says an American rocket blew off his arms and killed his family, and the boy doesn't yet know that his family is dead.

An American prisoner of war is interrogated on Iraqi TV. She keeps glancing to her right, as if someone is threatening her, off-camera. It's a violation of international law to interrogate prisoners this way. Several of her dead friends bear wounds consistent with execution.

An Iraqi prisoner of war undergoes surgery by American doctors, saving his life. The doctors say they're using medical triage, not political triage.

Mobs of young Arabs chant anti-Bush and anti-American slogans, burn effigies and American flags in the street, and beat their chests in anger.

Crowds of young Iraqis chant pro-Bush and pro-American slogans, burn portraits of Saddam and topple his bronze likenesses, and kiss photos of George Bush, saying, "Thank you, Mister Bush!"

A young woman at Baghdad University screams insults at an American soldier. He turn his head away.

The head of another young woman is found near a smoking crater which was once a restaurant and underground bunker. Four GPS-guided bombs made rubble of the building in hopes of killing Saddam and his sons.

Every day thousands of images pour into our homes. Does any one image tell the whole story?

Secretary of Defense Donald Rumsfeld compares the images to slices of pie. He tells reporters at a press conference that what they're seeing isn't the whole picture–only individual slices.

Sooner or later, however, with enough slices, it seems we ought to be able to tell what sort of pie it is.

Developing a balanced view of this war is no easy task. Opponents and proponents scream at each other across ideological picket lines. People opposed are labeled unpatriotic peaceniks. People in favor are labeled imperialistic warmongers. Some say they support the troops but oppose the war. Others say that's impossible.

A few things are becoming clear. One is that the world has entered a new era of warfare. Our satellites, bombs, and missiles are vastly more accurate than anything in history. The implications of this haven't yet become fully manifest.

Another thing that's clear is America's willingness to pre-emptively defend itself against nations that haven't actually attacked us. Most of the 9/11 hijackers were from Saudi Arabia, our ally. The old paradigm of waiting for the other guy to land the first blow is gone. This changes international relations considerably, and its implications here are still mostly undiscovered.

What is less clear is whether our actions in Iraq will make the world more stable or less. It's possible that Iraq will become a model of democracy for other countries in the region, and peace and prosperity will spread outward from Iraq in ever-increasing circles. This is the hope of the Bush administration.

Or it's possible that our actions in Iraq will catalyze our enemies and swell their power, the opposite of what we wished to accomplish, and violence and chaos will spread outward.

It's impossible to know which way things will go in the long run. At the time of this writing, there's jubilation, revenge murder, and looting in the streets of Iraq. Is this a glimpse of the Iraqi character, or a forgivable overreaction to "freedom"? Creating a stable government there will be tough but not impossible.

Now North Korea is pointing to Iraq as an argument for why it needs more nukes. Other nations are watching and learning. I wish I had the confidence in final outcomes that some of my neighbors seem to have.

We're told that success might take time. I believe this.

I also believe failure might take time. People don't want to hear that.

****

Nations Under Our Feet

One evening I was minding my own business, sitting on the back row at choir practice, when a lyric from the song we were rehearsing rose up and smote me:

"He shall subdue the nations under our feet."

On that same day a Palestinian suicide bomber had blown himself to smithereens along with a dozen or more Israelis. That horrible event was still fresh in my mind. It seemed connected to the song lyric about nations under our feet.

After choir practice I went home and looked in my Bible at Psalm 47: "Clap your hands, all you nations. Acclaim our God with shouts of joy. How fearful is the Lord Most High, great sovereign over all the earth!"

Next comes the line about subduing the nations under our feet.

If I understand correctly, the main idea of Psalm 47 seems to be that everyone ought to applaud because God has given the Promised Land to the Jews. This is land which formerly belonged to the Canaanites whom today we call Palestinians.

Pardon me if I don't feel like clapping.

When I was a child, I learned in Sunday School that God loved the Jews in a special way and promised to give them a land flowing with milk and honey.

We downplayed the fact that someone already owned that milk and that honey.

In order for the Jews to acquire the milk and honey, they had to move in with swords and skewer every man, woman, and child in the land of Canaan. I've never stopped to add up the numbers of Canaanites who perished, but surely it must have been in the hundreds of thousands, if not millions.

If this seemed like a violation of at least three of the Ten Commandments found in Exodus 20, not to worry–God himself wanted those people gone. At least that was the way it was explained to me.

Even to my childish mind, something seemed wrong with such a story. How could a God of unconditional love for every human person order such colossal mayhem and gore?

When I became a man, I put childish ways behind me and began to think about the traditions I'd been given. And here's where my thinking led:

Big fish eat little fish. History is written by the big fish.

The story of how the Jews conquered the Canaanites and took possession of the land has been handed down through the winners of that conflict, not the Canaanites who might tell it differently.

It's the old, old story. And it pertains not only to people far away.

Take Texas, for instance. Our culture took it from Mexico, who took it from Spain, who took it from the Aztecs, who undoubtedly took it from someone. I left out France because I can't remember when their flag was one of the six that has flown over Texas.

The point is that the strong tend to take from the weak. The Jews took Canaan because they had better weapons, better strategy, or better luck. It didn't hurt that they considered their cause ordained by God Almighty. Whether it was or not is subject to debate.

I consider the Jews a superior tribe of humans. Just look at all that's been done to them throughout history, and yet they not only survive but thrive. Where would our civilization be without their contributions in science, music, medicine, literature?

No wonder the Nazis burned with envy and tried to exterminate them. I suspect that deep down, Hitler trembled with the knowledge of which race was truly superior. He dealt the Jews a terrible blow, but they survived and he did not.

However, when people take sword in hand and attempt to appropriate what doesn't belong to them, I have to say Not So Fast. In order to be fair, I have to say this to anyone who tries to take someone else's property. Justice isn't justice if it's selectively applied.

I can imagine how the Israelis feel, with Saddam on one side, Syria on another, and Yasser Arafat walking to and fro. In a supreme irony, some of Israel's best friends are Evangelical Christians, who happen to believe that the Jews are going to hell because they don't accept Jesus Christ as the son of God.

Then there are the Palestinians. It was their land first. They lost it by the usual method, then got it back, then lost it again. Now they're living with an occupying army in their midst, which they like about as much as you or I would.

Where does this leave us? It leaves us with quite a mess on our hands.

Speaking only for myself, having nations under our feet is nothing to clap about.

****

March, 2003; Worrisome Specks on the Horizon

Although polls say that roughly twice as many Americans support the Iraq war as oppose it, my own feelings are more complicated than "support or oppose." I don't seem to fit in either group. Big surprise.

Before we invaded Iraq, I voiced the concern shared by many that President Bush was rushing into something that didn't need to be rushed into. Sooner or later, violence might have been necessary to get Saddam to tell the truth or die lying, but I didn't think we were to that point yet.

Our government felt otherwise, however, so in went the troops. I didn't like it, but I accepted it. Maybe Bush knew things that we didn't, and he felt that haste was necessary. I wanted to give him the benefit of the doubt.

This was described as a war of liberation. I don't mind saying I got a lump in my throat listening to Bush give his "the hour of Iraq's liberation is here" speech. I'm in favor of people being liberated.

This war could show America at its best: Brave men and women doing a dirty task which must be done, even though few nations would stand with us, to make the world safer and for the benefit of an oppressed people who would welcome us as liberators.

On the horizon I'm now seeing things that trouble me. Maybe they're just distant specks of little consequence. Maybe I'm just a worrier.

Or maybe they're the sort of specks that grow into oncoming disaster. While our space shuttle *Columbia* orbited the earth in January, a small piece of insulation striking the left wing was thought to be of no consequence. All the best minds said so. I don't want another catastrophe to surprise us.

One little speck on the horizon is the way our military planners underestimated the Iraqis' will to fight. I pictured Iraq as a persecuted majority held hostage by a brutal but tiny minority.

Now that picture might need adjusting. Maybe the Iraqis don't mind Saddam as much as we thought, or as much as we do. If they want to be liberated, they have a strange way of showing it so far. They seem to regard us as invaders on their home soil. Even Iraqis who dislike Saddam might fight us for driving tanks across their fields. I'm hoping that hiding in the basements are the millions of Iraqis who soon will cheer our troops.

During Vietnam we occasionally had to destroy a village in order to save it. Then as now, we had trouble telling enemy from civilian. I wonder how many Iraqi deaths our planners consider "acceptable," and what will happen if we have to kill a lot more than the "acceptable" number in order to achieve our goals?

It's possible that every Iraqi soldier we kill has a family somewhere. Spilling someone's blood has a way of hardening his relatives against us.

I know that in war we have to kill people. But at what point does killing more and more Iraqis become counterproductive to our own goal of making the world a safer place? What if it makes the world a more dangerous place, especially for Americans? If we instill lifelong hatred in more and more young Muslims in Iraq and beyond, are we moving forward or backward?

If Osama bin Laden is still alive, he's surely jumping for joy at what's happening in "the Arab street." Behold your next generation of warriors and suicide bombers. Orphans have long memories.

Another speck on the horizon is the way our military planners overestimated the "shock and awe" value of aerial bombardment. No doubt we could return Iraq to the Stone Age without causing many immediate American casualties. Our factories can make bombs until the cows come home.

Our bombs and missiles, however, haven't caused the wholesale surrender of Iraqi military units. The much-hyped "shock and awe" might just be "aw shucks" to tenacious Iraqi fighters.

A third speck on the horizon is money. I dislike the fact that the war figures were withheld until after it started: around $60 billion a month. That comes to roughly $300 per month for each American taxpayer.

I didn't like deficit spending when the Democrats were doing it, and it doesn't seem any wiser now that the Republicans are starting down that road. This war could suck our treasury dry.

Maybe these specks add up to naught. I hope to God that's the case, and my worry will signify nothing. I want to be proved wrong.

The thing that disturbs my sleep is this: What if our government has made a major miscalculation? What if Iraq becomes Mogadishu on a grand scale? Imagine house-to-house fighting in a city the size of Dallas. How many brave soldiers would die before the American people stood up and said, "We goofed"?

****

Monkey Dung

One year after our country's invasion of Iraq, the Square Peg Party assesses the war.

The Square Peg Party, you might recall, is made up of independent-minded citizens who've been kicked out of the Republican Party for being too liberal, kicked out of the Democratic Party for being too conservative, and are prevented from being kicked out of the SqPP only by the fact that no one seems to be in charge of the SqPP.

Square Peggers aren't swayed by political rhetoric or BS, don't attend meetings or caucuses, don't do polling or research, don't have a membership database, and the closest thing to "party headquarters" is a "party *at* headquarters," meaning each SqPP household is a sovereign political entity whose motto is, "Peggers Rhymes With Keggers."

Peggers aren't pacifists, but we need solid reasons for going to war. In this regard, President Bush has failed miserably. Even Bush loyalists admit that his primary rationales for "regime change" in Iraq haven't panned out.

The foremost rationale–that Saddam secretly harbored weapons of mass destruction–has so far shown that Bush was wrong and Saddam was right.

"Disarm, you ugly pile of monkey dung!" Bush kept telling Saddam.

"Been there, done that," said Saddam.

"Then how do you explain these nuclear reactors in this grainy but top-top-top-secret satellite photo?" Bush challenged.

"You myopic frat boy," Saddam retorted. "Those are my chicken coops. Go suck an egg!"

The other primary rationale–that Iraq was somehow connected to the 9/11 attacks–has proven equally false. Real terrorists cells proliferate across the Middle East, but Iraq's government was so repressive and dishonest that not even terrorists wanted to camp there.

Which brings us to our next point: the SqPP policy toward lying tyrants. As a general rule, Peggers despise a tyrant. At last count, 347 lying tyrants were in power around the globe.

As near as Peggers can tell, our government's attitude is to coddle tyrants who act friendly toward us, and to talk trash to tyrants who refuse to kiss Bush's signet ring.

"I'm not kissing that thing!" one tyrant is said to have declaimed. "There's no telling where it's been!"

"Very well," Bush said. "Your room is ready at Guantanamo Bay."

The SqPP would like clarification of our country's policy toward tyranny. We can't just invade every country whose leader we happen to consider monkey dung. There has to be a clear-cut philosophy involved, such as, "Would Donald Rumsfeld *himself* go there and be in charge of cleaning up monkey dung?"

In the interest of fairness, Peggers note that it's easy to criticize someone doing a tough job. Nobody said this Iraq adventure was going to be a cake walk–except maybe Dick Cheney–and probably we ought to reserve judgment until the job is finished in a few more months, years, or decades.

As for the Democrats who say they could do a better job than Bush, we Peggers doubt it. We doubt *anyone* could do this job and make it pretty. If Al Gore were president now, he'd be in the same pickle as Bush, except Gore would be claiming credit for inventing JDAMs–the smart bombs our military used to destroy Baath Party infrastructure–the only difference being we'd still have money to pay for the war without going in the red, because the words *lower taxes* are an oxymoron to Democrats, sort of like *bad luck*.

To sum up, then, Peggers aren't necessarily opposed to regime change in theory, but almost everything about how Bush has accomplished this particular one stinks. Hundreds of American boys have died since Bush declared an end to hostilities, Haliburton is making a sack of money, no weapons of mass destruction have turned up, global terrorism seems as potent as ever, and Iraq might be better off without Saddam but the real test–can the new, improved Iraq govern itself without a gazillion U.S. dollars and troops?– remains to be seen.

On the bright side, we captured Saddam and got Libya's Qadaffi to throw down his nuclear (a term Bush still can't pronounce) weapons program.

The SqPP gives our Iraq war a D+ rating so far.

Eager Young Minds

Upturned, Hopeful Faces

Chances are, while you read this page of the newspaper, I'll be standing in front of my English classes at Amarillo College for the start of the fall semester. Today is the first day of school. All summer I've been looking forward to today, and as usual, I have a slight case of butterflies.

I'm what's known officially as "adjunct faculty," a phrase that sounds more high-class than "part-time instructor." I'm trying to decide why I love this job so.

It sure isn't the pay. Adjunct faculty teach two or three classes instead of the four or five taught by full-timers, but hour for hour, our pay rate is about half what full-time faculty make, even if our education and ability are equal.

It isn't the benefits, either. Part-timers can't participate in the health insurance plan. The institution has barely enough office space for full-time faculty, so most part-timers carry their office in a briefcase. We don't get a computer, a telephone number, or voice mail.

No matter how good we are, we probably won't win any teaching awards. Our names often are omitted from lists of college faculty. We don't get invited to all the parties.

In fact, in educational journals discussing adjunct faculty, the word *exploitation* often comes up, usually in a resentful tone. Setting aside the question of whether a person who willingly participates in an exploitative system can claim exploitation (here women and pornography come to mind), any objective assessment of adjunct faculty would probably admit some degree of exploitation is occurring.

And yet we part-timers keep coming back for more. What are we, crazy?

In my case, yes. I am flat-out crazy about the feeling I get standing here on this first day of class, gazing out at twenty-five upturned, hopeful faces. They've been invited to participate materially in the American Dream, and they're showing up in droves.

Many of them don't yet suspect what heavy cost success will demand. They're young and full of vinegar and quite a few ridiculous ideas. So was I at that age.

Some will discover the cost of success to be too dear and will drop out. That's okay–college isn't for everyone. They can always try again next semester or next year.

Most, however, will reach down inside themselves and find discipline they didn't know they had. They'll stick to the task, sacrifice what must be sacrificed, and come away in two or three years with some things they can be proud of: a deeper knowledge of and confidence in themselves, an expanded and more flexible mind, a more mature understanding of the world and what's in it. And an associate's degree.

So yes, I'm crazy. Since I have a spouse who is the main support of our family, I cheerfully do this job for appallingly low pay. Even knowing all I know about exploitation, I count it a privilege to be standing here.

How can you spend time around nineteen- and twenty-year-old young people and not recall the springtime of your own life, when every morning was a spankin' fresh beginning? Being around youthful, hopeful energy makes me feel youthful and hopeful and energetic. For a guy in the late summer of his life, that's no small thing.

If a balanced view of adjunct faculty must include the positives as well as the exploitative dimensions of the work, I'd have to say there are more of the former, starting with the fact that being in the classroom is what I love best, and that's really all I'm asked to do.

Nobody ever asks me to head a committee or even *be* on a committee. I'm never invited to work overtime or nights, unless you count reading student essays, which I sometimes enjoy (I told you I was crazy). There is a bare minimum of meetings–maybe two per year–that require my presence, and these are generally lively and pass quickly.

Since I don't have any turf, I don't get drawn into turf wars. I don't know where one professor's turf ends and the adjacent turf begins. I don't want to know.

I teach with a fun team of colleagues, and I get free access to the fitness center.

So here I am on a fine, late August morning. A gentle breeze rustles the leaves outside the classroom window. Just a hint of fall is in the air. In front of me sit twenty-five expectant, anxious kids, and I'm feeling a little anxious myself but also excited. We're about to go exploring together, they and I, exploring both their inner worlds and the outer world of ideas.

I'm just happy to be here.

****

Wide River of Humanity

It's mid-December, and all across America, colleges and universities are winding down for the holiday. Instructors, hunched over stacks of final exams, defer shopping until grades are finished.

I'm a college English teacher. This is my story.

After fifteen weeks of being the advocate, personal trainer, taskmaster, and–one hopes–friend of students, we switch to judge mode and decree who passes and who repeats the course. The personal, subjective relationship of instructor to student ends with a tidy black circle on a computer-scan form.

Semester's end is always a mixed blessing. Closure is a comfort, but I miss my students already. Experience says their paths and mine probably won't cross again. They're like a flock of wild birds for whom I scattered a season's worth of grain. Now they're gone on a gust of wind.

While it's true that no two students are alike, patterns emerge as semester follows semester. The Dark Horse, for example, seems never to get it. His journey across writing assignments is littered with comma splices, abrupt tone shifts, and organizational chaos. He's Forrest Gump with a keyboard.

Then in the eleventh hour a miracle happens. Somehow it all comes together for him. The braces fall away, and Forrest runs. You read his final essay and blink away tears of–what? Joy? Happiness?

Maybe it's just gratitude. You were privileged to participate in a sort of birth. The Dark Horse, who previously couldn't string together three coherent sentences, discovers his voice. Language is power, and there's no telling how far it will take him.

Then there's the Hare. She's strong, fast, and writes circles around her classmates. With ease she zips through assignments, and, from luxuriant roadside grass, she greets the tortoises as they lumber past.

More talent resides in her little finger than the tortoises have in their whole bodies, but she finds it hard to show up for class. For the first time in her life, she's cut free from parental control. She seizes her destiny and drops it onto the floor with a splat, crossing the finish line behind the less talented but more disciplined plodders.

Then there's Immigrant Son. His family escaped political holocaust in El Salvador, Vietnam, or Chiapas. Or maybe it was an economic holocaust.

He's trying to discover his place in this New World. Your heart goes out to him as he struggles with the nuances of the maddeningly idiosyncratic dialect we call Standard English.

He thinks in one language but must write in another. Although he's more adept at your language than you are at his, now that he's in Rome your job is to teach him to talk like a Roman. He needs a running start to mount hurdles that American-born kids step over easily.

Older Student has returned to college after raising her family. Compared to nineteen-year olds, she's motivated and focused. What she lacks in language facility, she makes up for in dependability. It's a rare day when her chair is empty.

Older Student's main trouble is that a lifetime of nonstandard usage has transformed language problems into stone. Each petrified habit must be chiseled loose, tap by tap, and replaced. It's painstaking work.

Luckily her wild oats days are behind her now, so she's free to engage fully in the process. It's pleasant to see such determination. Plus, she knows the same songs you do. When you mention Woodstock, she says, "I was there."

Then there's Lemme Be man. He's not in English class by choice and considers it an affront to liberty that his degree plan forces thirty weeks of writing instruction down his throat. All he wants from you is 1) to be left alone, and 2) a *C* at the end.

More than he realizes, you understand how he feels–just like you would feel if, say, hydrology had been required for your degree.

He sits by the window in a feed cap and Carhart jacket. He doesn't interact socially with the class. He distrusts a "liberal arts" education.

In a few years, Lemme Be man will feed a hungry world with his agriculture degree and his combine. You can tell he's suffering now, so you try to avoid provoking him any more than necessary.

All these students flow through college like a wide river of humanity. No two need exactly the same thing. You get one chance to help them along, then it's time to say goodbye, turn in grades, and start planning what you'll do differently next semester.

Most Land Safely

Nine months ago I wrote about standing before several classes of hopeful, upturned faces and experiencing some fall semester jitters and joys. Today I stand at the end and reflect on a school year which is drawing to a close.

A balanced appraisal might begin by noting that there aren't as many upturned faces as I started out with. As I said back in August, college isn't for everyone, and the only way a student can discover if he's cut out for it is to try.

One thing I enjoy about the community college system is its fundamentally democratic nature. Amarillo College has open admission; whosoever will may come. The benefits of higher education are as accessible to the low-income student from across the tracks as to the doctor's daughter from the gated community. I like that.

Over the years I've come to think of college students in three rough groups. First are those who are so determined and focused that nothing short of unforseen catastrophe will derail their success. It's always good to have some of these in each class–the leaders and high achievers. You give them an assignment and know they'll work it until they've succeeded.

Another group is comprised of a small percentage of students who, for various reasons, I can't seem to reach. Some are damaged by life in ways I can't begin to imagine. Some just aren't a good match with my personal style of teaching. They come to a few classes and then drop off the screen, never to be heard from again. You try calling and find their number disconnected. They're an enigma.

The third group is the one I seem most drawn to: students who, with some help from instructors, might learn to succeed. They wrestle with motivation, with rolling out of the quilts for class. The law says they had to attend high school, but no law forces them to attend college. Once they are out from under Mom and Dad, some good things fall to the ground. It's called growing up, and it isn't always pretty.

Part of my job with them is salesmanship–to sell the idea of higher education. I try to convince them that the rewards of education will be worth the sacrifice. I don't reach them all, but I hope I reach some.

My notion about the few I don't reach has evolved. I used to wring my hands about capable students who drop out. Now my welcome on the first day of class includes a word about "failure." Discovering that he's not ready for academic work might be the single most important bit of self-knowledge a young man acquires. He's then free to take up some other line of work for a few years, and return a wiser and more self-disciplined person.

A few students find their learning skills inadequate, and they become discouraged. I believe that some who struggle in school have undiagnosed learning problems. Maybe they never learned how to study, or maybe they have conditions like dyslexia which prevent even their most dedicated effort from producing fruit. These I encourage to connect with appropriate resources.

Most of the students I started out with are crossing the finish line standing up, and for these I feel like cheering. They might be a little wobbly on their feet, they're sleep-deprived and cross-eyed from burning midnight oil, their social lives are hanging fire, but they're crossing the line on one more leg of the race.

I want to clap them on the back, especially when I compare my own college years–subsidized 100 percent by my parents and divided between Baptist Student Union, girls, touch football, and academics (in roughly that order)–to the life of my present students. I am awed and humbled. Almost all of my students work, many full time. Many have children. Some work two jobs and have children and spouses, and still manage to meet the challenges of academic work. I don't know how they do it.

A few years ago I watched a documentary about World War II aircraft carriers. The flagman was guiding fighter planes to safe landings after combat missions. Some planes had only one wheel down. A few limped in low, only to plunge over the edge of the deck and into the sea, and some missed the deck completely. Most landed safely, and the flagman shook their hand when they climbed down from the cockpit.

I know how that flagman felt. With a mixture of admiration and pride I've watched these students rise to the challenges I've placed before them. A few have missed the deck, but most are climbing down from the cockpit tired but wiser.

They know a lot more about how the world works now than they did just fifteen weeks ago. They've discovered that intellectual skills improve with use. They've cracked open some challenging texts and entered into the conversation of ideas.

More importantly, perhaps, they've learned about themselves. They've discovered boundaries and limits, and maybe seen a cause-effect relationship between hard work and success. Self-sacrifice and delayed gratification are not just empty concepts any more.

To students in their late teens, this could be the start of something big.

****

Here To-Day, Gone To-Morrow

One of my students at Amarillo College seemed miffed.

"How come you circled the ends of all my sentences?" she demanded to know.

I explained that she had failed to insert two spaces after each period, prompting my teacherly response. "It looks better my way," I said.

"Well," she countered, "my computer book says to put only one space after a period."

Of all the ridiculous things. Everybody knows the rule is two spaces after a period, not one. That's how Mrs. Eberle taught it in my eighth-grade typing class, that's how I write, and that's how I teach. One space just looks wrong.

"Show me," I said.

So she did. Right there in black and white, her computer textbook recommends only one space after a period.

Well, I'm not teaching from her computer textbook–I'm teaching from Kirszner and Mandell's *Literature: Reading, Reacting, Writing,* a heavy tome based on a thousand years of literary tradition. So merrily to Kirszner and Mandell we went, only to find this at the bottom of page 1,503: "The *MLA Handbook for Writers of Research Papers* shows a single space after all end punctuation."

Hmm. The plot thickened. Now our textbook was deferring to the MLA–Modern Language Association (the Supreme Court of English Usage)–to answer the question, and it appeared that I'VE BEEN WRONG ALL THESE YEARS! How could this be?

The short answer is that language and usage aren't set in concrete. Tastes change. What is right today might be wrong tomorrow.

Take the words *today* and *tomorrow*, for example. Not many years ago, those terms were hyphenated: *to-day, to-morrow*. If one of my students were to hyphenate *today* today, I'd circle it and ask her to remove the hyphen.

So to answer the end spacing question (and to save my reputation), I consulted the latest edition of the MLA Handbook. Nowhere could I find the answer. While it's true that the MLA Handbook *appears* to use one space after a period, it doesn't come right out and admit it. But we English teachers have other authorities to consult.

Page 232 of *Hodges' Harbrace Handbook* says, "The MLA and APA . . . style manuals state specifically that only one space follows all punctuation marks: the period, the question mark . . ." Well, shut my mouth.

Page 5 of the *Gregg Reference Manual* says: "As a general rule, use one space after the period at the end of a sentence, but *switch to two spaces whenever you feel a stronger visual break between sentences is needed*" [italics mine].

ARE YOU KIDDING ME? USE ONE OR TWO, DEPENDING ON HOW YOU FEEL AT THE MOMENT?

I went back to the MLA Handbook, trying to find where it addresses this question. I still couldn't find it. No wonder some students get frustrated and give up. Grammar can be a wonderful servant, but it makes a terrible master. Nit-picking questions such as spacing after punctuation must seem about as relevant as "how many angels can fit on the head of a pin?" And we wonder why composition instruction is so toxic to some students. Then when the teacher himself can't dig out the answer, what are students to think?

Hopefully they'll think that language is a fluid, living thing, and that very fluidity makes it a marvelous tool for expression. But not an infallible one.

In a recent column, for example, I typed the following sentence: "The felt hammers were moth-eaten, the wooden action broken, the soundboard split."

When this sentence appeared in the newspaper, my commas had been replaced with semi-colons. I called my editors. "How come you changed my commas to semi-colons?" I demanded to know.

"It looks better our way," they said.

It was hard to argue with that answer (although I did), because it was the very argument I use to require two spaces after a period, even in the face of mounting evidence that one space is becoming the norm. It just LOOKS BETTER my way, at least to me.

But anyone can see how this answer isn't going to satisfy a student with green circles all over her essay.

What should I tell her? Do it my way because I'm the boss? Do it one way for your computer teacher, and another way for me? Do it the Gregg way–however you feel?

If you were the teacher, what would you say? One space or two after a period?

****

End of the Line for Two-Spacers

In my column I don't shy away from difficult and serious topics. Over the years I've written about child abuse, accidental death, terrorism, parenting, war, spirituality, homosexuality, crime, and many other weighty subjects.

But I can't recall getting such an instant firestorm of response from readers, friends, and strangers on the street as I received last week after writing about how many spaces should go after a period.

Either a lot of people care deeply about this issue, or else a few passionate people have been sitting out there waiting for the chance to sound off. I don't know which.

For what it's worth, response is running two-to-one in favor of two spaces after a period. Typical of the "two-spacer" sentiment is a comment from my friend Bob Wylie, who, in answer to my request for a ruling and in defense of the two-space tradition, wrote, "Punctuation has but one purpose, to help the reader understand the writing. Double-spacing gives that help."

Louise Mulkey agreed: "In newspaper articles which only use one space, I sometimes miss the period or it blends onto the last letter of the word (trifocals, you know) and realize that what I've just read makes no sense at all. Then I have to go back and re-read slowly and decipher the intended meaning."

Ditto Larry Ellison of Dalhart: "TWO spaces must follow any punctuation mark that terminates a sentence. I know this fundamental rule to be true, because my high school English teacher, Mrs. Sorenson, told me so. I have practiced this rule for my entire life, and will argue to my death that it is proper."

Then there's John Ellis: "The truth: Here is a reference for you. Gavin and Sabin's *Reference Manual for Stenographers and Typists, Fourth Edition* (1970), [first edition 1951], Rule 298, page 57. 'Period: two spaces after the end of a sentence.' Can't get much clearer than that."

Mary Storm of Fredericksburg, Virginia, e-mailed this: "I did an informal survey today of coworkers and teacher friends. The unanimous result was 'of course you put two spaces after an ending mark of punctuation. Who changed the rules and when . . . and what do they know, anyway?'"

My favorite, which neatly sums up the argument, is from Marilyn House who wrote simply, "Two."

However. Living as we are in a post-modern, pluralistic, multicultural world, the inescapable fact is that "the times, they are a-changin.'" Several readers made good arguments for one space. Guess what machine is behind the growing one-space movement?

Right: the computer. Thoughtful readers have tried to explain to me why computers seem to prefer only one space. As near as I can

tell, one-space ideology is based on proportional fonts, molten lead, monospacing, and the history of typography–none of which I know diddly-squat about.

Computers, it seems, unlike my old Royal Standard typewriter, can adjust character spacing so that the letter "i" doesn't use as much space on the page as the letter "m." On a typewriter the "i" and "m" take equal space, so a double-space after a period is necessary to make the reader dead-certain she's reached the end of the sentence.

But computers have their own ideas about how type should look. Some programs, I'm told, won't even let the writer use two spaces. This is what we get for letting HAL 9000 drive that spaceship. (If you're old enough to understand that joke, you're probably a two-spacer.)

Joanne Stapleton sent an excerpt from a book titled, *The PC is Not a Typewriter*, in which typographic historian Robin Williams writes, "Use one space after periods, colons, exclamation marks, semicolons, question marks, or quotation marks–any punctuation that separates two sentences."

Who, we might ask, is Robin Williams and why should we listen to her and her ilk? The short answer: Because her ilk is gaining in number every day, and soon we two-spacers will be outnumbered, outdated, and outgunned.

One of her ilk, as John Ellis pointed out, is Bill Gates: "If Microsoft/Bill Gates says that is the way it is, you and I know better than to disagree, lest all files are suddenly lost and the big blue screen is all you can access forevermore."

Over all this din, Cathy Ricketts in Canadian asked a penetrating question: "Who is Miss Manners for the grammar world?"

We seem to be living in an age not unlike Israel's period of the judges, when everyone "did what was right in his own eyes." Instead of one final authority, the Supreme Potentate of English Usage, we have several–and they don't always agree.

Therefore, until we have firm evidence that usage has shifted away from two spaces after end punctuation, I will continue to practice and teach two spaces. I'll be my own potentate on this subject.

****

A Great But Perishable Gift

My speech to the graduates:

Congratulations, graduates. Thanks for inviting me to give your commencement address. I'll make this short and to the point.

Just look at you. Seriously. Look at your flat stomachs, your tight skin, all that hair. Take a good long look. Etch a negative in your mind's eye. You'll want to remember this night. When you walk out of here, time and gravity will kick in, like when a new car depreciates $3,000 the minute it's driven off the lot. Celebrate your beauty and strength–it's a great though perishable gift.

Your parents know almost precisely how you feel this evening, poised on the exhilarating cusp of life, but they lack the vocabulary to express it, and your ears couldn't hear it anyway. So they've asked me, since I'm not your parent, to send you off with our collective wisdom. Listen up:

Take risks. Teenagers have the risk thing partly right. You know that someday you'll be old and too safe for your own good, so you take risks now while you can. Note that the easy risks are the least meaningful. It's easy to get drunk and drive a car. It's easy to be casual with sex or drugs. The payoff is tiny compared to the potential for suffering.

If you want the most bang for your buck, take risks with ideas and relationships. Think outside the box, color outside the lines. Cultivate the art of original thinking. Expand your mind. Tell someone you love them. The danger here of dying tragically is small; the potential for reward huge.

Ask questions. Your head is full of ideas put there by others– friends, teachers, family. If you haven't begun examining these notions, what are you waiting for? Just because a thing is true for your friend doesn't mean it's true for you. Turn ideas over to see what's underneath. Caution is advised.

Question authority. History is splendidly littered with men and women who've challenged authority and were proven right. Galileo was under house arrest for questioning conventional wisdom.

Copernicus had the audacity to suggest that the earth whirled around the sun instead of vice versa, and the authorities were outraged.

Science, religion, medicine, the arts–all have been advanced by men and women who challenged The Wall. Don't take the president's word for it, or your professor's. Ask questions. A tip: When questioning authority, you'll get further if you do it with courtesy and humility.

Work a variety of jobs. Hire on as a flagman for a highway crew in Wyoming. Swab toilets one whole summer at the YMCA. Drive a truck. Pump gas. Work the wheat harvest, starting in Texas and ending in Canada. Sit at a desk, answer the phone. Do something on a horse. Be a park ranger or river guide. You'll never have as many choices as you do right this minute. Seize the day. Learn by doing. Expand your mind.

Unplug your television. Then, with a pair of wirecutters, snip off the cord close to the set. Clip the coaxial cable, too. Throw away the ends. Get up and live a life.

Buy a CD of music you don't like. Listen to it until you begin to understand why some people like it. Visit other churches. Go skinnydipping.

Sleep under the stars at least once. Pick a spot where coyotes are likely to serenade and shooting stars fall around you. Winter is best, when bugs and snakes are asleep and you'll wake with frost in your hair.

Start a daily journal, not a diary. Diaries tell what and when, journals why and how. It'll help define who you are. Write in it when you're feeling great and when you're feeling rotten. Bare your soul. Your children will read it someday and realize you were vastly more complicated than they imagined.

Visit someone in jail. Give your time at a homeless shelter. March in a picket line. Write letters. Read books for fun. Volunteer for missions in another country. Put your faith to the test. Be open to growth and change.

Pay attention to your dreams. I don't mean your aspirations. I mean your nightly dreams, the little one-act plays your unconscious mind produces for the benefit of your awareness. Write them down in your journal. In dreams, your mind is trying to tell you something you haven't quite grasped. Listen and learn.

If your car starts making a funny noise, don't keep driving and hope it's nothing. Same goes for your body.

Be a nonconformist. Get a feel for where the herd is running. Maybe it's headed for a cliff. To be a nonconformist requires great courage. Let the herd thunder past.

Some try to nonconform by wearing the Nonconformist Uniform: correct body piercings, official tattoos, regulation hair. Or maybe it's a black trench coat. Watch out that the Nonconformists Union doesn't dictate how you look or live.

Don't be a prisoner of fear. The world is astonishingly beautiful and corrosively dangerous. Be smart but shed that body armor. Trust God instead. Be vulnerable.

Seek advice. When you hit a dead end, ask directions. Your parents are vastly more complicated than you imagine.

Good luck. Thank you and good night.

Home and Garden

Alley Steward

So much meanness and strife in the world. So much ugliness where beauty should be. But what can one person do?

The answer came to me the other day as I was taking out the trash. Someone with bad aim had missed the Dumpster and scattered garbage all over the alley. Muttering a curse under my breath, I fetched my rake and cleaned up the mess.

Then I paused a moment and surveyed the alley–my alley. It was a tangled wreck of broken glass, spilled garbage, windblown litter, snarled tree branches and weeds. Suddenly I had one of those moments when the "scales fell from my sight" and I saw with different vision. When had my alley gotten this bad?

For example, across the alley and down the block from my home is a daycare center. Daycare centers tend to produce lots of disposable diapers. In my experience, the people who clean daycare centers have a casual attitude about putting their trash directly into the Dumpster.

You wouldn't think it would be too hard to hit a twenty-four-inch square hole with a sack of trash, especially from a range of twelve inches. But the litter tells a different story. Half a dozen squashed diapers decorated the ground around my Dumpster. Maybe daycare cleaners figure they already touched that diaper once–now it's someone else's problem.

I've put up with this sort of thing for years, sometimes raking them up and sometimes just ignoring them. After the trash truck runs over a diaper twenty or thirty times, it becomes virtually unrecognizable as an article of infant apparel. So why get worked up about it?

Granted, in the large scheme of things, an ugly alley is no big deal. But in that moment, as I stood with my hand on the rake, my new vision surveyed the ugliness all around me, and something snapped. In an instant I saw the universe, and I knew what I had to do.

I became the Steward of the Alley.

I can't control what goes on in Afghanistan or New York. I have little say in decisions made in Washington or Austin or even City Hall. But I resolved in that moment to clean up the mess in my alley and keep it cleaned up, world without end, amen.

With my trusty though seldom-used chainsaw, I went to work on trash trees which had sprung like unwelcome guests down both sides of the alley. Then I went to work on years of detritus packed into nooks and crannies of my alley's real estate.

Brickbats and lumps of concrete I piled next to the Dumpster. I've found over the years that although the city discourages placing rocks in the Dumpster–in fact prohibits it–if citizens use common sense, one rock per week won't choke the system.

Weeds, upstart saplings, and tree branches I piled for the chipper, thick ends pointing downstream. Bottles, trash, and leaves went into the Dumpster.

From one end of my block to the other, I cleaned that alley. I didn't seek or receive anyone's permission or approval. I'm not interested in starting a trend. Since I don't have to look at anyone else's alley, I don't care what others look like.

If your alley is an ugly mess and you're okay with that, fine. But mine is going to bloom like the backside of Eden. From now on, my alley has a steward and you're looking at him.

I'll plant flowers this spring. I'll strew buckets of mixed wildflower seed and watch what comes up. Tramps shuffling down the alley will think for a moment they've died and gone to heaven.

My little tiny bit of ugliness will become a thing of beauty, for no other reason than I prefer it that way.

In the future when someone shovels a truckload of old shingles into my alley (this has happened), I'll not stew and fuss. I'll just clean it up.

When someone drops off a pile of bald tires (this has happened), I'll not look for someone to blame. I'll simply address the problem.

When morons dump a pile of household garbage directly into the middle of the alley and then drive away, I'll not hop in my car and chase them down again (this too has happened). I'll look on such things as spiritual disciplines from now on.

When old refrigerators (ditto), wrecked lawn mowers (ditto), sofas (ditto), large tree stumps (those were mine), or other items too bulky to fit in the Dumpster appear, I'll take a cleansing breath and call the city's heavy trash pickup service.

Like Johnny Appleseed with an attitude, I'll create beauty where ugliness used to be.

God bless America.

****

You Say Tomato

Even though my family has been eating tomatoes this month like there's no tomorrow, at 2:41 p.m., tomorrow arrived. The production capacity of our garden finally exceeded our maximum consumption capacity. An alarm near the back door sounded, tomato-proof window and door grates slammed shut, and Phase 1 of our Tomato-Glut Protocol (TGP) action plan commenced. While the family scurried for gloves and insect repellent, I picked up the red phone and called our standby SPLAT team (Survival Per Lobbing All Tomatoes).

At 2:50 p.m., we rounded up every available plastic grocery bag and began picking tomatoes and filling the bags. We awarded season passes to Firewater Water Park to anyone who ate tomatoes while they picked. Fruit with the slightest blemish was hurled over the back fence. Unsuspecting transients walking down the alley had bags of tomatoes pressed into their hands.

By 3:30 p.m., the bulging bags were arrayed on the back porch. Phase 2 of TGP began. After I made a quick call to the police chief, a family of five from Kingman, Arizona, was pulled over on I-40 by uniformed Amarillo police officers. The officers filled the trunk of the family's car with bags of tomatoes, and instructed them to keep driving until they crossed the Oklahoma state line.

At 4:21 p.m., a back-to-school party was hastily arranged for neighborhood children, with sacks of tomatoes for party favors.

At 5:30 p.m., a bowl of tomatoes mixed with dog food was placed before Gus the dog.

At 5:40 p.m., we arranged a "Dumpster Layered Pie" in the alley: The bottom of an empty Dumpster was filled with six inches of ripe tomatoes, covered with a layer of grass clippings followed by another layer of tomatoes, another layer of clippings, then topped with household trash. (This is perfectly legal.)

At 6:43 p.m., a grain truck bearing a magnetic sign ("Big Boy Custom Feeding") pulled into a cattle feedlot west of town, quickly dumped its load of tomatoes while steers stared in disbelief, and drove away before feedlot operators could react. Authorities recovered the magnetic sign three miles east of Vega.

At 7:30 p.m., "SPLAT!", a new attraction at Wonderland Park, opened. Randall County's elected officials swung by the heels from ropes while taxpayers paid for the privilege of throwing tomatoes at them. Long lines quickly formed.

At 8:00 p.m., groups of volunteers fanned out across the city. Each volunteer carried two pounds of tomatoes in special "false bottom" pockets. Entering grocery stores, they casually approached the produce sections and, making sure no one was looking, emptied their loads. It was understood that we would disavow knowledge of anyone caught in the commission of this unauthorized donation.

At 9:06 p.m., Phase 3 commenced as dusk fell. We began distributing bags of tomatoes to neighbors in an action dubbed "Operation Reverse Halloween." Since postal regulations prohibit placing non-mail items in mail boxes, we hung sacks from door knobs, planter boxes, or light fixtures. Failing to find adequate places from which to hang sacks, distributors sometimes resorted to hooking sacks over car antennas, lawn furniture, and yard ornaments.

At 9:31 p.m., ten fifty-five-gallon drums of green tomatoes arrived at Palo Duro Canyon, where they were shot from cannons to simulate hail during the storm scene of the outdoor musical "Texas."

At 9:45 p.m., officials with the Panhandle Regional Ground Water Authority, using only ripe tomatoes, successfully plugged a brine aquifer feeding salt water into the Canadian River near Logan, N.M. Almost simultaneously, it was discovered downstream that the desalination of Lake Meredith could be speeded up by the addition to the lake of fresh tomatoes, which bind chemically with salt molecules and settle out to form an ideal spawning medium for bass.

At 10:00 p.m., two tilt-rotor V-22 aircraft lifted off from the airport, loaded with nebulizer tanks full of tomato puree. They seeded a promising-looking thunderstorm southwest of the city, producing widespread rainfall throughout the region. In addition, the puree-rain mixture reduced soil pH to levels more conducive to crops.

At 11:30 p.m., empty hopper cars leaving the coal-fired Harrington power plant were routed to a side-track and filled with tomatoes for the return trip, a gift from my family to the people of Wyoming.

At 11:45 p.m., all remaining tomatoes were trucked to a site north of town and dumped off a cliff, resulting in shock waves which registered 3.0 on the Richter Scale. Some people mistook this event for an earthquake.

At midnight, Gus the dog left home and hasn't been seen since.

****

Home Alone

A rare convergence of circumstances caused me to be alone recently. The three people I live with went out of town and left me in this big old empty house all by myself. It got mighty lonesome.

If a person grows accustomed to a certain level of interaction and noise, and then the noise ceases, the quiet can seem unsettling, even if the noise was Limp Bizkit or children arguing or the phone ringing thirty times a day. When my solitude began, I managed to keep busy during daylight but noticed the evenings were eerily quiet.

The thought occurred to me that the unnatural quiet might be more tolerable if I were to eat something sweet. I'm not allowed to eat ice cream directly from the carton when my family is around, even though I bought the ice cream myself and believe a man should be able to eat dessert however he wants. Members of my family dislike seeing tablespoon marks in the ice cream, although the marks made by a regular scooper don't seem to bother them. In the interest of harmony, I usually refrain from eating out of the carton.

Since the people with strong opinions concerning the right way to eat ice cream were gone, I stood in the quiet kitchen and, directly from the carton, ate as much as I wanted. I could hear the clock ticking. When the Blue Bell Vanilla Bean began to grow soft around the edges, I dug down deeper all around until I'd created a little mount of ice cream in the center of the carton, a pile of frozen goodness not touching the sides of the carton at all. For some odd reason, that pleased me and made me feel less lonely.

Next I decided to watch a little TV and see if I could reduce even further the feeling of isolation. Several old movies were on cable, and by deft use of the remote I managed to watch all of them simultaneously. When my family is home, flipping back and forth between several TV programs is verboten. They like to watch just one show at a time, including its commercials.

But since no one else was around, I flipped back and forth and was actually able not only to avoid seeing a single commercial but to follow the gist of four separate programs. I still felt lonely and sad, but not quite as much as before.

It was pretty late when the movies ended, but I wasn't the least bit tired. It might have been the two caffeinated soft drinks I had during the movies. I try not to drink soft drinks in front of the kids because they'll want one, and caffeine isn't good for children. Without them to complain, I drank one which went down pretty smooth, so I had another.

Normally my family practices quiet time during the hour before bedtime. With no one to take offense, however, I couldn't see the hurt in a little music. I put on some anti-depression songs written by a pair of classical composers named Lennon and McCartney. I cranked it up pretty loud and felt somewhat better.

A thought popped into my head. Earlier in the day I had been doing some work in the attic, getting ready to install a new air-conditioning system. I had knocked off work at suppertime as usual, but suddenly I couldn't think of a reason not to go back to work at 10:30 p.m. In order for the anti-depression music to reach the attic, I had to turn it up even louder, which disturbed no one except the dog, who retired to the basement.

It was well after midnight when I finished working and cleaned up for bed. Normally I don't retire late because it makes me sleep later in the morning. With no one to haul to school the next day, though, I couldn't think of a reason to get up early, so I read a book until 1:00 a.m. and slept until almost seven, which made my sense of abandonment less pronounced.

In hopes of reducing the isolation even more, the next night I decided to go to a movie. It's hard for four people to agree on a movie, but with just one person–me–to make the decision, it was fairly easy even in my depressed state. Popcorn is comfort food for me, so at the theater I got a large popcorn which doubled as supper.

During the show some people behind me were enjoying the movie a little too much–laughing, talking, making annoying noises with their straws–so I got up and moved. It's hard to move a family of four in a dark theater, but surprisingly easy for just one person. Doing so made me feel slightly less sad about being alone.

After the movie I went home and read in bed for a long time. Reading in bed while sipping a cold beverage did wonders for my suffering.

Right before my family returned, I went around the house flushing toilets and putting the seats down. They asked if I had missed them. I admitted I had but had coped with it as best I could.

****

Married and Contemplating Decks

Eleven years ago, not wishing to ever build another wooden deck as long as I lived, I installed onto the back of my home what I thought was The Deck to End All Decks. I used the best treated lumber and galvanized joist hangers and nails, and I poured twenty concrete footings to anchor the thing to Mother Earth.

I even went to the added expense of using "hot-dipped" galvanized nails, clearly superior to the "electro-plated" galvanized sort, the latter having only a microscopically thin layer of rust-inhibiting zinc, whereas the former have zinc so thick it sometimes glues two nails together like Siamese twins, rendering them useless as fasteners although interesting as a conversation piece. ("Would you like to see my Siamese sixteen-penny nail collection?") To prevent splitting, I pre-drilled holes for the nails.

The kids were small then and "helped" with the deck. Some of their hammer dings are still visible. Our new all-pine deck looked swell for a couple years. It was on the west side of the house and took a beating from the afternoon sun, and it locked up solid during a winter freeze, but what did I care? That's what treated lumber is made for.

The boards started to split and warp after about five years. One day my son was walking barefoot across the deck and slid his foot into a gigantic splinter. Pliers couldn't budge it, so we made a memorable trip to the hospital to have it removed surgically at a cost of approximately one-fourth the price of the deck itself.

I decided then to have the whole deck sanded down professionally. Although one reason we chose treated pine was to avoid having to paint or stain it, it seemed that stain might preserve the wood and keep it from deteriorating further. So I rolled on an oil-base penetrating stain.

"There," I thought. "I'll never have to do another thing to this deck as long as I live."

I should learn to stop saying that. At about the nine-year point, the boards were splitting, cupping, twisting, checking, and warping. Did I mention bowing?

"That deck has got to go," my wife announced. "Let's get a redwood deck."

Women think they can just snap their fingers and *voila!* things will appear. I had to explain my philosophical opposition to using redwood, the bottom line of which is that I don't care for the harvest practices of the redwood industry. I've been to the Pacific Northwest and seen how redwood forests are reduced to smoldering wastelands. Besides, if she thought treated pine was expensive, the cost of redwood would give her a nosebleed.

"Still, redwood would be nice," she repeated.

Fortunately there are alternatives to using real wood for decks. One is a synthetic lumber product made from sawdust and recycled plastic grocery sacks. I'm not kidding—I have a brochure that tells all about it. Sawdust is mixed with melted sacks and the "boards" are extruded like toothpaste from a tube.

To test these plastic non-boards, I bought several and let them weather for a year. They're heavier than wood and less rigid but are guaranteed not to split, cup, twist, check, warp, or bow.

After a year in the sun, the boards were examined. They hadn't done any of those bad things normal lumber does. But they didn't look like normal lumber, either. In fact, they weathered to a color surprisingly close to toothpaste.

"Yuck," was how my wife described it. I could always paint or stain the synthetic boards, but wouldn't that defeat the purpose of using synthetic? Back to the drawing board.

A second alternative to the toothpaste boards is a similar product but with wood grain embossed on the surface and a guaranteed fade-proof stain built in. It looks less plastic and more wood-like than the ungrained product. But the only manufacturer is in Maine. Might as well have the boards gold-plated before they're shipped.

In the end I did what any astute married person already has seen I would do: bought redwood. It's against my principles. I did it anyway.

It quickly became apparent why redwood is so popular. The stuff is plain gorgeous. I love working with it. It handles and cuts easier than pine and takes screws readily.

Yes, I said screws. No nail will ever touch this deck. I'm using coated screws and plenty of space-age exterior glue to fasten down the joints. I don't know what space-age exterior glue is, but it sounds like it ought to last forever. Maybe the International Space Station has a redwood deck made with this glue.

On the tube it says this glue will "outlast the application," meaning, I suppose, that after the deck itself has decomposed into a pile of splinters, the glue joints will be good as new. I'll be long gone then, but it's comforting to know that someone will walk past and remark, "Say, those are some pretty gobs of glue!"

****

Listen to the Wind

It seems only fitting, in view of the Panhandle's frequent windstorms, to spend a few minutes thinking about the March wind. Wind is such a big part of life here, and more so this month. It's said that the Eskimos have one hundred different words for snow, but here in the Panhandle we have one hundred different words for wind—most of them unprintable.

In my front yard is a flower bed that collects windblown debris. Something about the way last year's dried flower stalks—which I've been meaning to snip off and tidy up but haven't got around to yet—stick up seems to attract and hold trash. I call it the trash bed, for obvious reasons.

For two years I've been saving stuff that my trash bed has caught. In the interest of science, and in honor of the March wind, I'll describe just a few of these things:

• Two one-dollar bills. The second one blew into the yard a week after the first one. I'm still trying to figure out a scenario that explains why money would be blowing down Harrison Street. Only thing I can figure is that some bank robbers were passing along I-40 and throwing out the window of their getaway car anything smaller than a twenty-dollar bill. If that's true, I wish I'd gotten two tens instead of two ones.

• A page from a letter, on nice pink floral stationery. It includes these lines: "Liz wanted to come this weekend and I told her I needed more than two days notice to have someone visit. . . . Jerry and I are cleaning windows today and having mini-blinds cleaned so our day is cut out for us. He's gotta wash the siding on the house down. It's so filthy, I'm embarrassed. We need rain bad."

• A business card for "Justice and Righteous Roofing Service." They specialize in leaks.

• A post card from December 1998, from a church several blocks away, telling the recipient, "You have been selected to serve on the Lord's Table for the month of December."

I hope he read the postcard before it blew into my flower bed, or else the Lord's Table was short one server.

• A scribbled message on yellow note paper: "No one home call store for new delivery time on your two rugs–John."

John, if they still haven't called, it's because your note blew away. Please attempt redelivery at once.

• A full-page color photo of a nude woman with improbably large breasts. I'm no expert, but they don't look natural to me.

• A bill of materials from the City of Plainview, dated March 1995. It's pretty beat up, like maybe it's been traveling the wind all this time, back and forth across the prairie. Now its traveling days are over, and I doubt Plainview would mind you knowing that they ordered eight NOTA-BENE Technology 8 DI Exp. Mod. backpanels, Model No. AIXAII, in case you're interested.

• A legal document titled "Principles of Employment" that says, "The purpose of the above policies is to assure fair, safe, and pleasant working conditions for all of the Company's employees. However, we recognize that disputes may arise from time. . . ."

Uh-oh.

• A flier about a missing pet named Drake, a dog of the Rottweiler persuasion. At the time the flier was printed, Drake was a year old and weighed seventy-five pounds. Most of us know what it's like to have pets go AWOL, and we hope Drake's owners found him safe and sound. The flier mentions a "sizeable reward!" but doesn't say how sizeable. If anyone out there found a Rottweiler, call me and I'll give you the number of Drake's owner.

• A school handwriting practice page for the letters *T* and *F*: "Today is Thursday. Tomorrow is Friday."

• A notice from the manager to the residents of an apartment complex that a forcible rape has occurred within a two-mile radius: "As you can appreciate, no one can ensure your safety. Please remember that your security is your responsibility and that of the local law enforcement agencies."

In other words, don't sue us if you're attacked on our property.

• A business card for Don King, Goldsmith, on Historic Route 66. He also repairs.

• A page from the Generation Y section of the newspaper that includes a column by Amy Tao. It's a sad column. Amy and her best friend had a big falling-out, and Amy was not handling it too well. She gave me permission to quote from the column:

"For the next six months or so, I lived in the Great Garden of Grief. . . . Every day of my life was worse than the one before. . . . I was trapped in a whirlpool of despair with no way out."

Anybody who remembers being seventeen years old and losing your best friend can see that Amy Tao pretty much nailed the feeling.

I could go on but I'm out of space. If you want more, go read what's in your own yard.

****

Going Mental with Rental

Things in my life had been going a little too well, so I decided to buy a rent house. It's no accident, I've learned, that the term *rent* also means "torn in half," as in bank account, peace of mind, or bicep.

Buying rental property was no spur-of-the-moment decision. When the for sale sign first appeared in the front yard of the house, I gave the matter ten or possibly as much as fifteen seconds' consideration before calling to make an offer.

The reason I could decide so quickly was that for the past year, I'd been watching the house slowly slide into disrepair. The reason I could watch it slide into disrepair is because it's directly across the alley from my home.

How hard could it be, I figured, to be a landlord? Other people do it. The house seemed basically sound–after all, renters were living there. Their dogs had torn up the back yard pretty good and created an unmistakable doggy odor, but it was nothing that a little topsoil and a small thermonuclear device couldn't fix.

The plan was to spend a month spiffing it up, rent it to a conscientious, childless Mormon couple with no pets, then sit back and rake in the money. That was in May.

In June I noticed an outside faucet was crooked. When I tried to straighten it with a wrench, it broke off. A closer look at the pipes (why didn't I think of this sooner?) revealed that they were the original equipment, installed during the Wilson administration.

I added new pipes to my budget. No problem–I'd built in a little padding for just such contingencies.

The dogs had dug some big holes in the yard, so I brought in a couple of cubic yards of dirt. It became obvious that several additional yards would be necessary. Then a couple more and a couple more until I had spread TWENTY CUBIC YARDS of topsoil.

Usually people buy the lot and build a house. I bought a house and built the lot.

In July I noticed a loose foundation brick, and when I wiggled it, a big section of the foundation fell over. I wouldn't have thought it possible for a house to remain standing with the foundation removed.

Dutifully I dug down to the concrete footing, which was a lot deeper than you'd think. Where were those darned dogs when I needed them? I cleaned the bricks and neatly laid them back from whence they'd come, smoothing the mortar with a joint tool my mason grandpa had owned.

At least I thought I was neatly laying bricks. When I stood back to admire my work, the expression *crazy quilt* popped to mind. But what the heck–most of it would be hidden underground anyway, and at least it was tight and sound and wouldn't topple over when you looked at it.

During the hottest part of July, I scheduled a little concrete work. That was the only day it rained all summer. It not only rained but hailed as well. You don't often see hail dents in a sidewalk. The dents helped create the non-skid surface so coveted by professional concrete workers.

Next I visited the attic to see how much insulation was there. I was appalled to find a two-inch layer of dusty cedar shingle debris covering the entire attic. Apparently when the house was reroofed some years ago, the roofers let their trash fall through the skip sheathing onto the attic insulation.

That didn't look nice and possibly presented a fire hazard. So with a dustpan, whisk broom, and trash can, I began crabbing around atop the edges of the ceiling joists, sweeping up all that trash. TWO WEEKS and a box of dust masks later, I had the attic looking really fine. I know that will mean a lot to my renters, assuming I ever have any.

The old carpet presented a problem. It was saturated with doggy odor. Funny how a little dog hair will make a whole house smell doggy. I began pulling up carpet and pad. Odd–I'd seen pad glued to the floor or stapled to the floor, but never both.

Then I realized that the source of the doggy odor was the "glue" cementing the pad to the floor. Over the vociferous protests of the two teens helping me that day, we managed to get all the nasty carpet and pad out of the house. After a few hours of backbreaking scrubbing with bleach and water, we could breathe inside the house without gagging.

Now here it is August, and I'm still mending and painting. It's no accident, I've learned, that "rental" rhymes with "mental." As in breakdown.

****

A Study of Suburban Decay

For the past of couple of decades I've made an informal study of neighborhoods and how they change. While twenty years isn't long enough to get the whole picture, I've seen enough to form some tentative conclusions.

Imagine two hypothetical houses on two different streets in the same neighborhood.

Call them the Green House and the Blue House. They're both three-bedroom, single-story houses, listed on the tax roles at $75,000 each. Let's watch them for twenty years and see what happens.

The original owner of the Green House dies and wills it to a daughter who turns the house into rental property. The people who own the Blue House sell it to a man who owns other rental property in town. Renters move into both houses.

One day the Green House renters lock themselves out of the house and have to destroy a screen to get in. The owner replaces the screen and adds the cost to the rent. The Blue House renters also lock themselves out, except they don't tell the landlord they had to tear up a screen and, since the owner seldom comes around, the screen stays broken.

The Green renters own two cars. This being an older neighborhood, the driveway is narrow and it's a hassle to park. One day they park on the front yard to avoid having to switch cars around. The owner drives by and sees this, knocks on the door, and asks her renters to please keep cars off the grass. They agree.

But the Blue renters happened to see the car parked on the grass so they try it, too. Their landlord doesn't notice. After a few weeks the Blue renters realize how easy it is to park on the grass and it becomes habit. Their next-door neighbors decide to try it, too.

Although a lawn service mows the grass, it's hard to mow around the car sometimes so the Blue renters' grass starts to look a little ragged except for the dead spot under the car. Then another dead spot appears where they chain their Doberman. A neighbor complains, and the owner writes the renters a letter telling them to move the car and dog, but it's weeks before anything happens.

After five years, the Green House tenants move, and the landlord gets new tenants right away. The Blue renters move, too, but their landlord needs several weeks to clean up the yard. Since he spent extra money on the lawn, he decides not to fix the screen. But the broken screen and bare spots in the lawn make the new tenants feel it's okay to trash the place, which they do. More screens get ruined. These tenants aren't careful about their cats, either, so the carpet develops a rank odor.

Luckily the Blue renters don't stay long, but they leave quite a mess. The owner hates to put new carpet in a house with broken screens and an ugly lawn so he rents the house "as is," which gets some scary tenants who fight with the next-door neighbors. The police are called. After this happens a few times, other neighbors decide they've had enough. "For Sale" signs go up, but there aren't many lookers because realtors don't like showing that block.

After ten years, the Green House block looks pretty much the same—nothing fancy, just a block you wouldn't mind living on. Renters come and go, the owner fixes what needs fixing and keeps the trim painted. Her tax appraisals show a gradual increase in property value.

Appraisals on the Blue House stay flat. Several adjacent properties have followed the Blue House pattern and gone to seed. Landlords find they can no longer get the same rent as before, so they're forced to lower it. With less rent coming in, they don't want to spend as much on maintenance. The Blue landlord cancels his lawn service and puts a clause in the rental agreement requiring the tenant to tend the yard. Then, because he only gets one inquiry, he rents the house to a tenant who doesn't own a lawn mower.

After fifteen years, there's a noticeable difference between the Blue and Green houses. The Green owner puts hers on the market, and it's quickly bought by a young couple attracted by its well-kept appearance and the hospitable block. The seller makes a nice profit, and the couple gets a solid starter home.

The Blue owner decides to liquidate some of his less profitable properties, but the Blue House "doesn't show well." After watching it sit empty for nine months, he sees no other choice but to sell it to an out-of-town corporation. He takes a loss, because values on his block have shown "negative growth," but he's happy to be out from under the Blue House.

The out-of-town corporation hires a local management company to rent it out, but it's only a number to them. Soon the police are back at the Blue House, this time on a drug bust. On and off for the next five years, the Blue House is empty and trash sits around. Neighbors trying to reach the owner call the management company and are given an 800 number.

When they call that number, a machine puts them on hold.

****

Drano

Post 9/11, the president has told us to go about our business and get on with life. When I heard that, I immediately thought "science experiment."

I've always had a soft spot for science. Some say it's right between my ears. Others say it's wrong between my ears–what kidders. Hey, I already feel myself getting back to normal.

My fondness for science experiments can be directly traced to two influential biology teachers during my formative years: Mr. Eck and Mr. Peters.

I first fell in love with science the day Mr. Eck invited several of us boys to participate in a field trip. He took us to his place in the country and turned us loose with loaded shotguns. Looking back, it's not clear what he had in mind.

We performed twelve-gauge science experiments on anything that moved, including but not limited to songbirds, amphibians, and an unfortunate swarm of wild honeybees hanging from a tree branch. Science was a blast.

My enthusiasm was rekindled a few years later when Mr. Peters accidentally set ablaze the sleeve of his lab coat while demonstrating proper Bunsen burner technique. Later he gave me an *A* in biology for my work of discovering, digging from a prairie creek bank, and reassembling a buffalo skeleton–something I would have done anyway.

In fact, my life's course was aimed toward biology until I met a long-haired Italian girl in a college English class and came to prefer poetry over petri dishes.

Still, petri dishes exert an occasional tug. A happy confluence of recent events put me right back in the laboratory.

The tub in my kids' bath developed a "slow drain." The clog resisted every effort to dislodge it, and finally I resorted to taking apart the trap and drain pipe.

When I stood the pipe on end, what glooped out was a gelatinous black mass of hair, cellophane candy wrappers, orthodontic rubber bands, dental floss, and what looked like a pound of swamp muck.

I made a mental note to later address the issue of how these items ended up in the tub drain. What I wanted to do immediately was set up a science experiment to test several popular drain openers against this gunk. Science never quite leaves a person.

And so the scheme was hatched. The pile of muck was divided into three smaller piles, each containing equal portions of the various components.

Each of these piles was put in a separate Mason jar. Into one jar I added common ordinary lye powder, followed by a half cup of warm water.

Into the next jar I added a popular drain opener whose name I'm not allowed to use in this column, but it might rhyme with *Plano* (See? My training in English lit still comes in handy).

Into the third jar I added another popular drain opener whose name might rhyme with *Liquid Bummer.*

After installing tight-fitting lids, I shook all three jars for thirty seconds each, distributing the clog-eating chemicals. In real life, this would only happen if someone happened to pour in drain opener during an earthquake, but it seemed to hasten the violent chemical reaction which lies at the heart of why people do science in the first place.

The jar containing lye quickly became warm to the touch, so warm that I set it down and slowly backed away.

The other two jars did not become warm, but their contents became almost clear in only a few minutes, and their lids bulged slightly. I decided to get the heck out of there and let the chemical reactions continue unhindered.

Two days later I dumped out everything and sorted through it. The results were surprising, and I offer them to readers as a public service.

None of the three drain openers dissolved any dental floss, plastic candy wrappers, or rubber bands. This was strangely disheartening; I wanted to see foreign objects disappear. What good is a drain opener if it won't sizzle through the weird stuff kids put down the drain?

Furthermore, aside from turning all the black gunk clear, the "Liquid Bummer" did nothing to dissolve hair.

The lye solution and "Plano" liquid dissolved almost every strand of human hair.

This proves my hypothesis. Wait–I forgot to formulate a hypothesis. Guess I'll chuck (scientific term) this experiment and start over.

****

Mouse Tale

"Mine is a long but sad tail," said the dormouse to Alice.
– Lewis Carroll

The other evening I was working into the wee hours when, out of the corner of my eye, I saw something scurry across the floor. It had scampered into my study from the bedroom where a woman was sleeping.

At first I thought I was imagining. After hours of following little dark marks on a page, what's one more dark mark on the floor? But soon the mouse came out from behind a bookcase and sat by the wall, watching me. When I moved, it ran back into the bedroom by hopping over a shoe we use to prop the door open. (Without the shoe, the wind blows the door shut, awakening the woman. But never mind that.)

Scenes of the mouse jumping into bed with the sleeping woman played in my mind's eye. None of them was pretty. But I knew that my going into the bedroom to search and destroy would be almost as bad as the mouse in the bed, so I went back to my desk to think.

In a minute he came back into the study to explore. While he investigated, I got up and shut the bedroom door tight then waited to see what he would do. He continued wandering around the study, behind the fan, into and out of a closet, under the desk. He seemed unconcerned with me unless I moved.

I thought about getting my BB gun and shooting him. Years ago, dorm buddies and I would drive from Lubbock to the Abernathy, Texas, landfill with .22s and a box of Cheerios. We'd sprinkle the cereal on the ground and wait for the rat army to come running, then blast away until we had a large pile of dead rodents. I knew I could hit this mouse at close range with a BB.

But I no longer take killing as lightly as I once did, even killing a mouse. And I thought of the noise and the possibility of mouse guts and blood on the carpet, and I decided to see if I could catch him alive. In the kitchen I found a Sam Houston Middle School jug, dropped a gob of peanut butter into it, and brought it upstairs. Maybe I could lure the mouse inside, then quickly screw on the lid. (The reader is aware that my mind wasn't working too well at that late hour.)

When he saw me coming toward him with the SHMS jug, the mouse tried to run back into the bedroom, but, finding the door closed, he hopped and hopped frantically against it like he couldn't grasp that it was actually shut. He was a pathetic little sight. I thought he might have a heart attack and die. I laid the jug on the floor and waited for him to crawl inside, but he just sat and panted, staring at me. I noticed that one of his little ears was split, like he had been in a fight.

Next he scampered into the middle of the room and I chased him around and around until he ran into the bathroom. Instantly I saw this as a strategic mistake on his part.

I took the jug into the bathroom and closed the door and stuffed a towel under the crack. Now I had him. I could catch that mouse in the jug or maybe the trash can, quickly dump him in the toilet and while he was dog-paddling around, flush him down. He'd have a nice ride to the sewer, not unlike the Pipeline Plunge at Wonderland Park, and would emerge wet but unhurt somewhere on South Osage Road where the City of Amarillo could figure out what to do with him.

But I couldn't get the little peckerwood to cooperate. If it had been during the day, I could have caught him easily (I say now!), but since it was the dead of night, I knew that whatever I did must be done silently, which hindered my operational tactics.

Finally he surprised me by running under the towel on the floor. I trapped him in the towel, wadded it carefully so as not to hurt him, and carried him outside. When I shook out the towel, he went flying. End of story–almost.

The next day I was again sitting at my desk when the mouse scampered across the floor. Exact same mouse, same split ear, same defiant attitude. I swear to you that I thought I heard high-pitched laughter. How he found his way back into the house and up the stairs is a matter for military analysts to consider.

Obviously, my humane pacification and relocation program wasn't going to work, so I went to the store and bought a package of two mousetraps.

Like everything else lately, mousetrap technology has changed. I was surprised to learn that one no longer baits a mousetrap with cheese. Instead, the trip-pad part of the trap is a flat piece of yellow plastic in the shape of Swiss cheese. Maybe it's impregnated with fake cheese odor, too. It didn't take the mouse long to spring the trap and die an instantaneous death.

When I told this story to the females living here, the smaller of the two remarked wistfully that none of this would be happening if Rascal the cat would come home.

The Alternative Lifestyle

Sodomy Law Kaput

I'm not sure what "the homosexual agenda" is, but I'm probably part of it–whatever it is. I believe that in a free society, homosexuals ought to enjoy the same rights and privileges as heterosexuals.

I'm not sure what the "culture war," to which Supreme Court Justice Antonin Scalia referred in his dissent to the Court's June, 2003, landmark decision is, but–whatever it is–it's already been lost by Scalia's side.

I'm not sure what it is about Texas State Rep. Warren Chisum and his pronouncements on morality that makes me want to roll my eyes, but I have to keep reminding myself that he's in the majority– for whatever that's worth–and I'm not, and neither were the six Supreme Court justices who voted to strike down Chisum's sodomy law.

The U.S. Supreme Court said that government can't intrude into people's bedrooms and arrest citizens for giving and receiving certain types of pleasure. It seems like a conservative idea to limit government this way, but conservatives are on the other side of the issue–they want government to monitor the bedrooms of America.

Wal-Mart announced it has added language to internal policy statements to ensure that gay employees aren't discriminated against. I guess Wal-Mart is part of "the homosexual agenda" too.

Sooner or later–probably later–gays will get everything they want, and this is the way it should be. Full protection against discrimination, equal rights under the law, the ability to marry each other and form durable, legal relationships–whatever I can do to hasten these things, sign me up. As a heterosexual Christian man, I've always believed the church was on the wrong side of the gay issue.

The Southern Baptist Convention announced a new initiative aimed at helping gays convert to heterosexuality. I'm a firm believer in the right of any homosexual to pursue all avenues to become hetero. I'm moderately skeptical that it will work, but people ought to be free to try.

Reports I've read about gays trying to become straight seem mixed. A few gay men seem to have achieved a satisfactory level of heterosexual functioning. I don't know if they're officially hetero now, or bisexual, or just pretending.

Some have admitted that they want so badly to be straight that they've fooled themselves into believing they are. Others, it seems, have actually managed to become heterosexuals–at least in the short run.

Here's my question: What if gays try to convert and fail? Will the Southern Baptist Convention still be their friend? Will it bless them for who they are, if who they are is homosexual?

Of course not. It took the SBC a hundred years finally to apologize for slavery. Gays ought to look for an apology from the SBC in the year 2103 or so, give or take a few decades.

Some of the traditional arguments against homosexuality are based in Scripture, which is why the SBC holds so tenaciously to them. Baptists take the Bible seriously.

But what if we tried to build a case for or against slavery based on biblical statements? I suspect we'd conclude that slavery is sanctioned by God. Obviously, during the centuries since the Bible was written, the human community has learned a thing or two about slavery and has come to different conclusions.

We now see biblical statements about slavery within the context of ancient cultures, and we do not feel bound to uphold statements such as, "Slaves, obey your masters."

Similarly, a modern view of homosexuality transcends the ancient cultural mind-set of biblical authors. The real question becomes:

How does a thoughtful Christian faithfully respond to Scripture and decide which ideas are divine and which merely cultural influence?

That's a question about which I'd enjoy hearing from Rep. Warren Chisum or Justice Antonin Scalia or the Southern Baptist Convention.

* * *

My column about homosexuals brought some interesting and surprising responses. Typical of most letters was this from reader G.F.:

"What a great article appearing July 7. I'm a native of the Panhandle but now live in the San Francisco Bay area. My mother, who lives in Amarillo, sent me your article, and I'm always uplifted when I see examples of tolerance and open-mindedness in a part of the country I always considered strictly conservative."

Some readers addressed obliquely the religious question I posed: "Thank you, Mr. Horsley! As a gay Christian in America, it is a joyful thing indeed to see fellow Christians, especially my straight brothers and sisters, embrace me as one of God's kids, just like everybody else. If I ever could be accused of having an 'agenda,' it's that the Gospel includes all of us, with no exclusions based on sexual orientation." – J.B.

What is surprising was that neither Antonin Scalia nor Warren Chisum nor any representative of the Southern Baptist Convention attempted to answer the question I posed: How does a thoughtful Christian faithfully respond to Scripture and decide which ideas are divine and which merely cultural influence?

To me, this question stands at the center of any discussion about homosexuality and Christian morality. Start at Genesis and read all the way through Revelation and you'll encounter hundreds if not thousands of laws, commandments, divine edicts, and "thus saith the Lords." What should a serious reader think?

Fundamentalists will tell you, with a perfectly straight face, that there's no thinking involved: They simply follow every word of Scripture. Therein lies the central illusion of fundamentalism—it merely pretends to follow every word of Scripture.

Fundamentalists say they believe and live by every word of Scripture–and want you to do the same–when in reality they pick and choose which parts of Scripture to follow just like the rest of us do.

Given the vast scope and depth of subjects addressed by the Bible, the ones dealing with homosexuality make up only a tiny fraction. The Bible spends a lot more ink talking in detail about ritual purity–which no Christian fundamentalist takes seriously (though a Hasidic Jew might)–than about homosexuality.

Jesus himself had nothing to say about homosexuals, but he leveled a boatload of criticism at religious people who lorded their righteousness over others.

So until someone can explain what formula or principle they apply to sift through the myriad commandments, I'll assume they've never really thought about it.

****

Take Me Off Your List

Lately I've been getting mail from Virginia, as in the state of.

Bold print on the outside of one envelope announces, "YOUR CHURCH may soon be required by law to put homosexuals in leadership positions . . . UNLESS YOU ACT NOW to help save the Salvation Army!"

Here's another one proclaiming, "The Boy Scouts are under brutal assault by the anti-Christian, anti-family Left for its ban on open homosexuals serving as Scout Leaders. . . . This is a key battle in the 'Culture War.' That's why we need 'THE BOY SCOUT PROTECTION ACT OF 2001.'"

A third announces that "Anti-Christian liberals are now working around the clock to EXPEL GOD from America's armed forces."

I don't know who or what is behind these letters, but all three seem to be from the same outfit. All bear similar Virginia cancellations from the towns of Woodbridge, Dulles, and Merrifield.

If someone in Virginia is trying to scare me into giving money to fight homosexuality, he should save his breath. The "culture war" Pat Buchanan alluded to famously in his 1992 Republican National Convention speech is over.

The homosexuals won. Gays are now in a mopping-up campaign.

I'm not 100 percent certain if this is a good thing or a bad thing. I suspect it's neither–maybe it just *is*. To me, and probably to an ever-increasing number of ordinary people, the old arguments against homosexuality just don't seem relevant anymore. Gays have become part of the fabric of American life.

Similarly to the way the civil rights revolution caught fire in Selma and Montgomery and Memphis and gradually spread across the nation, it might take decades before pockets of resistance to homosexuality melt away. Here on the High Plains of Texas, we tend to be conservative in our social philosophies, so I don't expect many people to agree with my views about gays.

Isolated cases of hostility can be expected for years to come, but I see the day coming when being gay will carry no more stigma than having curly hair. It's just something that happens.

How did we get here? Gradually, for the most part. Every few months I notice small reports in the newspaper detailing how yet another American company has granted "domestic partner" benefits to gays. I'm not counting, but I'd guess the number of companies now offering such benefits is in the hundreds.

This sort of thing generally goes in only one direction: forward. The trend seems to be toward more and more acceptance of gays.

Homosexuality is also showing up in movies and on TV, mediums which both reflect and shape our culture. In 2001 a new TV series, *Queer as Folk*, surprised Showtime executives by succeeding beyond their wildest dreams, doubling the cable channel's primetime audience. Half of the show's viewers, according to network polls, are heterosexual women.

A movie about the life and violent death of Matthew Shepard, starring Stockard Channing as the mom of the gay man beaten to death by two gay-hating college students, aired in 2002. With every sympathetic portrayal of gays, a little more cultural resistance melts.

In just about any venue of American life you name–business, music, art, publishing, politics, religion–gays have managed through the past couple of decades to chisel out a foothold.

Politics? President Bush has several openly gay people as part of his government. There are probably lots more that nobody knows about simply because most gays–like most straights–don't need to publicize their sexuality.

Religion? I chuckled at the letter about homosexuals being in church leadership positions. If all the homosexuals in all the churches in America were suddenly raptured into heaven, those of us left behind would be scrambling to fill the vacant leadership positions. We'd probably pray for God to give us back our gays.

Like I said, I don't expect many to agree with my position on homosexuals. I'm not trying to win a popularity contest, but to call it like I see it. What I see is the tide of history shifting. People can either adjust or not.

Personally, I choose to adjust. Acceptance of gays is long overdue. Energy spent fretting about and railing against the gaying of America would be better spent addressing the serious issues our world faces.

And whoever in Virginia is soliciting my help in the war against homosexuals can scratch me off his list and save thirty-seven cents.

* * *

A few weeks ago I wrote that homosexuals are here to stay and we'd best get used to it. In response, the newspaper got quite a few letters from out-of-town readers, a few of which were published on the op-ed page. Then some other readers objected that we shouldn't bother reading the opinions of out-of-town writers.

In olden days, items printed in a local paper tended to stay local. Now, however, the very concept of "local" is evolving. Words on this page can be accessed this very minute by anyone in any country on earth. Our readership truly is global.

The reason so many out-of-town people responded to my gay column is because someone apparently posted the column on a Web site devoted to gay issues, and readers outside Texas saw it. This happens often with the Web–information gets shuffled and redistributed. You could call this process the free exchange of ideas. Generally we consider this a good thing.

One unfortunate implication of my gay column, however, was the notion that everyone who objects to "the gay lifestyle" is a gay-basher or a gay-hater. I didn't mean to give this impression, and I don't think it's accurate.

There are many thoughtful people who've considered homosexuality and arrived at conclusions which differ from mine. Just because they hold different views doesn't make them gay-haters.

Oh, there are gay-haters out there for sure. I recall a TV image of a man holding a sign saying "God Hates Queers" outside the funeral of Matthew Shepard, the young man tortured and beaten to death because of his sexual orientation. That sign-holder surely could be called, among other things, a gay-basher.

Someone e-mailed me suggesting that even "Jesus was a gay-basher." I doubt that, but never mind. My point is that plenty of people object to the gay lifestyle, and they aren't all bigots and rednecks. They have their reasons.

But I have my reasons, too, for believing that homosexuality isn't any more sinful than heterosexuality. The arguments against gays are familiar to me, and I think my arguments are better.

That's what it boils down to: The arguments against tolerance are weaker than those for.

Moments in History

When You Wish Upon A Star

Fate is kind–she brings to those who love
the sweet fulfillment of their secret longings.
  —"When You Wish Upon a Star" by Leigh Harline

Like millions of Americans, on the first Saturday in February, 2003, I was enjoying a quiet morning at home. A little past nine I flipped on the radio to catch *Car Talk* and heard the ghastly news from NPR: Our space shuttle had disintegrated on re-entry. I spent the rest of the day in front of the TV, almost too stunned to move, watching Columbia's fragments shoot to earth over and over.

The song lies when it says Fate is kind. Fate can be monumentally cruel. I can't imagine anything more sadistic than what happened to our brave astronauts that Saturday in the clear blue skies over Texas. No Greek tragedy can touch the grotesque irony of it: Our swiftest chariot deconstructed by its own speed and hurled back to earth in bits. No Icarus ever had so bitter a fall.

Some say God has a plan and infuses every event from the smallest to the grandest with his mysterious purpose. Some hold that there are no accidents, that Providence directs each moment in all its varied outcomes. Some people insist that everything happens for a reason, though the reason might be hidden from mortal eyes.

I am not one of those people. I don't believe the Almighty directs everything. Who could admire such a deity? I sooner would become an atheist.

It didn't take Iraq's politicians long, however, to invoke Providence and capitalize on our tragedy. God destroyed Columbia and its seven astronauts–so the story went–in order to punish America for plotting war against Iraq. For proof, we need look no further than this: Of all the places on the globe for God to accomplish his dire purpose, he picked the home state of Saddam's arch foe to scatter the ashes of our pride.

There is a certain grotesque logic to the Iraqi view. If the tables were turned and America awaited attack by a mighty foreign host, and suddenly the symbol of our enemy's superiority was inexplicably smashed to smithereens over its leader's home province, how long before our holy men would be thanking God on TV for such an undeniable sign of his favor? Not long.

Sorry, but I can't buy it. I believe in Providence, but I also believe in accidents. Without both, the world doesn't make sense.

Until that fateful Saturday, most of us had never heard of Ron Dittemore, NASA's shuttle program manager. I came to admire Dittemore and looked forward to his daily TV briefings. Although he never flew a space ship, his head is in the clouds and his feet are on the ground. Unlike some, Dittemore told us what he knew without overtelling. When he said NASA's "best and brightest minds" were looking into the accident, I believed him.

On the other hand, it was NASA's best and brightest minds who determined that a cold launch wouldn't hurt *Challenger's* O-rings eighteen years ago. It was the best and brightest who said a chunk of foam striking the left wing of *Columbia* was inconsequential. Now they're not so sure. We can't put blind faith in NASA scientists. Space flight is too young. Calamity dogs each and every launch, nipping at its heels, seeking advantage.

Our nation's fleet of space vehicles now has a forty percent rate of catastrophic failure. No passenger ever would use an airline with such a record. But people say manned spaceflight must go on. Cooler heads have prevailed and will permit science, not emotion or politics, to shape mankind's dream of manned space flight.

In so doing, we know we place our faith in an imperfect god. Science never claimed to be infallible. Fate, we know, can't be trusted–it will turn on us in a heartbeat. Providence might be kind but is no guarantor against mayhem and suffering.

As advised by Pinocchio's cricket friend, we still launch our wishes toward the stars, but we know that stars have a wrenching tendency to fall to earth. We know what the wooden-headed boy did not. Littering the forests and fields of Texas are the remnants of one star that arrived from the vault of heaven but is forever late to the tarmac.

For the sweet fulfillment of our secret longings, we'd best look elsewhere.

****

This Old House

A newspaper photo of a curious old light fixture caught my eye. Three brass dragon heads comprised the fixture. The story said the landmark Talmage Place had been purchased by Baptist Community Services and was scheduled for gutting and renovation. Everything of value in the six-story building, including fixtures like the one pictured, would be auctioned.

Old stuff draws me like a magnet. On a chilly day before the auction, I toured the Talmage with other scavengers, many of whom carried tape measures and note pads. Dozens of the dragon light fixtures–maybe they were duck heads, not dragons–hung in the halls. Figuring I could get one for ten or fifteen bucks, I signed an application and became Bidder No. 91.

The Talmage is an old-fashioned apartment house built in 1927, in its prime one of the finest buildings in town. Designed by Hawk and Parr of Oklahoma City, its construction was supervised by Amarillo architect Guy Carlander. Electric elevators, walnut doors, and the city's first parking garage were among its amenities.

Most large cities have thousands of such buildings. Amarillo has but one, its heyday long passed. In fact, the Talmage is hopelessly outdated. Previous owners understandably chose not to spend the millions required to maintain it in top condition.

Some of the vacated apartments reeked so powerfully it was hard to imagine humans living there. Tiny kitchens, corroded plumbing, stained bathtubs, ruined carpet, and a pervasive sense of decay greeted scavengers as we roamed.

Other apartments, though, seemed decent, and as I strolled from room to room, bumping into fellow bidders, I scribbled notes about light fixtures and glass-front bookcases I might buy. With a little paint stripper and elbow grease, the bookcases could be turned into attractive cabinetry. I decided to buy two at five bucks each.

Saturday dawned cloudy and raw, a good sign because I figured it would keep away the insincere. I was surprised to find several hundred people huddled in the dim light of Amarillo's first parking garage.

Auctioneers C.L. and Jeff Bentley warmed up the crowd by reading the terms and conditions (yawn!) and reminded us that everything would be sold "as it is, where it is, and what it is." In other words, no refunds. C.L. began his rapid-fire spiel and I fell into a sort of auction trance.

Maybe it was because I'd been reading Herman Melville's *Moby Dick*. Or maybe it was because I'd been listening to FM 94.9's Dick Estelle read *In the Heart of the Sea*, a true whaling story from the early nineteenth century. I began to feel we were members of a blasphemous whaling crew, carving away at a decrepit old leviathan until nothing remained but bones and gore.

Progress was slow as we sawed, line by line, through sixteen pages of inventory. After an hour I went home for coffee, returned, and saw the first dragon head fixture–it might have been sea horses, not dragons–sell for $60. No problem, I thought. Let them sell a few at that price, and the price will come down.

Besides, I'd found a prize which no one else knew about. Hanging in one of the upstairs apartments was a brass chandelier that matched the dragon head fixtures, except it had ten heads and weighed maybe forty pounds. I decided to lay low and wait for my secret fixture to come up.

Before I knew it, the five-dollar bookcases began selling for $80 to $100. More dragon head fixtures sold for $90. A glass chandelier exactly like one I once bought in a garage sale sold for $375. Another light fixture went for $700. I could see I'd have to wait until the high rollers went home.

The auction was a fine spectacle, anyway. Watching an experienced auction crew is high entertainment. The Bentleys seemed to enjoy their work, and they made the best of less-than-ideal conditions, joking, cajoling, and clowning with the crowd. One woman became confused and bid too much for something, then left to plead her case with the cashiers, who, I later learned, had mercy on her.

By midday, things were still ridiculously expensive to my cheap way of thinking, so I went home to eat and take a nap. Upon returning, I watched my "secret" ten-headed chandelier sell for $600. Book cases were still fetching $90, and some other old fixtures with crystal dangle-bobs went for $100.

I left the auction and walked in the dying light through the cold Talmage. Broken plaster crunched under my shoes. The odor of cigarettes and stale carpet hung in the halls. It was hard to imagine either the building's heyday or its future elegance. It seemed a sad, dead carcass.

Then a man said I had to leave–thieves were starting to pocket whatever they could carry out, so auction officials were locking down the Talmage. Buildings change, but human nature remains constant.

It's said that auction proceeds benefitted charity care for elderly Amarillo citizens. You have to commend Baptist Community Services for that.

In a year or so the Talmage will reopen with new everything. Wouldn't it be grand if one of the forty-two new apartments was outfitted with 1927 appointments: Pedestal sinks, cast iron tubs, renovated bookcases, and a brass light fixture comprised of three dragon heads?

****

His Honor's Garbage

Spend a moment with me going through His Honor the Mayor's garbage. Before me here is a curious collection of odds and ends gleaned from behind our mayor's home. I speak not of our current mayor, in whose garbage I have no interest, but former Amarillo Mayor J. H. Patton, who ruled city government during the years 1911 and 1912.

Patton was a liquor dealer whose home once stood where mine now stands. In those early years, trash disposal consisted of a "burn pile" behind each home, perhaps not far from the privy. Discarded items were thrown on the burn pile, and periodically the ashes (containing non-burnable leftovers) were scattered in the yard or garden.

Installing a sprinkler system recently gave me the chance to turn up soil which had been undisturbed for decades. With the soil has come a harvest of meager treasure, such as:

• Lots of glass shards and broken china. Here's a bottle bottom dated Sept. 20, 1898, another one marked, "Pat. June 30, 1925." Green glass, brown glass, glass crazed by heat or age. An old Dr Pepper bottle, part of a 7-Up. A large fragment of china in a pattern I recognize: Desert Rose. If my thin irrigation trenches pulled up this much glass, just think how much still must be down there.

I understand the presence of all the broken glass and china: boys. Imagine a turn-of-the-century mother cracking a favorite china cup. Sorrowfully she throws it on the burn pile. Boys of the home see that broken cup, formerly untouchable, lying helpless amid the other trash. They reach for a rock.

• A small metal snap from a woman's girdle, a common undergarment of yore. The girdle itself is long gone, leaving only the snap. I recognize it because someone I know well once wore such an apparatus.

• A brass plate from inside a harmonica. Can't you see some barefoot kid in knickers, wandering around his house, blowing into that device? I suspect only his mother knew how it got to the burn pile. A mystery solved after all these years.

• Coal. Before natural gas was discovered in our area in the '20s, most homes were heated with coal. The curious thing is that it's impossible to dig anywhere in my back yard without turning up lumps of coal. My explanation for all the coal is: boys again. Imagine a coal pile behind the house, where the coal truck dumped it once a month. Dad tells the children to stay off that coal pile or else. Boys being boys, as soon as his back is turned they play King of the Hill on the highest point in two counties, which degenerates into a coal fight. Hence coal everywhere.

• Buttons, buttons, and more buttons. Shirts became dust cloths which became oil rags which became fuel for the burn pile. Now only the buttons survive. There must be a zillion buried in my back yard. Maybe then as now, mayors were expected to dress well.

• Marbles, including blues, greens, reds, yellows, cat's-eyes and some strange clay-looking ones. I like finding marbles because they're as good as new even after all this time underground.

• A crumpled brass center-fire casing. Hard buffing revealed, "Peters .45 Colt."

• Copper pennies. Those dated between 1917 through 1964 are in great shape. The later ones, which I'm told are actually zinc with a thin coat of copper, are heavily corroded. Something in our soil doesn't like zinc.

• One of my favorite finds is the working end of an antique toothbrush, evidently made of bone or ivory. The bristles are missing, but four neat rows of holes show where they once stood. Do you suppose this was His Honor's own personal toothbrush? I prefer to think so.

• Before I describe my favorite thing, I'll list just some of the other items: a brass winding key for a clock or toy, a small hexagonal bathroom tile, tines from a garden fork, a copper-coated lead-backed photographic plate showing a seated woman drawing a stocking from a box, metal tags from hybrid roses ("asexual reproduction of this patented plant without license is prohibited"), fragile bottle caps, assorted nails so rusty they're easily bent by hand, mysterious metal objects whose origin and purpose I can't guess.

• Finally, a broken arrowhead. Finding flint points always excites me. The fact that this one came from my own back yard inflames my imagination. It's a lovely deep red, about an inch wide.

A man made it. He had a name, a family, a history. Maybe he shot it into a buffalo and watched as the beast galloped over the horizon.

Finding an arrowhead reminds me that in the big scheme of things, my tenure on this land is brief. It also reminds me that while I might think of J.H. Patton as belonging to antiquity, another man might have walked across my yard ten thousand years before Mayor Patton threw away his toothbrush.

****

On the Threshhold of the Millennium

You're floating blissfully in a silky bag of warm water. Sometimes you hear distant music, voices, the opening and closing of a door. But you don't worry because anxiety hasn't been invented where you live. Your every need is supplied. All that's required of you is to dream and stretch.

Then one day things seem to get upside down. You sense a change, something pushing, then squeezing you out of your comfortable little world into bright lights and cold air and terrifying noises. Things won't be the same for you. Ever.

Transitions are almost always hard. Besides birth and death–the Big Two–even the lesser transitions are difficult. A "For Sale" sign goes up in the front yard of your favorite neighbor. Someone spreads tar and gravel on your street. The phone rings in the middle of the night. An X-ray reveals a suspicious spot. Even "good" transitions can be trying, as anyone who's gotten married, started a new job, or sent a child off to school knows.

Now that I'm in my fifties, I seem to pay more attention to transitions and try to be open to their magic. Having been born a few days shy of this century's midpoint, and hoping to see the midpoint of the next century, I've come to feel myself standing with one foot planted curiously in each of two worlds–one old, one new.

For example, I'm young enough to understand how "frequent flier miles" work but old enough to remember "Please Do Not Flush While Train is Standing."

Young enough to connect a refrigerator's ice-maker by tapping a water pipe, but old enough to slip and call it the "icebox."

Young enough to appreciate Eminem but old enough to think "True Love" by Bing Crosby and Grace Kelly is one of the sexiest songs ever recorded.

Old enough to remember when soda straws were paper but young enough to think plastic is better.

Old enough to recall helping my grandmother wash clothes with a wringer, but young enough to understand why it was necessary to remove phosphates from laundry detergent.

Young enough to wait an hour outside the newest restaurant in town, but old enough to privately wonder why we don't just drive to Luby's.

Young enough to eagerly tune in to TV's Grammy Awards each February, but old enough to enjoy *The Lawrence Welk Show* occasionally, just to see how far entertainment has come.

Old enough to remember standing in line to receive the Salk oral polio vaccine, but young enough to see the implications of human genetic mapping.

Old enough to think most machines ought to be oiled regularly, but young enough to know cyberspace, e-mail, and have at least a vague idea where my motherboard is.

Young enough to figure out–eventually–how to program a VCR but old enough to remember frequently hearing, "We are experiencing technical difficulties. Please stand by."

Young enough to know the relationship between tartar and plaque but old enough to remember brushing with tooth powder.

Old enough to be comfortable talking with octogenarians about the good old days, but young enough to see a tongue stud on a person I'm talking to and not lose my train of thought.

Young enough to recognize the need for low-flow shower heads, but old enough to remember taking a bath once a week, on Saturday nights.

Young enough to know the four-digit suffix to my five-digit postal ZIP code, but old enough to understand what Elvis Presley meant when he sang, "Return to sender, address unknown; no such number, no such zone."

Old enough to remember when garden hoses had one and only one type of nozzle–a heavy brass device that twisted for various sprays–but young enough to own a pistol-grip type, a multi-spray type, a dial-a-jet type and probably others lost in the tall grass.

Straddling two millennia as we are, it's easy to get schizophrenic about the blizzard of choices and changes. Here in the final summer of this old age, which doesn't yet seem old and won't until we look back at it, we're tempted to kick and scream against this transition. There's plenty to be anxious about. We feel things pushing on us; everything seems upside down.

Maybe what we should do is relax and enjoy the distant music, the voices, the opening and closing of a door.

Or simply dream and stretch.

****

Bridge, Anyone?

A stone giant is falling to the ground, felled after thirty-six years by the sting of a scorpion and the bite of a turtle.

Most of us don't give bridges a second thought, or even a first thought. We hurry over them without noticing the fleeting instant they buoy us up. But every bridge in the world was planned and constructed by someone who gave bridges a lot of thought.

Some are works of art, like California's Golden Gate or New York's Verrazano Narrows, their graceful curves soaring into space to connect this thing with that. Others have historic significance, like the London Bridge, which was apparently so important to English history that someone tore it down and moved it to Arizona.

Most bridges, however, whether a single log spanning a creek or a loopy cloverleaf, are less artful and historic than functional–they just do their jobs day in and day out without ever being photographed for a post card. Such was the destiny of the I-40 bridge over Harrison and Tyler streets in Amarillo. Since 1963 it stood solid above the former prairie, with concrete muscle and bones of steel, to provide passage for east-west travelers.

I imagine if we had a way to list all the famous and infamous people who've used that bridge in thirty-six years, the names would amaze us: serial killers on the lam, governors and presidents, movie stars, rock singers, terrorists, escaped convicts, Pulitzer-prize winning novelists, assassins, TV personalities, war heroes, drug-runners. But mostly ordinary folks like you and I–truckers, travelers, and citizens.

Since the Kennedy administration, the Tyler-Harrison bridge has done exactly what it was designed to do, plus a few things never imagined by its builders: It was home to a perpetual flock of pigeons, and it saved countless cars from hail damage during spring storms. Several times in recent memory, these hail hideouts achieved near-party status, with all-night beer, music, and snacks. Or so I've heard.

Now the bridge's bones have become a problem. The reinforcement steel that makes bridges strong is rotting. Three decades of de-icing road salt have seeped into the concrete and corroded the re-bars. When steel oxidizes, it changes shape, literally bursting the concrete which surrounds it. Because I've walked under this bridge daily for the almost ten years, I've watched its slow decay. Slabs of concrete would periodically spall away and fall to the ground. Not good for pedestrians below or motorists above.

A few years ago taxpayers paid heavily to recondition the bridge, but that only postponed the inevitable. As Isaac Newton proved, what goes up must come down. And coming down is what the old giant is doing.

Like children everywhere, my kids and I are drawn to scenes of destruction. We videotaped the marvelous machines crews are using to deconstruct the bridge. One we call The Turtle is a man-sized set of hydraulic pincers, affixed to the end of a jointed arm extending from a huge diesel tractor-treaded base. If you've ever watched a turtle nip at a melon, you'll see the resemblance. It nibbles at the road deck precisely like a terrapin eating supper, effortlessly snipping inch-thick steel with its hardened jaws.

When The Turtle finishes with the pavement, the beams are lifted off by The Crane. Then The Scorpion clanks into place. It's a two-ton jackhammer with a stinger the size of a fence post mounted on a hydraulic arm similar to The Turtle. When the operator presses that steel needle against the bridge pier and pulls the trigger, concrete splinters like glass.

Once the bridge is gone, a new one will rise to take its place. According to Texas Department of Transportation Engineer Joe Chappell, several things about the new bridge will be different, which should give it a life span of seventy or more years.

First, Chappell says epoxy-coated reinforcement steel will be used instead of the bare steel used in 1963. The coating will prevent road salt from attacking and corroding the steel. Second, a different kind of concrete will be used, blended with additives and fly ash to make it resistant to penetration by salt-bearing moisture. You might wonder where this fly ash comes from: It's a byproduct of burning coal to make electricity. In other words, the light company has figured a way to simultaneously produce the light at your shoulder and the fly ash in your new bridge. Engineers are always thinking.

Finally, we've learned a thing or two in forty years of highway maintenance. Chappell says de-icing crews no longer use sodium chloride salt, which is so hungry for steel, but rather the gentler potassium chloride salt.

Seventy years from now, when this new bridge is being chipped down and my bones are nourishing a wheat field somewhere, perhaps your child or mine will watch and record yet a third structure rising above the former prairie, assuming there are still such things as cars and trucks to require one.

Holidays

Chaw Comments on "The Cowboy Way"

One winter a few years ago, with Valentine's Day fast approaching and no gift ideas springing to mind, I decided to pay a visit to my pal Chaw McCuddy, who runs beeves up on the Canadian River. I consider Chaw an expert on women, partly because–at last count–he's been married five times that I knew of.

A sharp February wind rustled the weeds along his driveway as I approached. Patches of orange-tinged snow lay in shadows along the bar ditch. Through his open barn door I heard music and saw flashes of light, indicating Chaw was welding. I waited for the dogs to catch my scent and shut up before I got out of the car. Then I stepped into the barn.

Chaw flipped up his visor for a second. "Hey, Old Son. Make yourself useful–wiggle that clamp, would you? I lost my ground." He adjusted his welding rod and bent over a mass of scrap steel.

Electricity makes me nervous, but I knew it was useless to argue. I wiggled the clamp. I asked what he was making.

"Oh, just a little Valentine's doodad for Veronica," he said over the hum and spit of the welder.

His Valentine's present looked like a cross between a fence stretcher and a rug beater, with hearts welded around the edges. I remarked as how that ought to make her happy.

Chaw snorted. "Happy? I gave up long ago trying to make that woman happy. I'm just trying to keep her from leavin'."

Oh. I tried not to look at the white flame. I noted with surprise that the music was coming from a CD player, new since I was last here. I asked him about it.

"My nephew give me that for Christmas. He makes CDs for me too. Took my whole record collection and put it on CDs. It's all right."

If Chaw says something is all right, it means he really, really likes it.

The Sons of the Pioneers were singing about the Red River Valley and a cowboy's love for a girl. I commented that was good music to make Valentines by.

"You know," he said, lifting his visor, "everything I thought I knew about love, I learned from the Sons of the Pioneers." He let the statement sink in a moment before adding, "Then I had to UNLEARN it."

I asked what he meant.

"Take that song right there," he waved a welding rod toward the CD player. " 'Come and sit by my side if you love me.' For God's sake, if you love her, go sit by HER side, you idjit! Don't wait for her to come to you. That lesson cost me my first marriage."

I said I'd never thought about it that way.

He went back to work but stopped when the next song came on. "There's another dumb idea about love I picked up from the Sons of the Pioneers: 'You'll never know I cried when I found out you lied, so I'll keep ridin', hidin' teardrops in my heart.' For crying out loud in church, what's wrong with letting a woman know you have feelings?"

We listened to the rest of the song.

A cowboy can't reveal a broken heart until he's all alone, someplace unknown, to play the part.

"Of all the stupid notions," Chaw fumed. "A woman breaks your heart, and you go tell your horse about it? And then wonder why there's so many divorced cowboys around? Bull manure!"

I suggested that was The Cowboy Way.

227

"Yes it is, and that's what's wrong with cowboys." He removed the visor and inspected his work. "The Cowboy Way–so called–is why we have so many alcoholic cowboys, drug-addicted cowboys, broke cowboys, cowboys cheating on their wives and abandoning their children, and cowboys behind bars. That's what The Cowboy Way has done for cowboys."

I saw we'd touched on a sensitive subject. The music played on.

But way down deep inside I can't give up my pride, so I'll keep ridin,' hidin' teardrops in my heart.

Chaw chipped at his doodad with a small hammer. "Men have to let go of the idea of being a tumbleweed, spilling seed across six counties."

As if on cue, that song played next.

Lonely but free I'll be found, drifting along with the tumbling tumbleweed.

"That's a coward's life," Chaw said. "I lost several good women before I figured that out. Lonely but free isn't free–it's just lonely. My lonesome cowboy days were my low. Hell, I wasn't free–I was cinched tight to my own misery, and I had to go wherever it took me. And some of the places I'd just as soon forget." He held his creation to the light. "How do you like that?"

I said it looked all right.

"Let's get some red on it," he said, reaching for a can of paint.

****

Dr. Valentine's Antique Road Show

Dr. Valentine: "Hello and welcome to Dr. Valentine's Antiques Road Show. Today we'll be looking at some fine historical pieces from all over the Texas Panhandle."

(Camera zooms in)

Dr. V: "First up is this luscious nude painted on a harrow disk. Tell me about this."

Woman: "Only a chauvinistic boarhead would call a nude 'luscious.' "

Dr. V: "Well, pardon my testosterone!"

Woman: "As if you had any!"

(Camera pans away quickly)

Dr. V: "Okay! Next up is a fascinating old love letter. What can you tell us about it?"

Man: "Well, I inherited this from my great-aunt, who told me that Colonel Goodnight himself wrote it to his wife from the rail head in Dodge City."

Dr. V: "Hmmm, interesting theory. What are these little perforations down the sides of the page?"

Man: "Perforations?"

Dr. V: "–where your printer's tractor strip was removed?"

Man: "I don't know what you're talking about!"

(Sounds of scuffle, camera pans away)

Dr. V (smoothing his toupee) : "Next I'm talking to this nice man who brought us a lovely Cupid statue. What can you tell us about this?"

Man: "Well, my grand–"

Dr. V: "–Hold on a second. Would you mind not starting with the word *well*?"

Man: "Excuse me?"

Dr. V: "Everyone always starts their little spiel by saying, 'Well, my grandfather blah blah blah,' or 'Well, I found this yadda yadda.' I'm getting tired of hearing it. Now go on."

Man (flustered) : "W– er, my grandfather left me this in his will. Grandma says he brought it back with him from overseas."

Dr. V: "Which seas, exactly?"

Man: "I dunno. What difference does it make?"

Dr. V: "We have to know which seas. Otherwise your priceless antique Cupid is a worthless trinket. Come back when you have all the facts. Next!"

Woman: "Okay, this love seat has been in my family for five generations."

Dr. V: "Whoa! I feel sorry for you! Your great-great-grandmother should have thrown it out while she had the chance!"

Woman: "Say what?"

Dr. V (choking back laughter): "It's nothing but a piece of junk. What did your great-great-grandmother pay for it, if I might ask?"

Woman: "Well, I have a receipt here for $125."

Dr. V: "Woo-eee! She really got taken for a ride! This thing wasn't worth twenty bucks NEW!"

Woman: "Thanks a lot, you big jerk! See if I ever come back on this show!"

(Stomps off)

Dr. V: "See if you're ever invited! Some people! Who's next?"

Man: "I found this in the Dumpster behind my house."

Dr. V: "You WHAT? Do you realize what this IS?"

Man: "I thought it was a box of chocolates."

Dr. V: "Yes, man, but not just ANY box of chocolates. This is the very first Whitman's Sampler ever produced! It's worth a FORTUNE–$20,000 at least!!"

Man: "Is that retail or wholesale?"

Dr. V: "Retail. Wholesale, it's worth $10,000."

Man: "Whaddya gimme for it right this minute?"

Dr. V: "Five dollars, cash."

Man: "Deal."

(They shake)

Dr. V: "Boy what a chump! Who's next?"

Woman: "I bought this in a garage sale for one dollar."

Dr. V: "I see. Looks like an antique apple peeler. Very nicely preserved, too."

Woman: "Shows how much you know, Dr. V. This is actually a Victorian birth control device for men."

Dr. V: "No way!"

Woman: "Way! Wanna see how it works?"

Dr. V: "Not really. Get that thing outta–"

Woman: "Actually, it's very simple. See, you take this part here–step a little closer, Sir– and you just pinch–"

Dr. V: "Hey, get away from me with that! You're out of your mind!"

Woman: "–squeeze these prongs out and then clamp–"

Dr. V: "HELP! SECURITY!!"

(Fade to closing credits)

****

Memorial Day

It occurs to me that I forgot to thank my friend Jim for something.

We grew up together, Jim and I. We were tent-mates in Boy Scouts, taught ourselves about snakes and girls and life. We'd seine the creek, not for minnows to use as fish bait, but just to see what would be in our net. We were inseparable for those early years and then we grew up and grew apart and finally left home. I went to college and he went to Vietnam.

Sitting in my dorm room, looking out across a manicured lawn where young men enjoyed a game of touch football, on clean paper I typed letters that circled the earth before reaching Jim in 'Nam. I was intensely curious about the war; I hated it but had half a mind to join up when I graduated from college.

He was equally curious about my world. He planned to enroll in college when he got home. On whatever paper he could scrounge– no two of his letters were on the same type paper–he wrote:

"I'm sitting in a cramped battered bunker, a cell block of scarred lumber and eroding sandbags, encircled by rifles, grenades, mines, detonators, machine guns and enough ammo for the king's army (MAYBE enough if the occasion arises for it to be used), enveloped with the acrid aroma of expended ammo, repugnant mire, and the dry sour odor of marijuana, smoking a cheap Hav-a-Tampa cigar, thinking of peace and enjoying the rare moment of meditative solitude in the early dawn of a truly beautiful morning. . . ."

"You can't begin to realize how bad it is here. The jungle is extremely hot and humid ALL the time. Humping a heavy pack, eating the same food continuously, and all the time surrounded by the deadly VC. It's enough to drive a person insane–especially since it's for one year, twelve LONG months. . . . Being hot and humid and constantly perspiring, you can imagine the germs, filth, and repulsiveness of not being able to shave, bathe, etc., so the whole concept is totally abominable. . . ."

"I have enclosed several articles on the onslaught at L2 Carolyn. . . . Our company really had the devil to contend with that night–a twelve-hour span that made a lot of men and broke just as many. Six hundred VC made a ground assault on the base and tried to take it–and they nearly had the upper hand. The next morning looked like a grave diggers' festival. Words can't describe it–it's something felt inexpressibly. . . ."

"The methods employed by both the VC and us for the taking of lives are so very unreal that I haven't fully come to realize I am participating in them. . . ."

"The monsoons have set in and naturally it's burdensome: high humidity, rains each night, extreme temperatures during the afternoon–really a pain. Everything is moldy or rotting. . . . If all goes well, next April should be my big day–out of 'Nam, out of the Army. . . ."

"Shrapnel imbedded in the back of your head is no fun. The only signal you have that mortars are coming is when you hear them in the distance being dropped in the tubes. So you are constantly at least half alert to mortar tubes. . . ."

"The sunsets here are beautiful but there are certain types which shouldn't be seen, like: The sun is a deep throbbing red, luminously burning slightly above ground level, giving everything a strange orange-red glow. It's captivating and you see everything with this translucent glow. You begin to mellow and appreciate the beauty, UNTIL, you look across the open field in front of you and see bodies of dead VC. Hands reaching up, fingers gnarled, grasping for ?, stiff with rigor mortis, a knee angled at the oblique, unsupported, black dried blood capping it. . . ."

"Or when it's just gotten dark, you're in the jungle, lying back, enjoying a refreshing breeze, looking at the moon and at how the light plays a game of silhouette with the plants, everything with a silvery tinge. You're full of water, not hungry, not thirsty, just feeling good and appreciative of life when a gust of wind brings the stench of dead bodies to your nose and you cringe. The offensive bitter repugnancy envelopes you and there's no way out. You just sit and gag until sleep and exhaustive fatigue relieve you. . . ."

"Let me know how life is where you're at and any feelings you have of college, i.e., demonstrations, peace movements, etc. Just your opinions and philosophies of anything–I'd like to hear some intelligent viewpoints on something noteworthy. . . . People really revert to illiterates and ignoramuses here. . . ."

Jim made it home and enjoys a successful career as an operatic baritone. On this day when we honor those who served, I want to say "thank you" to him. Thank you for going through an unimaginable hell. Thank you for putting your life on the line in an unpopular war, probably a wrong war, for no other reason than your country asked you to. Thank you for your service, for bearing the scars visible and invisible.

For all the Jims out there, some living and some with names chiseled in black granite in Washington, D.C., some buried under American soil and some whose bones are covered only by jungle vines, we salute you this day. A grateful country stands in silence, remembering your sacrifice.

****

Mowing on the Fourth of July

I sing of men and arms, arms sunburned from mowing before the gates of July's fiery hell.

Of the despair when it won't start, the burning biceps, the quickened breathing, pull after cramping pull, the muttered curses, the clear blisters where your skin meets the starter rope's 2handle, the drop of bitter sweat on the end of your nose, the grimy driveway exploration into its guts, the exultant cross-legged moment of discovery, the blast of blue smoke as it roars to life, the prickle of sand against your ankles, the rising cloud of dust.

Of the flood of mower noise washing over you, drowning out the world, reducing everything to you and it and the task before you, of the chlorophyll and gasoline incense connecting you with every other mowing, the spray of chopped foliage, the ricochet of pebbles, the gassy fatness of the turgid bag, the vibrations of whirring steel up the handle into your hands and bones and sinews.

Of how the grass shows a nap, a different hue in this direction from that, tracks of past mowings, the wheel paths coinciding year after year to form trails like wagon ruts in the everlasting prairie, guiding you while they surprise with their predictability, their routine, showing you the rut you're in–you are HERE.

Of the difficulty of walking a perfectly straight line while pushing the infernal machine, of how it scoops a donut in the turf when a wheel lurches into a hole, of the sweet bleat of the engine, the hum of the starter rope quivering in harmonic synchronicity with some impossible calculus of tension, length, and music; of the song that begins in your head and grows into a step-step-step mantra impossible to eradicate: *Rice* (step) *-a-Roni* (step) *the San Francisco treat!* (step) or *Key Largo* (step), *Montego* (step), *baby why don't we go?* (step), or *Remember when you ran away and I got on my knees and begged you not to leave because I'd go berserk?*

Of the puff of dust from the bag as a pine cone caroms inside; of the baleful eye of a toad accusing you from a toad fragment diced to slivers when he bolted from a hidden hole into sudden death; the pop of a dixie cup chopped to confetti; the blat of a shredded Cheetos bag; the bark of sticks beat into toothpicks; the dull crack of steel striking rock; the squatting inspection, lips pursed in disappointment; the socket wrench squeaking the hardened bolt loose.

Of the cool basement air, the sun-dimmed vision, cluttered workbench, whine of the grinder, spewing rooster tail of white fire, the peck of sparks against your fingers, the gleam of raw steel as a new edge emerges, the scent of motor ozone, the razor bite of blade on testing thumb, the click of the ratchet as the bolt goes home.

Of the memory of other mowings in other yards and pastures: of the lurch of a tractor trailing a brush hog, violence mincing everything in its path, throwing up plumes of stickers and stinging ants, invisible biting mites, furious hornets; of Grandpa's clickety-clickety push mower, more like scissors than a machine, its push gears distinctive from its pull gears to young ears; of cheap foreign import mowers, strange control arrangements, bad design, no design, the Edsel of mowers; of your first mower and the imaginary fortune to be made.

Of pausing to move a turtle out of harm's way; of how a dog will move again and again onto the uncut portion of the yard, never the cut; of a hierarchy that condemns crickets and moths but lets cicadas walk; of wondering how an underground grub winces as the machine thunders overhead; of cats' universal aversion to mechanized racket.

Of repetition's soothing rhythm–fill bag, empty bag, fill bag, empty bag–like a dairy cow, like payday, like breathing, like all other fill-empty cycles that let you finally think about the person you've become, or finally stop thinking and just be; of how the noise acts like a curtain drawn around your being so you can try things on, or drawn across the confessional booth–forgive me, Father, for I have sinned; of blood quickening in your veins, you and your machine working as one heart engine muscle fuel leg wheel, the task shrinking line by line; the fleeting uniformity you impose upon chaos and mayhem, knowing that chaos and mayhem will sprout anew forever and ever world without end after you grow old and quit, but while you are able you will tend your allotted patch.

Then of the silence almost theatrical in magnitude, the clatter of wheels on concrete, the shirt sticking crooked to your back, of settling back in the shade to spit grit and admire your handiwork, something big to drink, a taste of heaven. Finished, for now.

****

Turkey Terminator in Collingsworth County

I decided to shoot my own Thanksgiving turkey. Why pay grocery store prices for a fat, frozen bird when the whole state of Texas is teeming with wild turkey? Plus, I'm an experienced hunter of quail and dove, so how difficult could it be to shoot a bird the size of a small aircraft?

My friend Mel had assured me that his property was home to a large flock. Automatic feeders spewing corn twice a day would guarantee the birds would be nearby, so we wouldn't have to traipse all over the Panhandle to find them. As long as my old shotgun was in good working order, I should have no problem bagging my limit of two birds.

Let the reader note that I used the term *bagging*. This story will contain no politically correct hunter euphemisms such as *harvest, manage,* or *thinning the flock.* Rather, I will tell the plain truth using terms such as *blast, mangle* and *indestructible.*

We got out of the truck on a chilly, overcast day that threatened snow. We loaded up, Mel his large-bore pump-action scattergun and me my trusty little Sweet Sixteen auto. We could hear the turkeys down in a creek bed. It sounded like a convention, with everyone talking at once. Sneaking up on these gabby fowls shouldn't be a problem.

Mel and I split up. My plan was to follow the raucous noise until I either found the flock or scared them into the next county. I went into the creek bed and crept through the brush toward the racket.

I've always heard that wild turkeys were canny creatures, alert as eagles and smart as parrots, for which Benjamin Franklin tried without success to get them designated our national bird. I'd been advised to use No. 6 shot or larger, meaning pellets the size of BBs, because getting close enough for a clean kill with smaller shot was dicey.

After stalking awhile through the brush and weeds, I stopped for a breather. Already my shotgun was feeling heavy, as were the bulging pockets of my jacket. Unsure what the day might bring, I was carrying so much ammo that I couldn't close the pocket flaps. Shells kept bouncing out with each step. The turkey sound seemed to be getting closer.

It had been awhile since I'd used this gun. Thinking back, I couldn't recall my last hunt. Maybe during the 1990s or even earlier? It then occurred to me that the friction ring–the part that controls recoil–might be set wrong. Too late now.

It wasn't long before the birds came into view–a big flock of gangly, ghostly birds. I stood still. They came on, murmuring among themselves.

Knowing how alert turkeys are, I knew they'd bolt as soon as they saw me, so I crouched in the tall grass. Still they came. I flipped off the safety as my heart began to race. Man, there were a lot of turkeys–maybe twenty-five or thirty birds.

I foresaw a problem: how to shoot just two? I'm the sort of hunter who, if I can't make a clean shot with certainty of a kill, I don't shoot. This situation presented an inverted challenge to my ethos: how to kill only two without mangling a dozen more. Those birds kept coming.

Then I saw another problem. Obviously they were planning to step on me, and maybe peck out my eyes or gouge me with their spurs (do turkeys even *have* spurs?) as they passed. Mainly out of self-defense, I rose and aimed my weapon.

Blind luck had caused two hens to separate from the gang, and these I blasted. At such close range, I'm pretty sure the wad from my shells hit one of the birds in the head, killing it instantly. The other dropped dead, too, liberally perforated. I'd been hunting maybe ten minutes and already had my limit.

I picked up my Thanksgiving dinner and lugged it back to the truck. Mel had one bird and had nicked a second, and he examined my two birds with obvious envy. I mentioned that my friction ring might be set wrong, not that it mattered now.

"Let me see that gun," he said.

While he was fiddling with it, a long spring and at least one other piece went flying out of my gun and landed in tall grass. We found the spring; the other piece or pieces are still in Collingsworth County. Mel continues to claim it was an accident.

We followed the flock to try to recover that crippled bird, which would otherwise be coyote food by morning. I spied it peering at me through some weeds, and let fly with what remained of my shotgun. Funny thing–it seemed to work better without the missing parts.

The bird fell down, got up, and took off. I followed. When it stopped, I fired again, knocking it down once more. Again it stood up, glared at me, and high-tailed it through the trees.

We never saw that indestructible bird again. I'm sure that somewhere in the eastern Panhandle, a coyote slept well the next day, dreaming of giblets and gravy.

Ironically, I had to buy a frozen turkey after all, because my family threatened mutiny if I forced them to eat one of my wild birds. But come Thursday, I'm cooking a wild one just the same. I'll let you know how it tastes.

****

Like the Down of a Thistle

Ever since my kinsman John Calcott Horsley invented the Christmas card in 1843–the year Charles Dickens published *A Christmas Carol* and twenty years after Clement Moore published his famous poem–society has enjoyed a love/hate relationship with this seasonal greeting.

Horsley, a London illustrator, created the card at the request of a friend. It shows a family raising a toast, and it bears the inscription, "A Merry Christmas and a Happy New Year to You." One thousand copies were printed and sold for one shilling each. The idea caught on among Victorian gentility, the cards quickly sold out, and Christmas cards have been plaguing humanity ever since.

Besides the fact that a relative invented them, I feel partly responsible for at least some of the foolishness associated with Christmas cards because I've helped perpetuate it.

I used to buy boxes of cards and send one to everyone I knew, or to everyone who sent one to me, or both. It seemed the polite thing to do, but it created a feedback loop of ever-increasing burden. After awhile, you acquire too many acquaintances to send cards to everyone.

Most commercial cards, after all, receive only a glance before the recipient tosses them in the Christmas card basket, where they gather until being discarded or squirreled away in the attic.

I admit I'm a squirrel-away-er of Christmas cards. In half a minute I could produce every single card I received last year, because they've sat on my dresser for twelve months, en route to the attic. I also have cards I received five, ten, and twenty years ago. I really should throw them away.

Another bit of foolishness is what used to be called the form letter or Christmas newsletter. Early examples were mimeographed (if you're too young to know this term, think hand-cranked Xerox machine), later photocopied and sent via e-mail.

These Christmas newsletters almost have become a literary genre. Like other genres, it has its share of artless practitioners. I once knew a woman who filled two or three pages with dense, single-spaced minutiae from her recent life.

"TMI," I wanted to tell her, "–too much information!"

I used to enjoy sending out an annual newsletter, and I admit I've probably been guilty of leaving too little to readers' imaginations. Producing a newsletter every year became a chore, however, so now I only send one when the mood strikes–about every four years–and only to out-of-town friends.

This year I wasn't planning to send anything. It's too much bother, really, not to mention the expense.

Then I began to receive cards from friends, some of whom sent photos of children. I used to consider it bragging to send pictures of kids: See what beautiful children I have. Now that I have children, I look at it differently. It's not bragging–it's more like prayer: Can you believe what precious gifts I've received? String together ten or fifteen years of annual portraits and it's almost like watching loved ones grow from afar. Card by card and year by year, children grow up and friends grow old.

Several friends sent newsletters. Reading them, I felt strangely moved. After all these years, across all the miles and through every twist in the road, we're still friends. We still wish to connect, to share our joys and our sorrows. It's an amazing thing, and it prompted me to reply.

It's also amazing to sit and begin addressing envelopes and realize how many people are no longer married to their spouses of four years ago. It helps me appreciate the fragility of relationships.

A surprising number of people on my list from four years ago have passed away, which helps me stop and appreciate the fragility of life. While drawing a line through their names in my address book, it occurred to me that one of these days people will cross my name off their lists.

This year I experimented with some jpeg photo files on my computer, and I found a way to paste pictures into my newsletter. The result is pretty rough but gets the job done. Friends who haven't seen us for several years will get a general idea of how we're faring.

People who knew us when our children were born will be astonished at how they've grown. They'll look at those handsome kids–so beautiful–and remember how they looked only a moment ago through a hospital nursery window, or imagine how they'll look a moment from now with children of their own, grown up and flown, like we all will be someday, like leaves before the wind, like the down of a thistle.

****

Despised

"He was despised and rejected, a man of sorrow and acquainted with grief."

There's a good chance that at some point during the Christmas season, we'll hear or possibly even see a woman sing these lines from Handel's sacred oratorio, *The Messiah*. Chances are the singer will be pretty and nicely dressed and will have taken a shower and washed her hair a few hours before the performance.

The man who wrote the lines, however, wasn't anyone you'd invite into your home. If he were to ring the doorbell this afternoon, we'd take one look and call the police. He never took a shower in his life and rarely bathed. He probably had a long beard and stringy hair that we would call filthy by all modern rules of hygiene. Like most people living 2,800 years ago, he probably had a rank odor to him. His name was Isaiah, son of Amoz, and he was a prophet.

People today have some wrong ideas about prophets. They weren't fortunetellers. Predicting the future was not their main occupation, although our word *prophesy* has come to mean foretelling the future. Their main job was criticizing the government–trying to get it to do what was right and warning of catastrophe if it didn't shape up. They didn't mince words.

The closest thing our culture has to the prophets of old is probably newspaper columnists or syndicated radio commentators. Rush Limbaugh would certainly qualify as a type of prophet by the standards of 800 B.C., especially if he grew a shaggy beard and shed a few pounds.

Reading through the Book of Isaiah, you might be surprised how many passages sound familiar. Old Isaiah had a gift with words. My favorite of all Bible passages is found in Isaiah's writings, but it's not the passage most people think of during Christmas.

My favorite passage is from Chapter 55. It discusses God's word: "As the rain and snow come down from heaven and do not return until they have watered the earth, making it blossom and bear fruit, giving seed for sowing and bread to eat, so shall the word that comes from my mouth prevail; it shall not return to me fruitless without accomplishing my purpose or succeeding in the task I gave it."

At a time in history when people are slaughtering each other in the name of religion (and when hasn't that been the case?), or because they think God's word tells them to, or because they consider their enemies infidels (literally "unfaithful"), we might do well to listen to old Isaiah's thoughts on God's word.

Most people of faith would agree that God has many ways of speaking. Just about any medium is suitable, if the listener pays attention. In the words of the hymn, "In the rustling grass I hear him pass–He speaks to me everywhere." This notion that God speaks through a variety of means is found in all religions.

Although Christians refer to the Bible as God's word, we know his word—his purpose–extends far beyond the pages of any book, be it Testament, Torah, or Koran. God's word is wide.

Isaiah's idea about God's word being like water seems fairly radical. People living in a dry land understand well the cycles of hydrology. Himself a dweller of a semi-arid land, Isaiah uses an image as familiar as water to illustrate God's purpose. Water is constantly moving. It flows, seeps, spews, evaporates, boils into clouds, condenses as mists and rain, rushes in furious torrents and quiet freshets, gushes forth in geysers, pours off cliffs, mighty as unseen ocean currents and as delicate as drops of dew.

Water is the great sustainer of life. Every leaf and blade of grass, every creature from the smallest single-cell organism to the greatest whale is made mostly of water. Our very being depends on water, on its movement and containment through cell and vessel. Without water we quickly die.

Isaiah indicates that God's purpose percolates through all Creation, not just through the prophet's own faith culture. Like water, God's sustaining purpose nourishes everything. Religions which insist they have exclusive access to God or proprietary rights to divine purpose would be wise to heed Isaiah's message: God's word is in the world, in every inch of it, moving, flowing, stirring, and infusing in a constant cycle of refreshment and renewal.

God's word can't be controlled or managed or limited. It's everywhere, like water, and its defining characteristic is love. That's the main point which both the clean-haired, nice-smelling lady and Isaiah the reeking, woolly man are trying to get across.

This and That

It's the Little Things that Test Our Mettle

Today I'm feeling crabby. Things both large and small are wrong with this world. Strangely enough, the big things don't stress me too much–maybe because I can't do much about them: terrorism, corporate hog farms, wildfires, crooked accountants, aquifer depletion.

The little things, however, are driving me crazy.

Let's start with people in checkout lines at the grocery. I get behind a lady who has piled her cart a mile high. That's okay–people gotta eat. I wait patiently while the cashier rings her up then announces the total.

"$138.40," says the cashier.

Then–and only then–does the lady reach into her luggage-sized purse and start fossicking around for her checkbook. It takes her five minutes more to write one lousy check.

My question to her: Why the Sam Hill can't you GET OUT YOUR BLINKING CHECKBOOK AHEAD OF TIME and start WRITING THE BLINKING CHECK?? You could get at least half of it filled out so PEOPLE BEHIND YOU WOULDN'T HAVE TO STAND THERE AND WATCH THEIR ICE CREAM MELT!!

I warned you that I was feeling crabby today.

Here's another thing that gets my goat. It's summertime, right? The kids are home. They get bored and want to go to the movies. We get out the paper to check movie times.

But the theater we usually patronize has decided to pull its weekday listings. If you want to know show times, you have to call up and listen to a long infomercial about a bunch of movies you wouldn't see if they paid you.

My question to the theater people: What? You can't afford a TINY AD IN THE NEWSPAPER, TELLING POTENTIAL CUSTOMERS WHEN ALL THE BLINKING MOVIES START? YOU MAKE TWENTY BUCKS OFF EVERY MAN, WOMAN AND CHILD WHO ENTERS YOUR ESTABLISHMENT!! We buy overpriced tickets to movies we'll forget in forty-five minutes, consume tooth-rotting candy, fat-inducing soft drinks, and cholesterol-soaked popcorn, BUT YOU DON'T HAVE THE DECENCY TO PUBLISH THE TIMES OF YOUR FRIPPIN' MOVIES??

Let's talk about public radio. It's refreshing that the High Plains now has an alternative to the wasteland of commercial radio. I'm a big fan of public radio, and a modest financial contributor. In fact, I was a fan before most of the kids working the controls were even born.

My question to the people running public radio: Would it be too much to ask for you to READ OVER THE SCRIPT BEFORE YOU TRY TO READ IT ON THE AIR?? Chances are if you can't pronounce a word before you're on the air, BEING ON THE AIR WON'T SUDDENLY GIVE YOU MIRACULOUS POWERS OF PRONUNCIATION!! IF A SENTENCE DOESN'T MAKE SENSE AS YOU'RE READING IT ALOUD, YOUR LISTENERS WILL BE JUST AS FREAKIN' BAFFLED BY IT AS YOU ARE!!!

I'm starting to feel a tiny bit better. Maybe I should ventilate more often.

Let's move on to drivers. Most of the things other drivers do to make me crazy can be lumped into one category: acting like they are the only driver in the cosmos.

Here's a driver in front of me at my kids' school. Like me, he's dropping off his kids. Rather than pull all the way over to the curb, which would consume WAY TOO MUCH ENERGY ON HIS PART, he only pulls halfway over. The result is that he blocks in everyone behind him. No one can get around, over, or under his car.

My question to the above-referenced driver: Would it be too terribly much trouble for you to realize that THE EARTH IS POPULATED WITH MANY, MANY OTHER HUMANS BESIDES YOU?? AND MOST OF THEM ARE IN LINE BEHIND YOU THIS VERY MINUTE, WAITING FOR YOU TO FINISH YOUR EXTENDED GOODBYE RITUALS, LAST-MINUTE REMINDERS, THOUGHTS FOR THE DAY, ETC., WITH YOUR KIDS (FOR WHOM WE FEEL VERY SORRY, HAVING YOU FOR A PARENT!) SO WE CAN DROP OURS OFF AND GET TO WORK ON TIME??

Finally, we turn our attention to food products. Maybe I'm the only person this happens to: I'll find a food product I like, begin buying it every time I visit the grocery, build a nutritional habit around it, and then–with no warning–the manufacturer quits making it. I've lost count of how many times this has happened.

The most recent was with lime-flavored corn chips. Somehow I got hooked on those salty little snacks, could hardly live without them. Then one day, *ZAP!* no more lime-flavored chips. The muckety-mucks at Chips-R-Us are probably so busy cooking the books that they forgot to cook more lime-flavored chips!

My question to the chip industry: WHY CAN'T YOU PEOPLE MAKE UP YOUR WARPED LITTLE MINDS?? IF A PRODUCT IS GOOD ENOUGH FOR YOU TO SINK MILLIONS INTO RESEARCH, DEVELOPMENT, AND MARKETING, WHY CAN'T YOU LEAVE IT THE HELL ALONE? YOU'RE MESSING WITH PEOPLE'S LIVES HERE!! I WANT THOSE LIME-FLAVORED CHIPS BACK, RIGHT THIS MINUTE!! DO YOU HEAR ME?? GIVE! ME! BACK! MY! LIME! FLAVORED! CHIPS!!!

****

Attack of the Killer Beauty Queens

Call me weird. Things that seem to bother a majority of other people don't seem to bother me.

School prayer, for example. I've never thought officially sanctioned prayer belongs in public schools. Prayer is such an intensely personal thing, a dialogue between a person and his Creator. I don't want my children taught how to pray by some person whose integrity and faith is unknown to me. I don't think it's right for parents to have their kids exposed to models of prayer they might not agree with.

And the notion of asking the Almighty to bless a contest in which the participants try to knock each other senseless is . . . well, senseless to me.

But I realize most other people don't see it that way. Like I said, call me weird.

My weirdness works the other way, too: Things that bother me don't seem to bother other people. The Miss Amarillo Area contest, for example. A gorgeous, statuesque, leggy blonde from Dallas named Meranda Carter was crowned Miss Amarillo Area. No one except me appears to see anything unusual about Miss Amarillo being a woman who doesn't live here, has never lived here, whose parents don't live here, and whose dog–if she has one–is probably from Dallas as well. For all we know, Meranda Carter might be a vegetarian or a person who, like me, wants prayer *out* of the public schools. Do we want such a person representing us at the Miss Texas pageant?

While I have a policy of trying never to offend gorgeous, statuesque, leggy blondes, and would never speak ill of beauty contestants or others engaged in meaningful, socially relevant work, I'd prefer a rule that required Miss Amarillo to actually *live* in Amarillo, or at least to have spent the summers here as a child, or at the *very* least to have driven *through* on her way to New Mexico once in her life, or to know someone who did.

Having a Miss Amarillo from Dallas implies that we don't have an ample supply of gorgeous, statuesque, leggy blondes right here in Potter and Randall counties, which, we all know from spending time at the pool this summer, is patently false. There must be hundreds of qualified leggy blondes right here in town. Why didn't one of them win Miss Amarillo? I plan to get to the bottom of this, one way or another.

Having said that, I must confess that I'll be Meranda Carter's No. 1 Fan, rooting her on at the Miss Texas contest next July and praying (privately of course) that she'll make it to Atlantic City next year and ultimately become Miss America, Amarillo's own hometown girl!

* * *

A few weeks ago I commented on the fact that Meranda Carter, our new Miss Amarillo Area, is a Dallas woman who has never actually lived in the Amarillo area. Little did I know that I was stepping into a hornets' nest. If you haven't been brow-beaten by beauty queens, brother, you haven't been brow-beaten at all.

Blistering criticism began immediately. Current and former contestants and pageant supporters wrote to protest my suggestion that Miss Amarillo ought to be a woman who lives in the area.

Some of the letters seemed rather mean-spirited, like the e-mail message from Cynthia Puckett, who wrote, "Perhaps you should get your head out of whatever hole you are hiding it in and pay more attention to the news. I think that it is no more 'weird' for a woman from Dallas to hold the Miss Amarillo title than it is for a man with no brains to write a newspaper column."

I give Cynthia a low score in "Congeniality."

But not all the letters were mean. Some were thoughtful and well-written, like this from Caryann Wheeler:

"My point is that the Miss America Pageant changes lives. I'm walking proof. It hurts me to think that people can form uneducated opinions and live by stereotypes, but that is part of the unfairness I learned to accept so early in life. I hope Meranda Carter has the opportunity to experience the blessings that I have. . . ."

Let me try to clear up some confusion. First, I am not against the Miss America Pageant or any of its tributaries. I watch it every year on television. I'm pretty good at picking the top five. I didn't intend to insult the contestants by calling them leggy blondes; it's just that so many *are* leggy blondes or leggy brunettes. It seems that leggyness–which I define as having shapely, attractive, and preferably long legs–is a requirement for getting very far in the pageant system.

Indignant supporters of the pageant who insist, as one did, that "being a 'leggy blond' has nothing to do with it" are deluding themselves. Having shapely, attractive legs has everything to do with it, because it's part of our culture's definition of beauty. Even though the Miss America organization has dropped the term *beauty pageant* from its name in favor of the more politically correct *scholarship pageant*, it's still at least partly a beauty contest. Otherwise, why parade around in skimpy swimsuits and evening gowns?

Admitting that it's partly a beauty contest doesn't make it bad. Rather, it simply acknowledges that millions of dollars' worth of tummy tucks, breast implants, face-lifts, nose jobs, SuperGlue, duct tape, botox, baling wire and Lord knows what else go into the creation of the "scholarship contestants" we see in Atlantic City each year. Outward appearance is a huge part of success in the pageant business. Given a choice between a brilliant woman with average looks and a drop-dead gorgeous woman of average intelligence, the judges will never pick the average-looking one. Average-looking women aren't even allowed into New Jersey during the pageant.

Second, I would never suggest that some women's lives aren't enriched by participating in pageants. I'm sure many do gain self-confidence, learn teamwork, build relationships, and open doors of opportunity for themselves by competing. More power to them.

On the other hand, I wonder how many become disillusioned by failure or get tossed out due to cellulite or develop bulimia/anorexia and end up worse off than before except with a big debt to plastic surgeons? What about young women whose self-confidence is damaged? To get a well-balanced picture, we should examine the possible harm to some women's self-esteem as well as the benefit to others.

Third, I still think Miss Amarillo ought to be a hometown girl. You won't change my mind about this, so save your breath. I don't blame Meranda Carter for competing and winning Miss Amarillo

Area. She seems to be a fine young woman and it's not her fault that the rules are wacky.

But whoever made up those rules has been inhaling too much hair spray. If we allow women from outside the Panhandle to compete for Miss Amarillo Area, why not let women from Canada compete for Miss America? Can California women (of which there are twenty gazillion) compete for Miss Rhode Island? If so, how fair is that to eligible but native Rhode Island women, of which there were only seventeen at last count?

Opening up local pageants to women from other areas seems to suggest that the local women aren't good enough, and that pageant directors had to go "outside" for viable contestants. I prefer a residency requirement which would ensure that our local young women aren't upstaged by city girls who don't know calf fries from hush puppies.

Maybe I just don't understand the Miss America history or philosophy or theory. I'm sure someone will enlighten me soon enough.

****

Pariahs of Society

There was a local TV news story about registered sex offenders living too close to schools.

The news anchor reported that police had advised concerned citizens "not to take the law into their own hands."

Now, wait just a doggone minute.

Exactly which "law" were citizens supposed to avoid taking into their own hands? The "law" giving people permission to lynch their neighbors? The "law" that allows them to compound the misery already experienced by sex offenders?

Who are these registered sex offenders, anyway? They're people who've been tried and convicted of sexual offences, who are paying their debt to society under the law, and who are complying with requirements that they keep in touch with authorities.

I say leave the tormented souls be.

Registered sex offenders aren't asking to baby-sit, to coach Little League, or to be school volunteers. I imagine that most want to be left alone to live their lives. Lord knows they have enough problems without enduring the scorn of the self-righteous.

The sex offenders we ought to worry about are those who don't register, who fail to comply with the terms of probation, or who go on the lam and slip away from the watchful eye of authorities.

I have registered sex offenders living in my neighborhood–even on my block–and so, probably, do you. The ones I know seem to mind their own business. Why can't their neighbors do the same?

As a Christian, I ask myself, "What would Jesus do" about registered sex offenders living down the street? Would he spit on them? Would he advocate running them out of the neighborhood? Picketing their front lawns?

Or would he offer them forgiveness and self-respect? Look how he treated the lepers, tax collectors, and prostitutes.

Surely our sex offenders are the pariahs of society. They're easy to pick on because they don't fight back.

If you don't want to befriend the outcasts, fine–but for Christ's sake, leave them alone.

* * *

In a recent column I wondered how Jesus Christ would react if registered sex offenders lived down the street from him. Would he befriend them? Pretend they didn't exist? Condemn them?

Some readers–including at least one victim of sexual abuse–felt I was being too lenient with sex offenders. According to some, it's permissiveness such as mine ("tolerance run amok" is how one reader described it) that got society in this mess in the first place.

Another described my article as a "repulsive piece of trash" and went on to give statistics showing that sex offenders can't be trusted.

I'm not advocating we trust them. What I'm advocating is that people–even people who have done bad things—be treated like human beings.

Is sex abuse a problem in our society? Absolutely. Are people justified in feeling edgy about having registered sex offenders next door? Yes. Would we prefer to have someone else as our neighbor? Probably.

Are victims of sex crimes scarred in ways we can't even imagine? Yes. Are all registered sex offenders equally dangerous to society? Probably not. Is it easy to tell the truly dangerous ones from the less dangerous? No. Is that a good reason to treat them all like animals? Not in my book.

Should we hyperventilate when a registered sex offender moves into our neighborhood? No. Would anyone in his right mind fail to be watchful and cautious about such a person? I hope not. Is caution different from vigilantism? I hope so. Is a greater risk to children posed by the trusted uncle, Mom's boyfriend, or other *unregistered* sex offender? Yes.

Am I advocating that society let down its guard about sexual crimes? No. Should we do more to protect children? Yes. Would lynching a few registered sex offenders help make our neighborhoods safer? Get real.

I'm arguing that all men and women are created in the image of God. No sinner is beyond grace. Even convicted criminals are God's children and essentially worthy of respect and the possibility of healing, which is why churches have prison ministries.

This doesn't mean we pretend registered sex offenders are nice people, but neither should we vilify them as subhuman. The problem is they're all too human–fallen, broken, needy.

Our attitudes toward them should wise as serpents, innocent as doves.

****

I Am Curious, Big Brother

An Open Letter to Kenneth Prewitt, Director,
U.S. Bureau of the Census

Dear Mr. Prewitt,

As you will discover from our answers to your census questionnaire, the Horsley family believes in good citizenship. We vote, obey most laws, and recycle. We work hard, pay taxes, volunteer in the community and give to charity.

So when we received your booklet of census questions, we didn't hesitate to sit down and answer all 112 items pertaining to the four people living at this address.

We worked at the kitchen table after supper, which explains the jelly stains on the form. Although your instructions said it would take thirty-eight minutes, we needed almost two hours because some questions sparked heated discussion which temporarily got us off track.

Except for one or two questions that prompted a family member to shout, "THAT'S NONE OF THEIR BUSINESS," we were as truthful as possible. And now that we've answered your questions, Sir, we wonder if you would mind answering a few of ours?

1) Your cover letter of 13 March says that the purpose of the census is to "count every person living in this house." Obviously this statement is only partly true. If all you wanted was to count heads, you could have sent me a postcard on which I could have written *4* and returned it to you.

Why you didn't go into more detail about how my answers would be used? I would have liked more information.

2) Question 5 threw me for a loop. You seem to distinguish between "Spanish/Hispanic/Latino" and "Mexican, Mexican Am., Chicano." How is Chicano different from Latino? Hispanic from Puerto Rican? If I'm not mistaken, it was Spaniards who conquered and renamed the island nations of the Carribean in the sixteenth century. So what does Hispanic mean? It got me wondering what you were driving at.

3) Similarly, you seem to distinguish between "race" in Question 6 and "ethnic origin" in Question 10. Aren't these the same? Choices

under "race" include Korean, African Am., and Chamorro; choices under "ethnic origin" include Korean, African Am., and Cape Verdean. What the heck are Cape Verdean and Chamorro? I think you made up these "races" just to see if we were paying attention.

Question 10 was interesting, but for the life of me I can't see why it matters to you what my "ancestry or ethnic origin" is. I'm sort of a Heinz 57 of English, German, Irish, and Scot, with maybe some American Indian thrown in for color. I don't mind anyone knowing where I came from, but I'm trying to imagine how you will use this data.

Let's say you get everyone's answers and *voila!* prove that America is an ethnic melting pot. Didn't we already know this?

4) Question 17 wanted to know if, "because of a mental condition lasting six months or more," I have trouble remembering things. Funny you should ask. I spent the better part of yesterday searching this house for something I knew was here, but couldn't locate. I suppose you could call this a mental condition, since I've been this way for years. I'm always hiding things from myself, then I can't find them when I need them. Well, you had to ask.

5) I'm not a paranoid nutcase, but when my government wants to know what time I leave for work (Question 24), how long it takes me to get there, and how many people are in my car, it makes me sympathize with true paranoids. I'll bet you have a perfectly harmless reason for wanting to know such information, but questions like this stimulate the "paranoid" region of my brain, causing it to release chemical receptors which accelerate the re-uptake of serotonin resulting in malfunction of the radio transmitter implanted in my brain at birth by robotic doctors working on top-secret demographics analysis projects.

6) Personal income inquiries like Question 31 always put me in a quandary. On the one hand, how much I make is no secret. My earnings can be discovered by anyone with access to the IRS database, the Social Security database, or by anyone with a touch-tone phone.

On the other hand, it always makes me uneasy when people ask how much I make. It's sort of a private thing, I guess, like asking a rancher how big her ranch is. It's not a polite question. So I fudged a little on my answer. I'll bet ninety percent of all respondents enhanced or dehanced their answer to Question 31. If you want the exact figures, you'll have to hack into government databases like everyone else does.

Please use a black or blue pen to respond to these questions. Thank you for your cooperation.

****

Destiny Comes Calling

Do you believe in destiny? I didn't used to, but now I'm not so sure. I've been inclined to believe that we create our own destiny by the choices we make. But three little children in the news this week are causing me to reconsider my assumptions.

The first is tiny Rositha Pedro, a healthy baby girl born March 1, 2000, in a tree in Mozambique. It's hard to hear of her entry into the world and not wonder if she's destined for something special.

In case you missed the story, little Rositha's pregnant mother was forced by rising flood waters into a tree near her African village. Perched there for four days, her mother finally gave birth only moments before a rescue helicopter managed to hoist her and the child to safety.

Call me superstitious, but I'm keeping an eye on Rositha Pedro. Imagine a pregnant woman clinging to a treetop in Africa as one by one her neighbors and family grow exhausted and slip into the swirling waters. What odds of survival would you give that unborn child?

Based solely on the circumstances of her birth, it wouldn't surprise me if she achieves something unusual in her lifetime. Maybe it's her destiny for thousands of people in Amarillo, Texas, to be reading and thinking about her.

I don't want to make light of a tragic flood in which many have perished and many more surely will die from cholera, malaria, and dysentery. Rositha's great-grandmother was among those already lost in the muddy waters. But you'd have to be almost deaf not to hear a grace-note in her story.

Imagine Rositha telling her own daughter someday, "I was born in a tree while a helicopter hovered overhead. Your great-great grandmother died in the same flood that witnessed my birth."

If I can figure out a way to send her a birthday present, I plan to do so.

But I don't imagine a six-year-old first-grader at Buell Elementary School will be receiving many presents. The Michigan boy found a loaded pistol in the dilapidated crack house where he lived with his uncle, took it to school, and killed a classmate with it.

Do you suppose this tragedy was destined to happen? Does a six-year-old understand the difference between TV violence and actual violence? How must the parents of little Kayla Rolland, the murdered girl, feel?

This story disturbs me in so many ways, it's hard to know where to begin. Why was the boy living in that sort of squalor? What does it say about the rest of us, that we don't mind children living in inhuman conditions until the inevitable tragedy uncoils itself?

We don't have to go as far as Michigan to find children living in terrible and dangerous conditions. We have plenty right here in Texas. What are we going to do about it? What *can* we do about it?

As any social worker will tell you, our system for preventing the sort of circumstances which led to Kayla Rolland's death is deeply flawed. Parents don't want government authorities telling them how to raise their children. Removing a child from a dangerous home is a lot harder than you might think.

Our legal system is understandably schizophrenic on the subject. It supports the rights of social agencies to protect children from abuse but also supports the rights of parents, even parents who are proven losers by just about any standard you can name, to retain custody of their children.

So it seems inevitable, given a certain number of loaded guns lying around a certain number of drug houses where a certain number of small children live, that tragedy is bound to happen sooner or later. And it seems equally inevitable that given a certain number of people living along a flood-prone river, sooner or later disaster will strike.

This sense of inevitability brings me back to the notion of destiny. Maybe destiny is nothing more than the sum of all the tiny decisions made by every person in the world. Maybe somewhere in Mozambique, there's a civil engineer in charge of flood control who had it in his power to run some numbers on what might happen to the villages along the Save River if a certain amount of rain fell in a certain amount of time. Maybe he shelved the project as being too improbable, or was distracted by more likely scenarios.

Or maybe someone in Michigan suspected that something was wrong with the unnamed little six-year-old old boy's home life. Maybe a teacher, social worker, pastor, or neighbor should have said something, done something, gotten involved.

Maybe it's in the little boy's destiny to grow up with a sense of being touched by Fate. Probably he doesn't even understand what he's done, and won't remember it. Maybe he'll move to Texas someday and become your neighbor, or mine.

****

Through the Looking Glass with Pantex

Sometimes columnists write something provocative just to get a rise out of people. We deliberately take one side of an issue and run it up the flagpole to see who salutes and who throws tomatoes.

But it takes real talent to write something that elicits tomatoes from both sides of an issue, which is what I did in my column about Pantex, the nuclear weapons assembly and disassembly plant.

Thinking I was being fair to one and all, I raised the question of how ordinary citizens can tell truth from propaganda regarding safety at Pantex. Or put another way: can we always assume that government agencies tell the truth? The question was prompted by an article in the May/June issue of *The Bulletin of the Atomic Scientists* which voiced concerns about safety at Pantex.

One reader hammered me for being a naive stooge of the military-industrial culture: "I believe your article is written from the typical mind-set of propaganda in the Amarillo area. . . . It's all propaganda in your article and you present it very well."

This same reader took me to task for unnecessarily complicating the question of evaluating truth. To arrive at truth, she said, one need only to read; to talk to people and get their input of experiences, knowledge, and opinions; and then "I form my own conclusions, as I hope most other people do who do not have their thinking controlled, as is very prominent in the Amarillo community. . . ."

I'm not fond of the notion that my thinking is controlled by the government, even if it's true. Of course that would explain the tiny scar behind my right ear and the antenna sticking out of my head. But short of such obvious signs, how can we know if our ideas about truth are being fed to us by government agencies more concerned with damage control than veracity?

For example, I recall that when I first moved to this area, Pantex was admitting some groundwater contamination in the relatively shallow "perched" aquifers. We were assured the pollution hadn't reached the deep Ogallala Aquifer, source of drinking and irrigation water for millions of people on the Great Plains.

Now we're told that not only have Pantex contaminants reached the deep Ogallala, but officials knew about it months before telling the public. A front-page story in the Sunday, May 21, 2000 *Houston Chronicle* described this recent admission by Pantex, saying high explosives and TCE have now reached the deep levels of the Ogallala. Which means people were drawing, drinking, and cooking water from wells someone at Pantex knew were contaminated.

Officials at the plant claim their failure to warn the public quickly was merely an oversight. How can we judge that statement? It might very well be true–things do sometimes tend to get overlooked or buried in layers of paperwork. On the other hand, it seems a stretch that a company which disassembles nuclear bombs would overlook mentioning well water contamination to its neighbors.

But can I ever know for sure? No. I'm outside the system and ultimately shut out of participating in circles of knowledge needed to make such a call. There might only be a handful of people who know the truth, and there's little chance someone like you or me would ever uncover it if Pantex was determined to keep the lid on it. If push comes to shove, the government can always trump our desire for facts with the "national security" card. End of discussion.

On the other hand, maybe Pantex's mission is so important in the big scheme of things that a little groundwater contamination is a small price to pay. A few ruined farms and ranches are far outweighed, so the thinking goes, by the benefits of having Pantex here. This view is easier to hold if it's not YOUR farm or ranch being threatened by pollution.

Curiously, other readers thought I was being a lackey of the liberal peacenik culture. One called into question my quotation of an article in *The Bulletin of the Atomic Scientists*, claiming it took liberties with the facts: "It doesn't help to have bogus information passed off as fact, and so I hope this reference will help you in further deliberations of fact vs. postulation."

Another, whose letter was printed in the *Amarillo Globe-News,* thought the "inflammatory title of the article does a disservice to readers who live in the vicinity of Pantex." (I don't write headlines for my columns.) Furthermore, this reader thought that learning the truth is as simple as "getting the facts from Pantex and current DOE officials."

Pardon me, but getting the "facts" from Pantex and current Department of Energy officials is like asking Bill Clinton for the facts about Monica you-know-who, which gets us back to my original question: how to sift out conflicting versions of the truth.

"No one wants to see a 'catastrophe' at Pantex," the reader continued, "least of all the men and women who have dedicated their lives to making Pantex a safe and secure working environment. . . ."

True. But no one wants ever wants to have a car wreck, either, yet millions do.

So here's my question again in its simplest form: Should ordinary citizens like me put blind trust in Pantex? Yes or no?

If yes, then we automatically believe every single thing Pantex officials say, whether about safety or environmental issues.

If no, then we're faced with the daunting task of gathering data for ourselves and making an informed judgment.

****

Somewhere in the Hill Country

A chief of The People contemplates a morning star in the predawn darkness:

It's getting so I can't stay in the robes until first light. Sometimes gourds will do that to me, but we didn't have gourds last night. Maybe it's just forty summers.

Red Feathers is older than me, and he sleeps until the sun is high. If he would get up with the rest of us, he would get to go on more raids and would have nicer things. But his wives treat him like he was a big raider.

Wonder what Straight Teeth will cook this morning. I'm getting tired of deer. Roasted, boiled, fried, raw, smoked, jerked. What I wouldn't give for a buffalo hump. First buffalo I kill this fall, I'll ask her to cook it all day in coals with sweet grass and onions, like we used to do.

Maybe we ought to move camp early this year. The deer around here taste like acorns.

She's trying, though. She hates to look bad in front of the new wife. I'll keep on pretending small interest in the new one. She's not as pretty as Straight Teeth, but she's hard as a rock. I wish she showed more interest in cooking. All she wants to do is mate—morning, noon, and night. It's starting to wear me out. That's the trouble with young wives.

Wonder what is the name of that little star moving closer every day to Morning Star. I don't think they're going to bump. But the little star is full of energy. I'll ask Walks Funny what its name is, and if it means anything. I suppose he would have mentioned it if it were important.

Wonder if we really should move camp now. It takes the children all day to fill three bags with good flint. I remember when you could crack enough rock to fill three bags before breakfast. Now they come in when the sun is going down. They're not smiling. If they would work instead of playing, they could fill their bags by noon and still have time to play. But you can't tell them anything.

That reminds me that Crow Feet Girl has been disrespectful a lot lately. She makes me tired with her sass. Maybe if I marry her to one of the Blue Canyon clans, I'll get a few good horses for her. Then she can be disrespectful to her new family. Yes, I'll do that.

My good mare hasn't been too peppy all this moon. Hope she isn't coming down with something. That would be bad luck if she came up lame just when the buffalo arrived. Maybe I'll take her down to the big village and see what they say. My cousins are better about horses than I am.

I'll have to play that just right, though, to avoid looking humble. I'll tell them we're planning a raid and need some extra riders. And while I'm here, why don't you look at this horse for me? I suppose I'll have to smell their bad breath all day while they treat my mare.

How odd that no coyotes are singing today. I smell something in the air. Maybe a big fire far away.

Something just occurred to me. All these little annoyances could add up to a bad omen. Maybe I should talk to the spirits about it. Three Red Lances said he overheard the captives talking about a new enemy toward the rising sun. He thought they called them Horse Fathers. He asked the captives about it, and they acted like they didn't understand.

If they had been more cooperative, they might have lived awhile longer. I wish he hadn't killed them before we learned what they knew. You can't tell him anything, either.

Maybe I'll dream about this new enemy. The Grandfathers might tell me what they are. I can't imagine what is so special about these Horse Fathers, if that's what they're called. No one has better horses than The People, nor better weapons. If there really is a new enemy, I hope we get to fight them first, while they're still fresh. We'll teach them a few things about fighting. Let's see how their weapons stand up to ours.

That reminds me. I can't seem to find my good war club. I've looked all over, and it's just not here. Another piece of bad luck. I remember taking it with me that day we raided down around Fox Creek. It's not with my things now. Either I dropped it on the raid or on the way back, or else I put it aside and wasn't paying attention.

That's how I lost my favorite rattle last summer. Then I found it again when I went to my secret spring for a drink. It was right in the hole in the bank. As soon as I saw it, I laughed. I remembered putting it there. I'm surprised a porcupine didn't eat it.

There's a little light in the sky now. I think I hear Doesn't Like To Cook stirring. She mumbles while she's waking up.

If she comes out of that lodge, I'll pretend I'm asleep.

Acknowledgements

The author wishes to thank the following people for their help: Kay Brown, Debbie Dudley, Kerry Knorpp, and editorial page editor John Kanelis of the *Amarillo Globe-Ne*ws. Also, my thanks to *Globe-News* publisher Les Simpson for permission to reprint the newspaper columns which comprise this book.

About The Author

David T. Horsley lives in Amarillo, Texas, with his wife and two teenage children. Since 1992, he's written a weekly column for the *Amarillo Globe-News*. David also teaches English at Amarillo College, sings in the choir at Polk Street Methodist Church, manages rental property, and, for fun, hikes the remote canyons and prairies of the Texas Panhandle.

Raised in Missouri and Kansas, David received a Bachelor of Arts degree from Texas Tech University in Lubbock, a Master of Divinity from Southern Baptist Theological Seminary in Louisville, Kentucky, and a Master of Arts degree from West Texas Texas A&M University in Canyon.